AMERICAN AND CATHOLIC

profile: Georgetown (education, slavery)

earliest settlements: Florida, Great Lakes, New England

Tekawitha

Dominicans, Jesuits

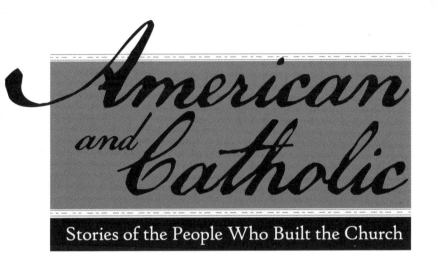

American and Catholic

Stories of the People Who Built the Church

C. WALKER GOLLAR

Franciscan
MEDIA
Cincinnati, Ohio

Scripture passages have been taken from *New Revised Standard Version Bible*, copyright ©1989 by the Division of Christian Education of the National Council of the Churches of Christ in the U.S.A., and used by permission. All rights reserved.

Cover and book design by Mark Sullivan
Cover images: © iStock | Lisa-Blue; (top) courtesy of the archives of St. John the Baptist Province, Cincinnati, Ohio. All rights reserved.

LIBRARY OF CONGRESS CATALOGING-IN-PUBLICATION DATA
Gollar, C. Walker.
American and Catholic : stories of the people who built the church / C. Walker Gollar.
pages cm
Includes bibliographical references and index.
ISBN 978-1-61636-878-4 (paperback)
1. Catholic Church—United States—History. 2. Catholics—United States—Biography. 3. United States—Church history. I. Title.
BX1406.3.G65 2015
277.3—dc23
2015003938

ISBN 978-1-61636-878-4

Published by Franciscan Media
28 W. Liberty St.
Cincinnati, OH 45202
www.FranciscanMedia.org

Printed in the United States of America.
Printed on acid-free paper.
15 16 17 18 19 5 4 3 2 1

To Ned

CONTENTS

When I decided to devote my career to the study of American Catholic history, a mentor suggested that I talk to priest-historian Clyde Crews. I made appropriate arrangements and met Clyde at his office at Bellarmine College in Louisville, Kentucky. Clyde asked if I wanted to go for a drive. I said, "Yes." Clyde pulled the car into Louisville's public Cave Hill Cemetery, and tuned the radio to classical music. Clyde explained that he always listened to classical music when visiting the dead.

Clyde steered up a hill toward the monument of Mamie and Lina Caldwell. These sisters had donated immense amounts of money to the Catholic Church. As Clyde and I got out of the car to take a few pictures, Clyde asked what I knew about the controversy of the Caldwells. The Caldwell sisters should have been buried in Louisville's St. Louis Catholic Cemetery beside their parents, Clyde explained. All I knew at that time, as I then shared with Clyde, was that some trouble involved the Caldwells and my great-great-uncle, Bishop John Lancaster Spalding of Peoria, Illinois.

Clyde marveled over what I did know about my rich family history. I am a seventh generation Kentucky Catholic and very proud of it. "Write down all that has been passed on to you," Clyde suggested, "both the good and bad. Everyone likes a story," Clyde said. "And never hesitate to buy a book you think you might someday need," he added.

In the twenty-five years since my first encounter with Clyde Crews, I have read a lot of books and gathered a lot of stories from countless forays into American Catholic history. I love exploring archives, libraries, and historical places. While traveling all over the country I have learned to read historical plaques real fast so my children won't get upset with me. I can drive for miles all alone, plant myself for hours amidst dusty old records, and happily search for that one gem which will make all my effort worthwhile.

When a former student of mine, and the managing editor of Franciscan Media, asked me to consider updating Clyde Crews's *American & Catholic—A Popular History of Catholicism in the United States* (2004), I could not say "No." As our conversation about the project grew, we decided a major reworking was appropriate. I proposed to focus the book more specifically around the stories that I have gathered through the years. I thank Clyde Crews for encouraging me to explore the American Catholic experience in this fashion.

Holy People

I recently drove a couple hours down the highway on a great adventure. I live in an old home. Previous owners had discarded the doors that once separated the downstairs rooms. I wanted to fill one large opening with something from an antique salvage store. I found two broken and beaten old French doors covered in dust that I figured would be perfect for my house. I called my wife to share the good news. Amy wanted to know how broken and beaten the doors were. I assured her that I could restore them.

With Amy's blessing, I purchased the doors, secured them in my truck, and drove a short distance to my cousin Ned's home. Ned is twenty years older than me. I love him very much. He and his wife, Jean, live in a 132-year-old schoolhouse, an historic landmark. Both Ned and Jean have many interests, most especially old stuff. Ned dusted off a pane of glass from my French doors, and much to his delight, found the waves and imperfections that dated the glass as late nineteenth-century.

"Have you read Charles Mann's *1491*?" Ned asked. I had not, but I explained that I had studied many of the original documents surviving from the Spanish Catholic era of Columbus. Ned invited me in for dinner. We talked about the beginnings of Catholicism in this hemisphere, noting that the story of the late-fifteenth- to early-sixteenth-century Spanish conquistadors was absolutely brutal. In God's name, whole peoples were wiped from the face of the earth.

Yet there were a few edifying parts of that story, as well. I told Ned how I remembered watching the movie *The Mission*, which appeared when I was teaching high school religion in 1986, and then saw *Black Robe*, which came out five years later as I began doctoral studies. I learned a lot from these depictions, which inspired me to conduct some serious scholarly research on that era. Ned remembered how much he enjoyed the music from both films. "A lot certainly happened before Catholics finally landed in Maryland," Ned mused. I agreed.

Then the issue of slavery came up. Ned and I always seem to talk about this. Slave cabins owned by our ancestors still stand, while our family tree includes slaveholders and slaves alike. Ned and I know this. Most other relatives don't, or simply prefer not to talk about it. Years ago Ned encouraged me to write about it. Other historians have mentioned slavery as part of the Catholic story, usually in some kind of Civil War chapter. I have come to realize that the contribution of enslaved persons, along with many indentured servants, began the moment Catholics landed at Maryland in 1634 and extended well beyond the Civil War.

Ned grew up near those slave cabins in the heart of what many Catholics call the Kentucky Holy Land, that is, the area in central Kentucky in and around Bardstown. So did my mother. She taught me early on that Kentucky Catholics contributed mightily to the early growth of the American Catholic Church, second in influence only to Catholic Marylanders. After dinner, Ned and I moved into the original section of his home, the room that was used as the school's classroom. Ned and Jean have decorated this space with family heirlooms from our early Catholic pioneers. We began to talk about the institutional growth of the United States Catholic Church. I now knew I would have to spend the night. I called Amy, and she said it was OK.

I grew up and still live in northern Kentucky, where nineteenth-century Irish and mostly German Catholic immigrants built the Church. Well into the evening, Ned and I marveled over how much the Church changed after the United States moved from a largely slave-based to an immigrant-based economy. I attend Covington, Kentucky's St. John Church, which was an early extension of Covington's German *Muttergottes Gemeinde*, the Mother of God parish. As seen in the beautiful architecture of St. John's, along with countless other immigrant churches spread out across the country, immigrants from various nations brought and still bring tremendous skills to the

United States and to the Catholic Church. I invited Ned to see St. John's at Christmastime.

Amid the early waves of European immigrants, Catholic leaders tried to address the injustice of slavery, Catholic sisters cared for the wounded on Civil War battlefields, wealthy Catholics donated freely to Catholic causes, and Catholic bishops stood beside the poor and working class victimized by the industrial age. Ned recalled that the portrait of our great-great-uncle, the bald-headed scary-looking Bishop John Lancaster Spalding of Peoria, Illinois, hung above the family fireplace as Ned grew up. I reminded Ned that Bishop Spalding was an incredibly influential Catholic leader from the turn of the century whom Blydie, our grandmother and Spalding's niece, lovingly called "Uncle Bishop."

Jean went to bed about the time Ned and I landed the conversation in the twentieth century. We raced through two great wars, pausing to retell how a water mine killed our uncle (my namesake) days after D-Day. Throughout such horrors American Catholic bishops, along with some prominent lay Catholic leaders commanded all people to respect the dignity of all human beings. Then dawned the 1950s, which Ned lived through, and the experience of Vatican II, which constituted the Church I was raised in. As I fell asleep in Ned's extra bedroom, I marveled over the wonderfully complex and grace-filled American Catholic story.

The next morning Ned offered me a small Victorian couch. It had belonged to Blydie, our grandmother. Blydie had inherited it from her mother, Nannie, who had gotten it from her mother, Mary Jane Lancaster Spalding. I was thrilled to receive the piece. After some restoration, it will live on in my daughter Caroline's bedroom.

I grew up with antiques, including items carried by my Catholic ancestors from Maryland into Kentucky some eight generations ago. My little brother and I once played baseball with pillows in the living room. The game ended when my homerun dislodged a hundred-year-old porcelain teacup. Mom picked up the pieces. Friends recommend that I have the cup restored. I prefer to keep the pieces in the same bag Mom placed them in. It helps me tell the story, and helps my children learn to not play baseball in the house.

In grade school, I memorized the family tree seven generations back. One relative, Mother Catherine Spalding, helped to establish the Sisters of

Charity of Nazareth, Kentucky, in 1812. During the Civil War, my great-great-great-uncle, Martin John Spalding, served as archbishop of Baltimore, the first Catholic diocese of the United States. And Archbishop Spalding's nephew, Bishop John Lancaster Spalding of Peoria (that is, Uncle Bishop), founded the Catholic University of America in Washington, D.C. in 1888. The portrait that he signed for his "beloved niece," Blydie, hangs near the couch where I read stories to my children.

Pictured above the same couch are numerous other relatives, including my Grandmother Blydie. Of all the ancestors, Blydie may have best embodied the Catholic faith. Widowed at thirty-six years of age, Blydie lost two (and almost lost four) of her six children, but she carried on with the dignity of a faithful Catholic who believed that death was not the end. Ned often escaped the turmoil of his childhood to find peace in Blydie's home down the street. Heirlooms were sacred to Blydie. My caring for Blydie's things, along with, now, the memories of Mom and Dad and many other relatives, helps keep my Catholic communion of saints alive. Preserving the past is in my blood.

While earning a Ph.D. in American Catholic history, my professors equipped me with the critical tools of storytelling, insisting, for example, that historical investigation tell the whole truth, good, bad, and everything in between. Four years teaching high school religion and twenty-one years teaching university theology has further convinced me that religious history must involve more than recounting old events. Catholics proclaim that God lived on this earth as Jesus and that God continues to guide the church through the Holy Spirit. In other words, God lives in history. Part of me has known that since I was a child.

In this book I do not offer a comprehensive history. This is not *the* story of American Catholicism. This is *one* collection of stories that I hope will stimulate further conversation. I touch upon some key themes that arose throughout the lives of Catholics living with the land we now know as the United States of America. Through the stories of the people that I choose to tell, I offer glimpses into the long, sometimes painful, and always holy lives of the people who built the Church.

CHAPTER ONE

Spanish Conquistadors and Native American Martyrs

*N*o one knows the name of the first person to live in America. Scholars figure that people inhabited this land maybe fifteen thousand years ago. These first inhabitants probably had migrated from Siberia to Alaska across the Bering Strait, though some historians contend that the first Americans sailed over the Atlantic Ocean. Christian convert Leif Eriksson perhaps landed in North America when taken off course near Greenland around 999, but his efforts produced no permanent Christian presence in the New World. The first continuous Catholic settlement in the Americas came about five hundred years later.

After thirty-four days at sea, the morning of October 12, 1492, Catholic explorer Christopher Columbus sighted land somewhere in the Bahamas, perhaps at a small island that natives called Guanahaní (now known as San Salvador Island). After Columbus's flagship, the Santa Maria, ran aground on Christmas Day, 1492, his men built an encampment called La Navidad (or Christmas) south of San Salvador Island, on the much larger island natives called Haiti, "the land of the Mountain."

As word of Columbus's crossing spread across Europe, Pope Alexander VI charged King Ferdinand and Queen Isabella with leading "the peoples dwelling in those islands and countries" to the Catholic faith. On the feast of San Matteo, or St. Matthew, September 21, 1496, Ramón Pané baptized the first convert, a Taino man named Guatícaba. In honor of the feast day, Pané renamed Guatícaba as Juan Matteo. All of Juan Matteo's family joined

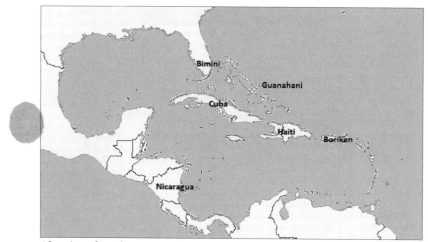

After thirty-four days at sea, the morning of October 12, 1492, Columbus sighted land somewhere in the Bahamas, perhaps at a small island natives called Guanahaní (now known as San Salvador Island). After Columbus's flagship, the *Santa Maria*, ran aground on Christmas Day, his men built an encampment called La Navidad (or "Christmas") south of San Salvador Island on the much larger island of Haiti (in what is now the Dominican Republic). Subsequent conquistadors explored Boriken (Puerto Rico), Bimini (Florida), and Nicaragua, among many other places in the area.

the Catholic Church. Columbus renamed Guatícaba's homeland Haiti, *La Isla Española*, "The Spanish Island," or more simply, Española.[1]

The following spring, some of Juan Matteo's family buried a few Catholic images in their cassava fields. The Tainos routinely placed sacred objects under the ground to ensure fruitfulness of the land. Columbus's men thought the Tainos mocked the Catholic Church, and thus rounded up those who had buried the Catholic images and burned these people at the stake. Other Tainos then seized Juan Matteo, denounced him for embracing Columbus's worldview, and killed him. Thus, the first American Catholics died the first American Catholic martyrs.

Though hardly appreciated by Columbus, the Tainos may have been the most advanced of all peoples living in the islands, displaying strong family ties, profound religious beliefs, and complex social structures. Tainos sometimes exploited natural resources, replacing trees with cassava fields, for example, but typically put back as much as they extracted from the land. Tainos certainly considered themselves more intelligent and more resourceful than Columbus's men. Columbus and his strange, hairy, Spanish-speaking companions paid little attention to nature and, as a result, struggled to survive.

Columbus called the Tainos "Indians" because he believed he had landed near India. He considered Indians ripe for conversion to "the holy faith of Christ, to which indeed, as far as I can judge, they are very favourable and well-disposed." (Columbus was less sure about other natives who reportedly were "born with tails.") Columbus began to sign his name, "Christoferens," or "Christ-bearer," confident that he had begun a new era in Christianity. Columbus also named many islands after the crown or Christian holy days.[2]

After the Europeans heard that the island which natives called Cuba "abounds in gold," many conquistadors crossed the Atlantic not so much to spread Catholicism but, as one adventurer bluntly put it, "to get rich."[3] Few conquistadors actually got rich, others died in conflict with natives, and more perished unprepared for the unfamiliar environment. Queen Isabella did not support the enslavement of the Tainos, but she did encourage the relocation of indigenous persons near gold mines. The Catholic crown needed resources to extend the empire, and conquistadors could use whatever help they could find.

Conquistadors rarely established means to sustain themselves. After encountering another indigenous group on the mainland, Columbus's men supposedly reappeared just as these natives prepared their noontime meal. The natives shared what they had made, but after Spaniards kept showing up day after day always asking, "What's in the pot?" the leader of the indigenous people, an old man named Nicaragua tried to dissuade the conquistadors from coming back by suggesting that he was cooking "an old Indian." Repulsed by the thought that Indians were cannibals (which they were not), the conquistadors quit showing up begging for food. (To this day the descendants of Nicaragua in the Central American country named for him tell the story of their namesake turning away the conquistadors, and also routinely cook a stew called "Old Indian.")

In 1502 a conquistador's greyhound killed a Taino in eastern Española, which prompted Tainos to ambush and murder some conquistadors, which provoked conquistadors to retaliate, which drove Tainos to kill more

Theodor de Bry depiction, in Bartolome de las, *Casas Brevisima relación de la destrucción de las Indias* (1522)

conquistadors. Some four hundred "gentlemen volunteers," that is, Spanish-speaking fortune-seekers, next descended upon Española to "pacify" (a euphemism for "extermi-nate") the Tainos. Outnumbered four to one, yet equipped with steel, horses, and dogs, conquistadors murdered thousands of Tainos in and around Española. As soldiers prepared to burn one defiant Taino named Hatuey at the stake, a priest offered to baptize him. Hatuey asked, "Where do [the baptized] go after death?" "To Heaven," said the priest, adding that Spanish speakers also enjoy eternal life in the same place. "Then I don't want to go there," concluded Hatuey. "I prefer to go to hell." Soldiers lit the fire.[4]

Queen Isabella died in 1504, Columbus passed away in 1506, and Italian explorer Amerigo Vespucci announced in 1507 that the mainland that he had explored was not India, but a New World. German mapmaker Martin Waldseemüller next coined the term, "America," named from the Latin and feminine form of Vespucci's first name. By this time, conquistadors had begun to import enslaved Africans to fill the void left by the dwindling number of natives. Conquistadors also introduced plants and animals that destroyed the island ecosystem.

In 1510 Dominican priests refused the sacrament of confession to one of the fortune-seekers, Bartolomé de las Casas, for his mistreatment of Tainos and Africans. This censure prompted las Casas to regret his collu-sion in the violence. Las Casas then joined the Dominicans as the first man to be ordained a Catholic priest in the New World. He next begged King Ferdinand "In God's name, [to] consider what sort of deeds are these, and whether they do not surpass every imaginable cruelty and injustice...and whether it could be worse to give the Indians into the charge of the devils of hell than to the Christians of the Indies." The following year, 1511, Pope Julius II established the Diocese of Puerto Rico (now the Diocese of San

Bartolome de las Casas

Juan) as the first American Catholic diocese.[5]

Another fortune-seeker, Juan Ponce de León had meanwhile built profitable plantations in eastern Española and on a nearby island that natives called Boriken, "the great land of the valiant and noble Lord." Columbus had renamed the island the Isla de San Juan Bautista, the Island of Saint John the Baptist (now Puerto Rico). But after Columbus's oldest son, Diego, claimed Ponce de León's holdings as part of the Columbus inheritance, King Ferdinand commissioned Ponce de León to colonize Bimini, a vaguely known island to the north. The sixty-year-old Ferdinand was intrigued by rumors of a fountain of youth called the "secret of Bimini" supposedly located on the island. Ferdinand had just married a twenty-five-year-old French woman with whom he had hoped to conceive a male heir.

The Development of Florida

On March 27, 1513, Ponce de León first sighted Bimini. He renamed it "La Florida," or Florida, "The Flowered One," in honor of the day of discovery, Easter Sunday, or the "day of flowers," as Spanish speakers called it. A week later, Ponce de León landed somewhere on the east coast of Florida. Ponce de León's landing party included a Spanish woman, two free Africans, two indigenous slaves, one European slave, and about sixty other Spanish freemen. Ponce de León tried to make a "good first impression" with indigenous persons he met, but when one of the natives hit a sailor on the head with a stick, Ponce de León supposedly "had to fight [back]," which began another cycle of violence. Ponce de León eventually named an island on the west side of Florida "Matanza" or Slaughter, in memory of the numerous natives his men had killed there (now known as Pine Island near Fort Meyers). Ponce de León explored Florida for two hundred thirty days, and discovered the Gulf Stream (which became the favored route back to Europe), but always thought Florida was an island, and never found Ferdinand's fountain of youth.[6]

While Ponce de León was exploring Florida, about two hundred Caribs, that is, enemies of the Taino from southeast of Española (and from whom the name "Caribbean" is derived), destroyed Ponce de León's home at San Juan Bautista. Ponce de León's wife and children barely escaped with their lives. King Ferdinand ordered Ponce de León to destroy the Caribs. Then return to Florida, Ferdinand instructed Ponce de León, where "by every way and means…[you should] bring [natives] to understand our Catholic faith." But if they do not obey, Ferdinand added, "make war and seize them and take them away as slaves." Upon Ferdinand's death on January 23, 1516, Ferdinand's successor, his grandson Carlos, suspended hostilities against the Caribs. Carlos also united what had been a myriad of Spanish-speaking kingdoms into one country called Spain. Upon the death of another grandfather in 1519, Carlos inherited more of Western Europe, the Hapsburg monarchy, which granted Carlos unprecedented power and authority in the Catholic Church. Catholics thereafter hailed Carlos as Charles V, the Holy Roman Emperor.[7]

Still in 1519, Catholic conquistador Hernán Cortés marched some three hundred fifty Spaniards across the central American mainland carrying a holy card in his pocket and a sword at his side, tearing down temples, erecting altars, and killing anyone who got in the way. Cortés also formed strategic alliances and intimate relationships, including with a woman named La Malinche (after her conversion to Christianity sometimes called Doña Marina). In 1521 La Malinche helped Cortés conquer the wealthy Aztec capital, Tenochtitlán, which Cortés renamed Mexico City. (To this day some Mexicans still call a person who turns their back on their own culture a malinchista after Cortés's mistress.) In addition to La Malinche, Cortés's most powerful weapon may have been disease. Before Cortés had begun his march, thousands of natives had died of smallpox that other conquistadors had unintentionally brought to the mainland.

Hoping for Cortés's type of success, Ponce de León chose the site of the Matanza to establish his colony in west Florida. But this time natives gained the upper hand. In brutal combat, an arrow pierced the thigh of Ponce de León. He died a few days later. Most of his men perished, as well.

The handful of Spaniards who survived the battle abandoned Florida and joined Cortés in Mexico. The Holy Roman Emperor next elevated Cortés to governor of the "New Spain of the Ocean Sea," and Mexico City grew as the epicenter of the Spanish Empire in the New World. By this time Spaniards

Cortes and his translator, La Malinche, holding court

had reduced the one to two million Tainos originally found on Española to a few thousand. The number of enslaved Africans brought over to take their place had grown to about thirty thousand. In 1533 Cortés's distant cousin, Francisco Pizarro conquered the Inca Empire of Peru. Four years later, Pope Paul III declared that the "Indians" already encountered, and those yet to be found "are truly men" deserving liberty and land. But subsequent adventurers paid little attention to the pope.[8]

After Hernando de Soto had amassed a fortune as a subordinate officer in the conquest of Peru, the Holy Roman Emperor granted Soto permission to conquer Florida (at Soto's expense). Soto sighted Florida on May 25, 1539, the feast of the Holy Spirit. Soto anchored at what he called "Espiritu Santo", the Bay of the Holy Spirit (probably Tampa Bay). Nine ships unloaded six hundred men, hundreds of slaves, twelve priests, three hundred horses, and

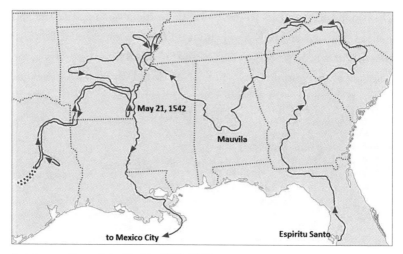

Soto's army through La Florida, 1539–1543

countless pigs. Soto's army marched across what they called the Kingdom of Florida (modern-day Florida, Georgia, South Carolina, Virginia, Tennessee, Alabama, Mississippi, Arkansas, Louisiana, and Texas) not to survey the country, but to find silver and gold, all the while intending to "spread the gospel [only after] they had won and pacified the land."⁹ Soto's army entered many towns, and encountered a wide range of people, some of whom fought each other, and many of whom hated Spaniards. Spanish slave catchers had recently terrorized the land.

Natives asked Soto, "Do you seek peace or war?" Soto claimed peace, though his men carried little food and thus pillaged whatever stocks they could find, and then used the three hundred sets of iron collars they carried with them to enslave natives as porters. "Spaniards [also] threatened to burn the Indians alive if they did not surrender," according to one account. War ensued. One soldier reported that Soto was "much given to the sport of hunting Indians on horseback."¹⁰

At the town of Mauvila (from which Mobile, Alabama, gets its name) Soto's men killed thousands. "The streets could not be traversed," noted an eyewitness, "because of the [number of dead] bodies." Though natives outnumbered Spaniards, horses, dogs, and steel again swung the odds in Soto's favor. Yet Spaniards suffered significant losses, as well. During this and other campaigns, Soto's priests received "the confession of those

"The Burial of De Soto in the Yellow Floods of the Mississippi," unknown artist. Soto's men felled an immense oak, carved a space large enough for his body, nailed planks over the opening, and sunk the tree in the middle of the river.

[Spaniards] who were dying and...[gave] them courage to die well." Soto caught a fever and passed away on May 21, 1542. Attendees claimed, "He died as a Christian Catholic, beseeching mercy of the most Holy Trinity, invoking in his favor and protection the blood of Jesus Christ Our Lord, and calling for the intercession of the Virgin and all the Celestial Court as well as the Faith of the Roman Church." Natives wanted to tear apart Soto's body, which caused Soto's men to sink his remains in the Mississippi River. Bartolomé de las Casas remarked, "We do not doubt...that...[Soto] was buried in hell."[11]

Immediately after Soto's death, his army vowed to "leave [the land of the Indians] as quickly as possible." Natives concluded that Soto's men were "sons of the devil," "professional vagabonds who wander from place to place gaining...livelihood by robbing, sacking, and murdering people who have given no offense." Less than half of the original Spaniards (including none of the clergymen) and twenty-five of the original slaves survived, limping back to Mexico City the middle of 1543. The only riches these Spaniards ever found were pearls stolen from an ancient burial ground. Soto had encouraged his soldiers to use this plunder "to make rosaries on which to pray." Natives shot like wild deer the few surviving horses the Spaniards had left behind, but let pigs wander in their midst and thus allowed pestilence to spread among the estimated five million Native Americans then living in North America. The indigenous population quickly plummeted. In 1549 the Holy Roman Emperor sent five Dominicans to evangelize Florida. Natives slew their leader, Luis Cancer de Balbastro as soon as he stepped ashore.[12]

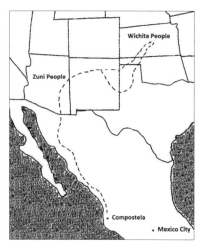

(left) Route of Coronado's Army, 1540–1542.
(below) La Caroline (San Matteo or Saint Matthew), San Agustín (Saint Augustine), and site of the Matanzas.

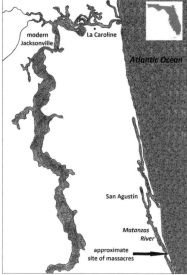

THE SPANISH FRONTIER

Another conquistador, Francisco Vásquez de Coronado, meanwhile led about three hundred soldiers, six Franciscan priests, eight hundred servants, and over a thousand horses from Mexico through the hard, dry terrain of the Rio Grande Valley (into what is now Arizona, New Mexico, Texas, Oklahoma, and Kansas). Coronado sought what a scout had described as one of the seven great cities in the Zuni region. A popular Spanish myth claimed that "Seven Cities of Gold" lay somewhere overseas. Coronado only found small towns. After Coronado's soldiers plundered native food reserves and raped local women, the Pueblo people rebelled. Coronado counterattacked, destroying thirteen villages and killing hundreds of natives, including one hundred warriors who were burned at the stake. Coronado then fled to Mexico, leaving behind a Franciscan priest, Juan de Padilla, who evangelized the Wichita people for a brief time before another group of natives put him to death.

Spaniards for the most part stayed away from the Rio Grande Valley and from Florida for the next decade and a half, that is, until they learned that French Protestants in 1564 had established along the east coast of Florida a settlement called La Caroline. Pedro Menéndez de Avilés immediately led a Spanish armada up the coast to wipe out this "heretic camp." The French intended to surprise the approaching enemy, but a hurricane wrecked the French ships in waters south of La Caroline (near modern Daytona Beach). Menéndez anchored his vessels, marched his men overland through the storm, and murdered every resident of La Caroline over fifteen years of age. Menéndez then renamed the settlement San Mateo, Saint Matthew.[13]

A couple of weeks later, bedraggled French sailors surrendered some forty miles south of Saint Matthew. Spaniards bound the prisoners and ran swords through each captive in what became known as the Matanzas. On the Matanzas River, Spaniards then established on August 28, 1565, that is, the feast of St. Augustine of Hippo, a settlement called San Agustín, or Saint Augustine. Yet Spaniards also maintained Saint Matthew, which thus became the first permanent European occupation of North America. But few Spaniards populated these, and other early Florida settlements, several of which natives destroyed. Menéndez concluded, "It would greatly serve God Our Lord...if these [Indians] were dead."[14]

Spaniards eventually reentered the Rio Grande Valley with royal orders to proceed "peacefully and charitably." In 1598 conquistador Don Juan de Oñate formed a settlement called "New Mexico" with about five hundred colonists, including one hundred twenty-nine soldiers and seven Franciscan friars. Oñate quickly grew obsessed with hope for "extraordinary riches and monstrosities never heard of before." Conflict ensued. Oñate's soldiers raided local food stocks and killed hundreds of men, women, and children "without rhyme or reason,"[15] as one Franciscan moaned. Spanish authorities in Mexico City removed Oñate, and his successor, Don Pedro de Paralta founded a new town, Sante Fe in 1609. By this time the Pueblo people increasingly fell victim to disease.

Over the next several decades, Franciscan friars formed fifty missions in and around the Rio Grande Valley, and gained some converts, but also alienated Spanish authorities with charges of corruption and brutality. By 1638 violence, disease, and famine had cut in half the indigenous population of sixty thousand from forty years before. In 1680 a charismatic shaman named Popé (or Po'pay) led what by then had dwindled to seventeen thousand Pueblo people in an organized revolt at Santa Fe. One historian described what happened: "Venting their rage at eighty years of exploitation, the rebels took special pains to desecrate churches, to smash altars, crosses, and Christian images, and to mutilate the corpses of priests." Natives temporarily recaptured their land.[16]

THE AFTERMATH OF VIOLENCE

The intentional brutality of Spanish conquistadors was horrific, especially since it was committed in the name of God. The retaliation from indigenous peoples was sometimes just as mean. But the unintentional violence was worse. Far more Native Americans died of infectious disease than in combat.

In the end, however, the greatest and longest suffering may have occurred on the first island of encounter. Spanish interest in the Caribbean dissipated as the conquest spread inland, opening the door for France to seize Haiti. In early 1804 the slave population of the western part of the island rebelled and gained independence as a new country named Haiti. But the United States and many European powers refused to recognize this country, fearing that such recognition would excite further slave rebellions. Moreover, France demanded significant compensation to French investors in Haiti who had lost their slaves. The Vatican did not acknowledge Haiti until 1860. As a result of all this abuse and neglect, Haiti became the poorest country in the Americas. (The eastern part of the island progressed more slowly, and with more economic success, eventually as the independent country of the Dominican Republic.)

Nineteenth-century American Catholics acclaimed Christopher Columbus a champion of the Church and hero of the country, "the First Minister of the Christian Religion in America" who had "deemed the salvation of a soul of greater moment than the conquest of an empire." Columbus had followed the will of God by blazing the path for the "heroic" and "gentle" missionaries who "toiled among the Indians…that they might win them from savage ways and lift them up to higher modes of life."[17] In truth, very few Caribbean natives joined the Catholic Church, or even survived Spanish conquest. Into the twentieth century, Haiti descended further into poverty.

"The Landing of Columbus and the Planting of the Cross," unknown artist.

Pope John Paul II visited Haiti on March 9, 1983, boldly proclaiming from the Port-au-Prince airport, "Something must change here." To the chagrin of some observers, however, the pope did not admit to any Catholic complicity in the island's impoverishment. Four years later in Phoenix, Arizona, Pope John Paul II noted the "deeply positive effects" of the first meeting with indigenous persons. This encounter enriched native peoples and the Church, alike, the pope proclaimed. He nonetheless also acknowledged that the encounter included a "harsh and painful reality," oppression, injustice, and disruption of life. Alfretta M. Antone, a local indigenous leader of the time simply prayed that the pope respect "our sacred ways."[18]

In 1992 the American Catholic bishops marked the five-hundredth anniversary of Columbus's landing as a "time of remembering, reconciling, and recommitting ourselves as a Church to the development of the people whose ancestors were here long before the first Europeans came." Insisting that historians "tell the truth," bishops apologized for the "catastrophic consequences" of the first encounters and pledged to fight for social justice on the behalf of indigenous persons. At the same time, bishops echoed the assessment of Pope John Paul II when they acclaimed the significantly positive effects of having brought "to the peoples of this land the gift of the Christian faith with its power of humanization and salvation, dignity and fraternity, justice and love."[19]

By 2000, the number of Catholic Native Americans remained "largely invisible," as the American bishops lamented, comprising a small portion of the total indigenous population. Native Americans constituted, at that time, the fastest-growing segment in the United States and lived everywhere in nearly every diocese, but they were not adequately represented in the Catholic Church, at least in the eyes of American Catholic bishops. Bishops thus concluded that "the oldest ministry of the Church in the United States," that is, outreach to the first peoples of the Americas, had largely been unsuccessful.[20]

On January 12, 2014, the fourth anniversary of the 2010 earthquake that killed 250,000 Haitians, Pope Francis announced the appointment of the first Haitian cardinal, Bishop Chibly Langlois of the southern diocese of Les Cayes. On that occasion Langlois promised, "I'm bringing the reality of the Haitian church to the heart of the College of Cardinals." Langlois added that the Church's reality "is also Haiti's reality." To this day many Haitian Catholics, and some Native Americans, find solace in the Catholic Church. A great many others, especially those who have descended from the first violent encounters with Catholicism in the New World, feel damaged by the history of oppression and neglect, and they consider any affirmation of Christ in the Americas another imposition of colonial control.[21]

CHAPTER TWO

French Black Robes
and a Little Lame Girl

*F*rench, English, and Dutch sailors occasionally attacked colonial towns in New Spain but more often navigated far away from Spanish territory. After King Francis I of France authorized explorers to find new lands to extend the Catholic Church, Jacques Cartier on July 24, 1534, planted a thirty-foot cross bearing the words, "Long Live the King of France" near a native village in the Gulf of St. Lawrence (at what is now called Penouille Point). Cartier asked natives what they called their land, and they said "kanata" which meant "village," but which Cartier misunderstood to mean all the land, and which he consequently called "Canada."

In 1541 Cartier attempted to establish a colony called Charlesbourg-Royal (present-day Cap-Rouge, Quebec), but frigid temperatures, scurvy, and angry natives ran Cartier back to France, where in 1542 he displayed "glittery stones" that he had stolen from natives. Cartier thought the stones were diamonds and gold. They actually were quartz and iron, giving rise to the French expression, *faux comme les diamants du Canada* ("As false as Canadian diamonds").[1]

Subsequent explorers focused on other commodities. Fishermen set up bases at Newfoundland and Acadia (now Nova Scotia), sending salted fish back to Europe in part to satisfy the Catholic prohibition of meat on holy days. Traders also cooperated with native hunters to supply furs for the European market, which had been depleted by overhunting in Europe. Natives grew to covet European goods they received in exchange. One hunter explained,

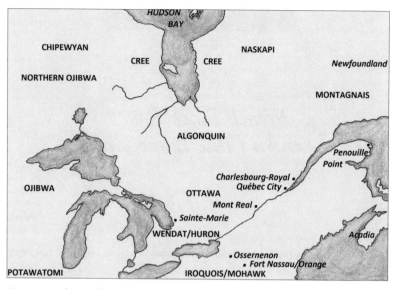

Native peoples and French encounters

"The Beaver does everything perfectly well, it makes Kettles, hatchets, swords, knives, bread [guns and alcohol]; in short, it makes everything."[2]

As the fur industry grew, animals became commodities, natives hunted year round, hunters competed with each other, the environment suffered, and many natives lost their religious conviction that "not only men and other animals, but also all other things, are endowed with souls."[3] In short, holistic sensibilities of Native Americans were threatened by the market economy of Europe.

In the summer of 1608 Frenchman Samuel de Champlain built a small fortified trading post where the St. Lawrence River narrows at the point of Quebec (now Quebec City). Catholics Louis and Marie Hébert built a home and raised a family near the fort, making the Héberts the first real colonists, the "Father [and Mother] of Canada," according to some.[4]

Champlain formed an alliance with the highly organized Wendat, or Huron hunters, and thus alienated Huron enemies to the south, the Five Nation Iroquois. Mad that the Hurons now had a powerful ally in the French, one of the Five Nations, the Mohawks, connected with a Dutch colony called Fort Nassau (later Fort Orange near modern Albany, New

Hébert Monument, Québec City

York) out of which Mohawks sent raiding parties armed with Dutch rifles against the French and against the Hurons.

Hoping to introduce civility among the natives, in 1615 Champlain installed at Quebec four Récollect priests, called "grey friars" because of their dress. According to one account, this most austere of the Franciscan orders quietly went about their business working with natives and Frenchmen alike, "barefooted, save for heavy wooden sandals, coarsely clad in gown and hood, enduring a rigorous climate, to which they were unused."[5]

THE BLACK ROBES ARRIVE

After little success, in 1625 the Récollects invited to Quebec the highly educated Society of Jesus, or Jesuits. Wearing black robes, the first Jesuits to arrive included Jean de Brébeuf, a large and remarkably strong man who soon left Quebec to work among the Hurons to the west in what was called Huronia, eventually establishing what became the hub of Huron evangelization, Sainte-Marie Mission among the Hurons (on the banks of the Isaraqui, now called the Wye River on the southeastern tip of the Georgian Bay of Lake Huron).

With "sincere affection for the Savages" Brébeuf and fellow missionaries studied local customs and learned the native tongue, hoping someday to supplant "savagery and paganism" with civility and Christianity. "Let it be enough," one of the Jesuits remarked, "to keep before our eyes the vision of these poor natives, these images of our God as we are, and as capable of enjoying Him, these companions of our own species, and almost of the same quality as we."[6] Jesuits used words and pictures to convey to natives the pleasures of heaven, the torments of hell, and the life of Jesus. They also taught formulaic prayers, rituals actions (like crossing oneself), and good moral behavior (especially shunning sexual promiscuity).

Jesuit missionaries endured incredible hardship, and displayed unbelievable zeal, all along finding, as one of them put it, "[in] the air of New France the air of Heaven." Brébeuf confessed that, "I was sometimes so weary that the body could do no more, but at the same time my soul experienced very deep peace, considering that I was suffering for God."[7] For seventeenth-century Catholics, especially for Jesuits, struggles on earth meant nothing compared to the rewards of heaven. Hurons were impressed by the spiritual strength and moral character of the Jesuits, who unlike French traders, did not exploit women. Moreover Jesuits cared little for fish and fur.

Brébeuf attributed much of the challenges that he faced to widespread illness. As had been the case in New Spain, in New France, Europeans unknowingly brought infectious diseases. During the 1630s, influenza, measles, and smallpox wiped out half the Hurons, reducing their number to around eleven thousand. Survivors wondered why they died in such great number, especially since the widespread deaths began right after the Jesuits had moved among them. Natives also asked why the Jesuits did not similarly fall ill.

Though not understanding how disease was transmitted, Jesuits surely recognized that illness was often associated with their presence, with one priest confessing that, "No doubt we carried misery with us, since, wherever we set foot, either death or disease followed us."[8] While Brébeuf considered one of his greatest assets to be his good health—like most Europeans he was immune to the diseases—many Hurons began to suspect that Jesuits were sorcerers who spread death especially while dispensing their so-called life-giving waters of baptism.

Dutch traders communicated smallpox to the Mohawks in 1634. At least half and likely three-fourths of the Mohawk population perished over the next year, dropping from around twelve thousand to perhaps three thousand, that is, twenty-five deaths per day. To appease their grief, Iroquois warriors searched for captives to replace the dead, particularly targeting Hurons. Through the 1640s and 1650s Iroquois attacked and killed with unprecedented ferocity.

Isaac Jogues

In August 1642, Jesuit Isaac Jogues paddled with two Frenchmen and thirty-seven Christian Hurons up the St. Lawrence River toward the Huron mission when Iroquois warriors attacked. Jogues safely hid but came out of hiding after the Iroquois captured about half of Jogues's companions. "Could I indeed," he said to himself, "abandon our French and leave those good Neophytes and those poor Catechumens, without giving them the help which the Church of my God has entrusted me."[9] Jogues willingly surrendered.

RAMPAGE, CAPTIVITY, AND DEATH

The Iroquois marched their captives to the village of Ossernenon (now Auriesville, above Albany, New York), where they ripped out Jogues's fingernails, cut off his left thumb, and chewed off most of his right index finger. As was true throughout much of Europe at that time, brutal torture was common in certain parts of the Americas. On September 29, the Iroquois killed René Goupil, a French surgeon and Jesuit lay brother, after he had made the sign of the cross on an Iroquois child. The Iroquois subsequently tortured other native and nonnative prisoners, including some captives from the newly established French fort of Mont Real (now Montreal).

After more than a year of captivity, Jogues wrote a letter to the governor of New France explaining that, though Dutch traders from Fort Orange were bargaining for his release, "I become more and more resolved to dwell here as long as it shall please Our Lord, and not to go away, even though an opportunity should present itself. My presence consoles the French, [and] the Hurons.... I have baptized more than sixty persons, several of whom have arrived in Heaven."[10]

The Dutch eventually ransomed Jogues from the Iroquois, and gave him passage to New Amsterdam (now New York) and then to France. On January 5, 1644, Jogues knocked at the door of the Jesuit College at Rennes. The porter informed the rector that an unidentified man had news of Canada.

The rector came down to ask the man, "Are you acquainted with Father Isaac Jogues?" "I know him very well," the man said. The rector continued, "We have had word that he was taken by the Hiroquois; is he dead? is he still captive? Have not those Barbarians slain him?" "He is at liberty," the man answered, "and it is he, my Reverend Father, who speaks to you."[11]

Catholic Europeans heralded Jogues a "living martyr," and Pope Urban VIII designated the Sainte-Marie Mission "a place of pilgrimage," the first of its kind in North America. The pope also granted Jogues a dispensation to say Mass. Church law of the time dictated that the Eucharist could only be touched by the thumb and forefinger. Jogues's badly mangled hands were missing at least one of each of these digits.[12]

Physically broken yet spiritually undeterred, in the spring of 1644, Jogues returned to Canada. Jogues eventually led a party into Iroquois territory to negotiate peace, but was captured and marched again to Ossernenon. On October 18, 1646, an Iroquois warrior tomahawked Jogues's head in two. When a Jesuit brother named Jean de Lalande attempted to recover Jogues's body, the Iroquois killed Lalande, as well, and then threw both bodies into the Mohawk River.

Iroquois warriors later stormed numerous Huron villages, including Saint Joseph Mission, twelve miles from Sainte-Marie, on July 4, 1648. Jesuit Antoine Daniel hastily baptized Hurons who thronged around him and then ran to the church screaming, "Today we will be in Paradise; believe this, hope this, that God may forever love you." French Catholics were obsessed at this time with experiencing what they called a "beautiful death."[13] A musket ball took Daniel's life, Iroquois pummeled his body, and set fire to the entire mission, including the church, which consumed Daniel's remains.

The morning of March 16, 1649, Iroquois warriors descended upon Saint Ignace, six miles from Sainte-Marie, seized Jean de Brebeuf and a newcomer to the missions, Gabriel Lalemant, and set fire to the village. An eyewitness recounted that the Iroquois then "proceeded to vent their rage on those two Fathers." The Iroquois beat every part of Brebeuf's body, during which he encouraged "all the new Christians who were captives like himself to suffer well, that they might die well, in order to go in company with him to Paradise."[14]

MORT DES PP, LALEMANT ET DE BRÉBEUF.

The death of Fathers Gabriel Lalemant and Jean de Brébeuf

A Huron who had been baptized by Brebeuf and who had been previously captured and adopted by the Iroquois, next supposedly proclaimed, "thou sayest that Baptism and the sufferings of this life lead straight to Paradise; thou wilt go soon, for I am going to baptize thee, and to make thee suffer well, in order to go the sooner to thy Paradise." The Huron dumped a kettle of boiling water three times over Brebeuf, who kept praising God. This provoked the Iroquois to cut out his tongue.[15]

Brebeuf breathed his last when the Iroquois tore out and ate his heart. The Iroquois explained that Brebeuf "had been very courageous to endure so much pain as they had given him, and that, by drinking his blood, they would become courageous like him."[16] No one recorded the details of Lalemant's death, but fellow Jesuits subsequently gathered up and revered both Lalemant and Brebeuf's bones.

FLIGHT FROM TORMENT

Jesuits at Sainte-Marie assumed the Iroquois would attack them next and thus abandoned the mission, set fire to everything, paddled into the lake, and relocated the besieged Hurons nearby at what the Jesuits called Sainte-Marie

II on Saint Joseph's Island (now Christian Island in the Georgian Bay). "In times of dire distress," one Jesuit reported, "we should flee with the fleeing."[17] The Jesuits dug up the remains of Brebeuf and Lalemant, preserved the bones, and took them with them.

As a safety precaution Jesuit authorities also separated missionaries who remained on land, sending Noël Chabanel, for example, away from the remote mission of Saint Jean, some thirty miles from Sainte-Marie II. At three o'clock on the afternoon of December 7, 1649, the Iroquois descended upon Saint Jean, set homes on fire, killed many Hurons, and took some captives. The lone Jesuit still at the mission, Charles Garnier, ran to the church where he instructed the Hurons hidden there, "May death find you with God in mind." Garnier baptized as many Hurons as he could before two bullets struck him down. One woman later reported seeing Garnier dragging his dying body toward another injured man "in order to assist him in dying well."[18]

That night, Chabanel heard Iroquois parade Saint Jean captives through the woods in which Chabanel was resting. Chabanel awoke his fellow travelers, seven or eight Christian Hurons who scattered to avoid detection. After the Iroquois passed, Chabanel's companions reversed their course and marched back to Saint Jean. Chabanel walked with them for a while before falling exhausted, saying to the Hurons, "It matters not that I die; this life is a very small consideration; of the blessedness of Paradise, the Iroquois can never rob me."[19]

Chabanel had already suffered what he called a "bloodless Martyrdom" enduring six trying years in the missions. He could not speak the Huron language and reportedly saw in natives "scarce anything that pleased him; the sight of them, their talk, and all that concerned them, he found irksome." Chabanel detested the food, the work, and the living arrangements. He lived in constant fear of the Iroquois. To his blood brother, a fellow Jesuit, Chabanel confessed that he longed for martyrdom, only lamenting that "to merit the honor…a virtue of another stamp than mine is needed."[20]

The Hurons heading back to Saint Jean left Chabanel in the woods, after which Chabanel changed his course and walked toward Sainte-Marie II. On the banks of the Nottawasaga River, still twenty-five miles from his destination, another Huron saw Chabanel lay down his bag evidently to ease his burden while crossing. No one knows what happened next, but the Jesuits guessed that the Huron, who had been baptized but had since left the faith, wanted Chabanel's bag and thus murdered him. Chabanel's body was never found.

After a bitter winter during which many natives starved, the Jesuits abandoned Sainte-Marie II and the entire Huron mission, fleeing the summer of 1650 with a few hundred Christian Hurons back to Quebec. By this time the Iroquois had destroyed nearly every Huron village. Due to war and disease, the Huron population had fallen by this time over 70 percent, down to perhaps 6,500 persons. The Iroquois nation meanwhile rose with the adoption of war captives, who soon outnumbered old-stock Iroquois.

KATERI TEKAKWITHA

Not finished grieving, that is, with vengeance still on their minds, Mohawk warriors turned to the east, capturing among many others an unnamed Catholic Algonquin woman near Three Rivers, between Montreal and Quebec. Mohawks marched the woman to the Iroquois village near Fort Orange. She married an Iroquois man and gave birth to a son and, around 1656, to a daughter called Tekakwitha. Six years later, smallpox took probably all of Tekakwitha's immediate family. Smallpox shattered Tekakwitha's health, scarred her face, and rendered her eyesight so sensitive that Tekakwitha wore a blanket over her head the rest of her life.

In 1666, French soldiers gained control of the area where Tekakwitha lived. French Jesuits moved in, but after six years conceded that the Iroquois could not be converted as a people. Iroquois continued their violent campaigns, with Tekakwitha routinely horrified by Iroquois warriors running captives through the gauntlet. Jesuits focused on a minority of converts, sending dying Iroquois who were willing to be baptized to heaven and living Iroquois who had embraced the church to a Christian settlement at Kentake (later Kahnawake) near Montreal.

In 1675 Jesuit priest Jacques de Lamberville told nineteen-year-old Tekakwitha, still in New York, about the joys of heaven. For someone who had suffered so much on this earth, word of a better life beyond must have brought great consolation. Tekakwitha thereafter routinely prayed with some other Mohawks, mostly women, in the mission chapel. On Easter Sunday 1676, Lamberville baptized Tekakwitha. She took the name Catherine in honor of Catherine of Siena, the fourteenth-century saint whom the Jesuits had made popular among native peoples.

The following year, Catherine moved to Kahanwake, where an old friend of her mother's, an Iroquois convert named Anastasia, taught Catherine "the way of life of the good Christians." But in early 1678 an Iroquois woman accused Catherine of having sex with her husband while on a hunting trip. One of the Jesuits thought the accusation might be true.[21]

Another Iroquois convert, Marie-Thérèse, meanwhile harbored another, more certain "guilty secret": after most of her hunting party had starved to death, Marie-Thérèse had survived by eating the flesh of the dead, including that of her husband. Marie-Thérèse thereafter beat herself, perhaps mimicking the self-inflicted punishment of some of the Catholic saints, and also reflecting the violent practices of grieving Iroquois.[22]

Marie-Thérèse shared her secret with Catherine, and the two women began to beat each other until their shoulders bled. In time, a few other women joined in these mortifications. Catherine, or "the little lame girl," as admirers started to call her, also slept on a bed of thorns—the Jesuits had told her that Aloysius Gonzaga, the sixteenth-century Italian Jesuit (later canonized a saint) had done this. Catherine's mortifications undoubtedly hastened her death on Holy Thursday, April 17, 1680. It was an extraordinary death, at least according to subsequent accounts, during which Catherine's corpse released the pain of a lifetime and was miraculously transformed into some kind of angelic state.[23]

Over subsequent days Catherine supposedly appeared to former friends, including Jesuit Claude Chauchetiére. Chauchetiére heralded Catherine a saint, wrote a glorious account of her life, and insisted that her bones be buried in the church. Pilgrims began to visit Catherine's remains, with miraculous events occasionally associated with her relics. Similar reverence grew for the legend and the remains of the eight French Jesuits whom the Iroquois had martyred.

Veneration of Catherine and of the Jesuit martyrs increased over time. Catherine was acclaimed as the "Lily of the Mohawks," and after the early twentieth century her name was rendered as "Kateri" Tekakwitha. The National Shrine of the North American Martyrs was meanwhile dedicated at Auriesville, New York, in 1885. In 1907, Archbishop Dennis O'Connor of Toronto consecrated a small chapel near the site where Iroquois had killed Brébeuf and Lalemant.

In 1925 Pope Pius XI beatified all eight Jesuit martyrs. Jesuit John Filion thereafter oversaw construction of a new Martyrs' Shrine at the site of Sainte-Marie, now Midland, Ontario. The stone exterior reflects the Belgian Gothic style, and the dark cottonwood interior looks like a Huron residence or longhouse. The ceiling resembles an inverted canoe. When storms hit during early Canadian history, traveling Hurons found refuge on land under overturned canoes. On June 25, 1926, Cardinal William Henry O'Connell of Boston consecrated the shrine, which has since become a site of refuge for countless pilgrims from around the world. In 1930 Pius XI canonized the eight Jesuit martyrs.[24]

In 1980 Pope John Paul II declared Kateri Tekakwitha blessed. The pope acclaimed Kateri for her dedication to Christ as well as for "always remain[ing]...what she was, a true daughter of her people, following her tribe in hunting seasons and continuing her devotions in the environment most suited to her way of life." Four years later, John Paul II visited the Martyrs' Shrine, where he honored the sacrifice of the Jesuit martyrs and also pointed out the contributions of Hurons such as Joseph and Aonnetta Chiwatenwa, early converts who "became evangelizers and provide even today eloquent models for lay ministry." With Brebeuf, John Paul II "dreamed of a Church fully Catholic and fully Huron," explaining that "not only is Christianity relevant to the Indian peoples, but Christ, in the members of His Body, is himself Indian."[25] John Paul II then prayed over the fractured skull of Brébeuf. Pope Benedict XVI canonized Kateri Tekakwitha on Sunday, October 21, 2012.

CHAPTER THREE

English Gentlemen
and Their Servants

Shortly after France began to invest in North America, England laid its claim. Anglicans founded the first permanent British settlement in the Americas at Jamestown in 1607, and Puritans landed the *Mayflower* at Plymouth, Massachusetts, in 1620. Both Anglicans and Puritans disliked Catholics, partly due to a general misunderstanding of what Catholicism was all about. Since Henry VIII had separated from the Catholic Church the previous century, many English citizens had come to believe that Catholicism represented the anti-Christ. British Catholic investment in North America was a bit complicated.

George Calvert was baptized Catholic, but British authorities removed him from his parents' home when he was a young boy after his parents had failed to attend Anglican services as the law had prescribed. Calvert was thereafter raised by Anglicans. As a young man, Calvert won over the royal family, eventually serving as secretary of state and a member of the king's advisory council. These positions earned Calvert enough money to invest in North America.

In 1620, Calvert purchased from the King of England the middle of the Canadian island of Newfoundland. Calvert commissioned Anglican Edward Wynne to settle this purchase. In August 1621, Wynne landed twenty-five men and seven women on a small peninsula that French fishermen had called Forillon or Foriland, which meant "standing out from the mainland." Wynne anglicized the name to Ferryland.

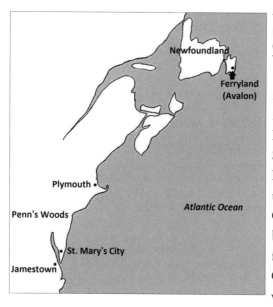

The settlements of Ferryland and St. Mary's City

Calvert then tried to negotiate the engagement of King James I's son, Charles, to a Spanish Catholic bride. Parliament balked at the prospect of a future Catholic queen, and blackballed Calvert for his promotion of Catholicism. Calvert's wife next died, and a series of personal troubles ensued, which prompted Calvert to revert back to his childhood faith. In 1624 Calvert proclaimed that he was Catholic. He then resigned all his political appointments. The following year, King James I rewarded Calvert for past service to the crown by appointing him Lord of Baltimore, in County Longford, Ireland.

Ferryland's new association with Catholicism meanwhile prompted the colony's Anglican Governor, Edward Wynne, to leave the settlement. British authorities had recently charged many priests with treason. Priests were not loyal to the state, British authorities had claimed, because priests followed a foreign pope. The few priests who survived this persecution tended to serve wealthy families, while laywomen, especially Catholic mothers, assumed greater responsibility for transmitting the faith. Assisting the Calvert household, Catholic priest Simon Stock recommended that Calvert pick as Wynne's replacement Sir Arthur Aston, "a Catholic knight and dear friend, who for many years has fought in the wars against Turks and infidels."[1]

After Calvert appointed Aston governor of Ferryland, and after Aston sailed with about twenty Catholics to Ferryland the end of May 1625, Father Stock begged his religious order, the Discalced Carmelites, to send missionaries to Calvert's colony, now called Avalon. Missionaries had first preached Christianity at a place called Avalon in England. From Avalon, in Newfoundland, Stock hoped to spread Catholicism. "English heretics have [already] sown their heresy in all the northern parts of America," Stock had warned.[2]

About a year later, and amidst glowing reports from Governor Aston, the Discalced Carmelites asked Stock to go to Avalon. Anti-Catholic persecution had risen in England with two Discalced Carmelites who had been slated for Avalon thrown in jail. About the only priest left in England who could possibly serve Avalon was Stock. But Stock refused to go, claiming that he was needed in England. In late 1626 Aston returned to London with his Catholic colonists, leaving some Protestants to defend Newfoundland against possible attacks. Looming French pirates were less than pleased that British folks were laying claim to Newfoundland.

CALVERT IN THE NEW WORLD

George Calvert decided to take matters into his own hands, arriving at Avalon the summer of 1627. After a pleasant few months, Calvert returned to England where he secured from King Charles I permission to establish permanent residence at the colony. (Charles I was King James I's son, whom Calvert had unsuccessfully tried to marry to a Catholic.) Aiming to relocate the Calvert family manor in the New World, in June 1628 Calvert returned to Avalon with his family, about forty Catholics, and two unnamed priests.

Calvert insisted that Catholic colonists live side by side and even worship under the same roof as the larger contingent of sixty or so non-Catholic settlers. Calvert could hardly expect to make money if the work force was segregated along religious lines. Calvert first of all wanted to turn a profit and consequently butted heads with the two priests, as well as with the leaders of the non-Catholic majority, who did not approve of Calvert's open religious policy.

French pirates continued to threaten the colony, but in the end, weather foiled Calvert's investment. "From the middle of October to the middst of May," Calvert reported, "there is a sadd face of wynter upon all this land... no plant or vegetable thing appearing out of the earth...nor fish in the sea...

the air so intolerable cold as it is hardly to be endured."[3] Calvert's residence became a hospital, with as many as fifty settlers sick at one time. Nine or ten persons died.

Charles I advised Calvert to return to England, explaining that "men of yor condition and breeding are fitter for other imployments, than the framing of new plantations." Before the next cold season, Calvert, some of his family, the two priests, and the forty Catholic colonists sought a warmer climate, eventually eyeing open land just north of Jamestown. Calvert returned to England hoping that the king would grant him that land, but then Calvert died on April 15, 1632.[4]

Two months later, Charles I granted Calvert's son Cecil, the second Lord Baltimore, a charter for the uncolonized land his father had spied north of Jamestown. Charles I bestowed on Cecil Calvert more power than previously issued to other investors in Virginia and Massachusetts. Calvert was to be the absolute "Lord and Proprietary" empowered to recreate a new society using England as the model. Calvert was required only to deliver two Indian arrows to Windsor Castle every Easter Tuesday.

Calvert named his colony "Maryland" in honor of the King's French wife, Henrietta Marie. Consistent with earlier Calvert investments, Maryland was to be an economic adventure with profit, not religion, the primary impulse. Though Catholic, Calvert did not intend to found a Catholic refuge and never put the interests of the Catholic Church above the interests of the colony.

Calvert nonetheless did invite Catholics to Maryland. He put his brother, Leonard, in charge; talked other family members into supporting the enterprise; and readied two ships for passage. But few Catholics were willing to leave England at that time. Anti-Catholicism rose and fell in England often in conjunction with the nation's general well-being, and the 1630s were a prosperous, and therefore peaceful, decade.

English Jesuits, on the other hand, were keenly interested in the religious prospects of Maryland. Two Jesuit priests and one Jesuit brother agreed to go overseas and then secured funds to pay for the trip of about thirty other passengers. Explaining that they intended to bring salvation to Maryland natives (and probably promoting the possibility of amassing wealth in North America) Jesuits also convinced about twenty or so wealthy, but younger,

Matthias de Sousa, from Old Saint Mary's Monument, Old Saint Mary's, Maryland

sons to agree to move to Maryland. These sons stood to inherit little from their fathers' estates. These sons, so-called "gentlemen investors," covered expenses for the rest of the travelers as well. Two wealthy women also agreed to come. Though no passenger list survives, of the 140 or so estimated colonists, these wealthy ones probably constituted almost all the Catholics on board.

The rest of the travelers came over mostly as indentured servants. In payment for passage, each servant, generally young men from fifteen to twenty-four years of age, agreed to work free of charge for his wealthy benefactor for a period of about five years. After this time, the servant would be awarded "freedom dues," which often included some land, a plough, and a new suit of clothes. The Jesuits imported an indentured servant named Matthias de Sousa who probably was Catholic, and who was listed as a "Molato," or mulatto, that is, a person with mixed (likely African and Portuguese) heritage.[5]

Calvert's brother, Leonard, also may have brought an African slave named Jowett. Slaves certainly were part of the Maryland experience early on, though they constituted a very small segment of the population and were often confused with indentured servants. In theory, at least, indentured servants had fixed terms. Slaves were generally bound for life. But many indentured servants never enjoyed freedom (many died before the term of indenture ended), while some slaves seemed to live as if they were free.

DIFFERING OBJECTIVES

Although Jesuits had grand hopes for spreading Catholicism, Calvert did not. On the eve of the ships' departure, Calvert admonished the Catholics on board to "be very careful to preserve unity and peace...suffer no scandal nor offense to be given to any of the Protestants…and…for that end…cause all Acts of Romane Catholique Religion to be done as privately as may be, and…instruct all the Romane Catholiques to be silent upon all occasions of discourse concerning matters of religion."[6]

Calvert did not display a systematic understanding of religious matters, yet was attuned to the mixed religious reality of his new community. Calvert hoped that the same type of reserved Catholicism that had survived in England could provide the necessary privacy and safety for Catholic investment in the New World. By promoting religious tolerance, Calvert (along with his father before him) advanced the same type of openness that William Penn some fifty years later would advance in his "Holy Experiment" in Penn's Woods (now Pennsylvania).

Yet Maryland was more than an investment. Whereas Avalon had been conceived as a small fishing station with little social cohesion, from the start, Maryland was to be a grand British manor. Calvert was to be the lord of the manor, and below him would spread out a hierarchy of power controlled by the landed aristocracy. As in England, strong family structures and a diverse economy would be put in place in Maryland. Profit remained the objective, though survival in Maryland, especially for Catholics, would take place in the same complex manner as it had in England.

Calvert's 360-ton *Ark of Avalon* and forty-ton pinnace, or supply ship, the *Dove*, entered open seas on November 23, 1633, the feast day of Saint Clement. After navigating across the Atlantic, the ships entered the Chesapeake Bay, moved up the mouth of the Potomac River, and on March 25, 1634, landed on a 400-acre sandbar that was covered with herons. Jesuit Andrew White celebrated Mass later that day. "This had never been done before in this part of the world," White beamed.[7]

Hardly heeding Calvert's instructions to keep Catholicism private, some of the travelers next planted a large cross and christened the sandbar Saint Clement's Island in honor of the feast day of their departure. They then moved ashore. For a "trifle," that is, for some hatchets, axes, hoes, and cloth, the newcomers purchased thirty miles of land from the native Yaocomicoes people, including some half-oval shaped huts. Colonists took up residence in the huts, and a new economic adventure was underway.[8]

Conflicts with Virginia merchants, struggles with local leaders, lack of settlers, and various other inherent difficulties, including religious conflict, threatened the colony early on. Insisting that Maryland be governed by a loose plan of religious freedom, Leonard Calvert converted one of the Yaocomico huts into a place of worship for all Christians—Catholics and non-Catholics alike. But some of the Catholic gentry and, more emphatically, the Jesuit priests argued that they deserved special treatment, including the benefits that they would have received in a European Catholic country. Calvert wanted to offer some sanctions to Catholics, and eventually granted a few immunities to the Jesuits, but also felt committed to a system without religious favoritism.

CONFLICT WITH THE JESUITS

Lacking special favor from the state, Jesuits learned to sustain themselves. Jesuits ministered to the Catholic gentry and tried to reach out to natives, but more often slipped into the role of "English gentlemen," as one early observer noted, "well informed and of sterling virtue." Jesuits went to great lengths "to import from England, all their shrubs, fruit trees and garden seeds...[keeping] their garden in a very flourishing state." In about 1636, Leonard Calvert sold to the Jesuits the slave Jowett, along with a few parcels of land in the newly laid-out Saint Mary's City in what was called Saint Mary's County.[9]

In 1637 Jesuits acquired three thousand additional acres that they christened Saint Inigoes in honor of the founder of the Jesuits, Ignatius Loyola. The Jesuits entrusted Saint Inigoes to a local Catholic, Cuthbert Fenwick, who rented out some of the property to former indentured servants. Jesuits relied on income from Saint Inigoes (augmented by donations from Europe) to allow them to pursue their primary reason for coming to America, namely, the conversion of indigenous peoples. But Jesuits did not have much success in bringing natives to Catholicism.

Jesuits certainly did not minister to working-class Catholics. Jesuits figured that the religious needs of these people were the responsibility of secular priests. But Jesuits were reluctant to allow secular priests to come to Maryland, and even prevented their migration. The population of working-class Catholics nonetheless increased. Their ranks soon outnumbered the original gentlemen investors nine to one.

Arguing that clerical service was everyone's "birthright," the early Maryland Assembly legislated that Jesuits serve common people. Still dominated by a small but powerful number of Catholics, the assembly outlawed priest ownership of property and prohibited priest involvement with Native Americans. The assembly also ordered Jesuits to give lectures and perform Sunday services, baptisms, marriages, and burials. Some Jesuits considered the newly legislated ministerial duties "inconvenient," and others got around the prohibition against owning land by transferring all Jesuit assets to lay trustees.[10] A few Jesuits nonetheless also began to minister to the common people.

In 1638, Protestants and Catholics built Saint Mary's chapel on land in Saint Mary's City held by Jesuit trustees. The chapel was designated for use by all Christians. Yet virtually no Protestant clergy were present at this time, and Jesuits primarily led services. As a result, many of the formerly non-churched Marylanders, along with nearly all the hundred or so Protestants who migrated to Maryland the year the chapel was built, became Catholic. Catholics remained in the minority, even though they certainly were the best served by any institutional church.

After Oliver Cromwell's Puritans seized control of England in the early 1640s, in 1645 Puritans in Maryland joined Anglicans in Virginia to run Leonard Calvert, the Jesuits, and a few other leading Catholics out of Maryland, plundering Catholic property in Saint Mary's City and at Saint Inigoes along the way. Order was eventually restored, and Leonard Calvert resumed his role as governor, but as a result of this crisis, Calvert removed certain privileges previously enjoyed by Catholics. Jesuits could no longer screen property under the cover of a trust, and no Marylander could thereafter transfer any property to the Jesuits. Jesuits in Rome meanwhile assumed that Maryland had been lost, especially after Leonard Calvert passed away in June 1647.

On January 21, 1648, the executor of Calvert's will, a prominent landowner named Margaret Brent, asked the Maryland Provincial Council for the right to vote. Brent actually asked to vote twice, once as an independent landowner and once as Calvert's attorney. Brent's petition constituted the first such request put forth in the Americas by a woman. Governor Thomas Greene refused Brent's petition, declaring that such privileges for women were reserved for queens. Brent stormed out of the assembly declaring that she "protested against all proceedings...unless she may be present and have vote as aforesaid."[11]

In August 1648, Cecil Calvert installed the first Protestant governor, William Stone, but also promoted the Act Concerning Religion, the so-called Toleration Act, which the Maryland Assembly passed in April 1649. This act aimed to protect Catholics (and other non-Anglicans) in the colony. What Calvert had earlier implied, he now made clear, namely, that all Christians would be welcomed in Maryland, even though no individual group would enjoy special rights.

Catholics were not free from persecution, but one of the ousted Jesuits, Thomas Copley, nonetheless reclaimed some of the Saint Mary's City property and all of Saint Inigoes. The slave Jowett returned to Copley as well. As compensation for Jesuits having brought a total of sixty indentured servants to the colony, the Maryland Assembly also granted Copley four thousand acres on the Potomac River near Port Tobacco. The Jesuits christened this property Saint Thomas Manor. Copley and the handful of Jesuits who succeeded him developed Saint Inigoes and Saint Thomas Manor into profitable farms.

That development was not easy. In 1655 a large influx of Puritans made Maryland overwhelmingly Protestant. Maryland Puritans ousted Calvert's government and again plundered Saint Inigoes. The Jesuits escaped to Virginia, where they reportedly had "no servant either for domestic purposes, or to guide them through unknown and suspected localities, or to row and steer their boat when that is used."[12] Other accounts similarly described Jesuits as helplessly lost when traveling alone, especially when navigating through unknown and sometimes unfriendly territory. One Jesuit actually lost his life when trying to cross a swollen stream all by himself.

Assistance came from a handful of Jesuit brothers, and indentured servants also helped out, but the last servants known to have been imported by the Jesuits probably had ended their indenture a decade ago. Jowett and his family must have provided the most reliable and consistent service.

After Cecil Calvert recovered Maryland in 1657, the Jesuits returned, again reclaiming Saint Inigoes and Saint Thomas, and again reuniting with Jowett. As Jowett's descendants put it, Jowett was "always loyal to the Fathers."[13]

With an increased number of slaves in the colony, Maryland began to define slavery. In 1661, Cecil Calvert sent his twenty-four-year-old Catholic son, Charles Calvert, over from England to govern Maryland. Under Charles Calvert's rule, the colonial government declared that "all Negroes and other slaves already within the Province And all Negroes and other slaves to bee hereafter imported into the Province shall serve *Durante Vita* [or for life]."[14] While other English territories enslaved only non-Christians, in Maryland, lifelong service would be guaranteed regardless of the professed religion of the slave. In other words, baptism would not constitute grounds for manumission in Maryland.

Maryland slaveholders were not only obligated to baptize slaves but were reprimanded for failing to instruct slaves in the Christian faith. Slavery never constituted a huge part of seventeenth-century Maryland, with only 10 percent of the known three hundred or so slaveholders of southern Maryland owning more than ten slaves. Emerging legislation nonetheless suggested that slavery was becoming a more recognizable part of the Maryland landscape.

SERVANTS AND SLAVES

Indentured servitude also remained part of the Maryland scene. A tailor at Saint Mary's City named John Shirtcliffe paid traveling expenses for his cousin, an eighteen-year-old illiterate laborer named Thomas Spalding of Suffolk County, England, to work Shirtcliffe's property on the west side of Bretton's Bay in Maryland. Each year from 1650 to 1690, Maryland colonists like Shirtcliffe imported about one thousand indentured servants like Spalding. Indentured servants arrived from various locations in England. They brought diverse skills and usually were in their late teens or early twenties.

Upon Shirtcliffe's death in 1663, Spalding received fifty acres of land, which constituted at that time about the minimum size for a viable farm. The average landholder in Saint Mary's County held about two hundred and fifty acres. In all likelihood, Spalding's new land signaled part of his freedom dues and the end of his indenture. Opportunities for freed servants to advance had been abundant. Many former servants had acquired large tracts of land and had participated in government, with some freed men becoming prominent leaders in the community. By the time Spalding was set free, such opportunities still existed, but were harder to come by.

Like many former servants, Spalding moved slowly into his freed state, for some time continuing to work for his former mistress, the widow Ann Shirtcliffe. In 1667, she compensated Spalding with one hundred and sixteen acres. Shirtcliffe may have employed Spalding after this time. Spalding also began to attend to his land, what he called "Saint Giles," named after an eighth-century hermit who initially was associated with France and who had become popular among English Catholics.

In about 1673, Spalding married Catherine Hall, another former servant. Lieutenant Colonel John Jarboe, a prominent Frenchman who had been in the colony for nearly thirty years, had brought Hall to Maryland perhaps four or five years earlier. Throughout the seventeenth century, male servants outnumbered female servants three to one, while women in general consti- tuted a little less than a quarter of the total population of Maryland. Probably serving as a household servant to Jarboe, Hall would have prepared food, washed clothes, and occasionally worked the fields.

Hall must have been a few years younger than Spalding, that is, in her mid-twenties, if she were typical for a female servant bride in colonial Maryland. Spalding was thirty-three-years-old at the time of his marriage. Both men and women who had been servants tended to marry later than did persons who arrived in the colony totally free. The relative lateness with which former servants married, along with the high infant mortality rate, generally limited their number of children. Against the odds, Catherine and Thomas Spalding raised five sons and an unrecorded number of daughters.

Catherine and Thomas Spalding invested earnings in more land, and climbed the economic ladder, though they were never rich. Like couples with similar backgrounds, the Spaldings probably lived simple lives. They almost never showed up in public records. Land and livestock accounted for their worth. Clothing and household furnishings would have been meager. They worked the fields and passed down property to subsequent generations.

Children of former servants rarely exceeded their parents' economic status. While initial profit from new property was significant, once major improvements—such as clearing the land, acquiring livestock, and cultivating orchards—had been completed, income tended to level off. In southern Maryland the early growth spurt ended in the 1680s. Children inheriting land after this time typically did not rise up the economic ladder. Catholic offspring nevertheless proved more apt to prosper, with association to the close-knit Catholic community evidently rendering a person less vulnerable to economic hardship.

In spite of the increased legislation that distinguished servants from slaves, personal motivations sometimes kept the distinctions blurred. To wash his clothes, Charles Calvert had brought with him to Maryland an Irish girl named Eleanor Butler. "Irish Nell," as Butler was called, boarded with Calvert's friend, a prominent Catholic slaveholder named Major William Boarman of Charles County. In time, Irish Nell fell in love with Charles, a slave owned by Boarman. Charles and Irish Nell planned to marry in 1681 in a thirty- by twenty-foot chapel that Boarman had built two years earlier right on his property. Such house churches were common among wealthy Maryland Catholics.

But the morning of the wedding, Calvert cautioned Irish Nell against marriage. Colonial law stipulated that a white woman marrying a black man enslaved not only herself, but all of her descendants. Irish Nell did not care, supposedly retorting that "she had rather marry the Negro under them circumstances, than to marry his Lordship with his Country." Calvert next told Irish Nell "she might go marry him, and be damned."[15] Richard Hubbert, one of the few Franciscan priests to live in colonial Maryland, performed the ceremony. Numerous white people attended.

Charles Calvert afterward worked on Irish Nell's behalf to pass a hastily written law that repealed prior legislation by implying that the offspring of a black male voluntarily wed to a white female would be free. But this law was widely ignored, even in the case of Charles and Irish Nell. Irish Nell spent her remaining years free, but Charles and their six children, along with what would become hundreds of descendants, were enslaved to Major Boarman and his offspring. Other persons joined through, or descendants from, so-called mixed marriages similarly were enslaved.

CATHOLICISM IN MARYLAND FLOURISHES

Assisted by fewer indentured servants but a growing number of slaves, Jesuits kept in tune with the rhythms of farm life, appreciated the character of farm people, recognized the social inclinations of Marylanders, and even encouraged their amusements, including dancing. Jesuits often celebrated Mass in private homes where they spoke positively about the human condition. Much to the delight of the people, Jesuits stressed virtuous living as a key to happiness. In essence, Jesuits affirmed the quiet, withdrawn spirituality of Maryland Catholics.

Jesuits also helped Maryland Catholics more clearly articulate their spirituality, what scholars call "devout humanism." Jesuits obtained for the Catholic gentry books on scripture, theology, apologetics, and the spiritual life and also circulated the popular works of John Gother's *Instructions for Particular States and Conditions of Life* and Richard Challoner's *The Garden of the Soul*, both of which encouraged the humanist tradition that emphasized the power of the individual to make a difference. Jesuits eventually published their own *Pious Guide to Prayer and Devotion*, which fit the social conditions and private nature of Maryland Catholicism. This publication grew popular in large part because it presupposed Catholics were in charge of their devotional life.

Jesuits acknowledged that they constituted a small clerical force and thus relied heavily on non-priests or laypeople to maintain the faith. Mothers and daughters routinely gathered in the manor house those Catholics in the neighborhood wishing to learn more about the faith. In this way, women exercised the same critical religious role in Maryland that they had in England. The focus of the Catholic life was the home, and women became the principal instructors in religion.

Catholics circulated freely with non-Catholics in Maryland but formed special bonds with fellow Catholics. Catholics often partnered in financial transactions and served as witnesses for each other on legal documents. Catholics frequently rose in economic stature, and gained political power, together. Catholics oversaw the disposition of estates of deceased Catholics, paying special attention to the well-being of Catholic orphans. Widowed Catholics seeking remarriage usually remarried other Catholics. Catholics socialized with each other and even knew their priests, the Jesuits, outside as much as inside of church. The Catholic community was strong, and an intense family spirit emerged.

When economic hard times again hit in the late seventeenth century, the Protestant majority indicted Cecil Calvert's successor—his son, the third Lord Baltimore, Charles Calvert—and the mainly Catholic advisory council for enriching themselves at the expense of the colony. These accusations were not altogether unfounded. In another part of the country in the spring of 1682, French Catholic explorer Robert Cavelier de la Salle claimed the lower Mississippi Valley for the Catholic Church and for the French king.

In 1685, the Catholic King of England, James II, promoted widespread religious toleration in England, which only provoked many English parliamentarians to unite with William of Orange and his Dutch forces to overthrow James II in the so-called Glorious Revolution of 1688. William and his wife, Mary (James II's Protestant daughter), became the new king and queen and thus ended any outside chance that Catholicism might be reestablished in England.

In 1689 Anglicans in Maryland overthrew Catholic leaders in the colony, including the Catholic Proprietor, in another so-called Glorious Revolution. Subsequent anti-Catholic legislation denied Catholics the right to worship in public, to vote, and to establish schools. In 1691 Maryland became a royal colony, and the Church of England became the established church. The Maryland Catholic community abandoned any lingering hopes for an exclusively Catholic colony and settled in as a minority group with a strong yet private home-based spirituality.

After the uproar of the Glorious Revolution settled down, wealthy Maryland Catholic Charles Carroll I purchased seven thousand acres outside Baltimore. Carroll named the land "Doughoregan" after a Carroll family estate in Ireland. In 1727, Carroll's son, Charles Carroll II, built an impressive Georgian plantation house at Doughoregan. Local Catholics used the detached brick chapel Carroll built beside the house as the community's primary place of worship.

In 1832, Charles Carroll V enlarged and remodeled the home in the Greek Revival Style and incorporated the chapel into the main structure. Nearby parishes were soon thereafter established, but the Carroll family continued to open their chapel to the public for Sunday worship until the 1990s. The Carroll family still lives at Doughoregan. "Only God, the Indians and the Carrolls have owned this land," one family member recently remarked.[16]

CHAPTER FOUR

Maryland Masters
and Slaves

Most Maryland homes remained simple and small, maybe two rooms and a loft, but after 1700, a growing number of Maryland homeowners grew concerned for manners, social ceremony, and fashion. Middle-class farmers, including many Catholics, started doing things that only the rich used to do, including drinking tea. The second son of Catherine and Thomas Spalding, William Spalding and his wife, Ann, used utensils and fine dishes for the first time. Such items were widely advertised and more readily available to Maryland Catholics.

Whereas Maryland's founders had envisioned a stratified, hierarchical, feudal society, colonial Maryland evolved with less rigid economic boundaries. Free people climbed the social ladder with distinctions defined not so much by inherited states as by economic success. At the same time, the elite Maryland Catholic families, including the Brookes, Neals, and Carrolls, continued to enjoy both inheritance and wealth and thus remained in a class of their own.

After farmers established tobacco as a successful cash crop, Marylanders began to import large numbers of African slaves to tend the labor intensive tobacco fields. Slaves soon outnumbered servants almost four to one, which constituted a complete reverse of ratio from just twenty-five years before. Most of these slaves lived in southern Maryland where Catholics were concentrated. Most slaveholders, including William and Ann Spalding, owned one or two slaves.

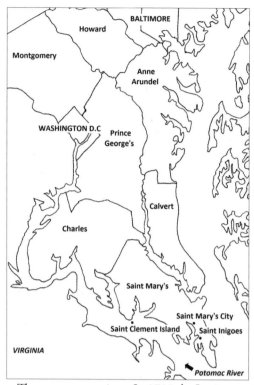

Colonial Maryland

For the next hundred years more than 90 percent of the slaves brought into the Chesapeake Bay area arrived directly from Africa, with three-fourths stolen from West Africa (extending from present-day Sierra Leone to Ghana). These Africans struggled to maintain social cohesion, especially since the small number of slaves per household meant that slaves did not usually live with their own relatives.

There were exceptions. In 1711 the Jesuit superior in Maryland purchased fifteen slaves. James Carroll of Prince George's County then willed his White Marsh estate, along with seventeen slaves, to the Jesuits. Richard Isaac next sold his farm adjoining White Marsh, along with "a whole family of Isaacs," that is, a group of slaves who had taken the last name of their former owner, to the Jesuits. Individual slaves also joined the growing Jesuit community when, for example, a parent of a child who attended an early, short-lived Jesuit school paid tuition by delivering a slave boy named Jacob to the Jesuits.[1]

Jesuits soon ranked among the largest slaveholders in the colony, and certainly the largest among Catholics. Through the 1720s, about a third of Maryland slaveholders owned one or two slaves. More than three fourths owned fewer than ten. By 1730 the Jesuits owned about fifty slaves, most of whom resided on two farms in Saint Mary's County, Saint Inigoes and another early Jesuit acquisition, the so-called Newtown Manor located about twenty miles up the Potomac River. Slaves provided basic necessities and thus allowed Jesuits to continue their religious ministries.

Jesuits claimed to have gotten along with their slaves, treating them as part of "our family," or as "One of Ours," as the Jesuits commonly put it. Jesuits typically did not educate slaves but tried to keep slave families together, which explained in part why Jesuits invested in large groups of slaves and also why Jesuits occasionally sold slaves who had married outside the farm. Jesuits cared for the physical health of their slaves, routinely employing physicians. Jesuits trained some slaves as artisans such as carpenters, shoemakers, and seamstresses. And Jesuits permitted several slaves to earn their freedom (though Jesuits otherwise opposed emancipation).[2]

Probably more than the average Catholic and non-Catholic slaveholder in Maryland, Jesuits cared for black family life. After an old Jesuit slave named Enoch asked permission from the Jesuits to marry a woman who lived across Saint Mary's River, one Jesuit said he "did [his] best to purchase the woman" but could not get her owner to agree. On another occasion, Nelly wanted to marry Harry, a slave who similarly lived on the other side of the river. This time, a Jesuit determined that Harry was an immoral man who would corrupt the Jesuit slaves. Nelly was not permitted to marry.[3]

The Spiritual Well-Being of Slaves

The Jesuits felt that enslaved persons should be respected, but only before God were they considered equal to free people. While Maryland Jesuits promoted a humanistic spirituality that fostered basic good behavior, what really mattered for Catholics at this time was not how a person lived on earth, but whether or not that person had secured a place in heaven. And access to heaven was granted through the sacraments.

Jesuits encouraged Catholics to attend to the spiritual well-being of slaves by issuing "Regulations Concerning the Observance of Holydays in Maryland" at the end of 1722, which insisted, among other things, that Catholic slaveholders ensure that slaves have steady access to the sacraments and to religious instruction. Jesuits regularly offered baptism, confession, and Eucharist to slaves.

After early efforts with Native Americans had failed, Jesuits spent an inordinate amount of time with African Americans. Jesuits considered slaves "members of Jesus Christ, redeemed by His precious blood. They are to be dealt with in a charitable, Christian, paternal manner, which is at the same time a great means to bring them to their duty to God and therefore to gain their souls." Following the lead of the Jesuits, young Catholic women instructed slaves about prayers and the catechism, as well as about good moral behavior.[4]

In a different part of North America, Marie Tranchepain and her French Ursuline nuns similarly cared for free and enslaved African Americans. Almost immediately after arriving in New Orleans in 1727 (thus making the Ursulines the oldest female religious order in what would become the United States), these Ursulines opened a school that educated European, Canadian, Native American, and African girls (in what is now the oldest Catholic school in continuous operation in the United States).

Ever since Maryland had outlawed the public celebration of Mass, Jesuits had begun to extend their ministry beyond Maryland, ultimately sending Joseph Greaton in 1729 to Philadelphia where he built Saint Joseph's Chapel (on Willings Alley where the 1739 Old Saint Joseph's Church now stands). Saint Joseph's was the only public place in the English-speaking world at that time where celebration of the Mass was permitted by law. William Penn's Charter for Pennsylvania guaranteed religious and civic freedom to "all who worshiped one God."[5]

Evangelical preachers Jonathan Edwards and George Whitefield inspired a rebirth of religion across the British colonies through the Great Awakening of the 1740s, and Catholic fervor grew, as well. A small group of German Catholic immigrants who had settled a little to the west of Philadelphia at Goshenhoppen and Conewago requested German-speaking priests to celebrate devotions and hear confessions. In 1741, Maryland Jesuits sent to Pennsylvania two German Jesuits, Theodore Schneider and Wilhelm Wappaler.

By 1750, thirteen Maryland Jesuits owned nearly thirteen thousand acres spread largely over five Saint Mary County farms. The number of Jesuits in colonial Maryland never exceeded a couple of dozen men, and usually was much less. With Catholics scattered across the colony and a little beyond, Jesuits often rode three to four hundred miles per week on horseback. They rarely saw each other. Some Jesuits complained of loneliness. They nonetheless were supported by a significant workforce. By 1765, thirty-nine tenants (mostly former indentured servants) and 192 slaves worked Jesuit farms.

Jesuits considered some of these slaves "loyal and trustworthy" companions. These trusted slaves often lived in the same house, or glebe, as the Jesuits. Glebe slaves, including descendants of Jowett, frequently stayed on with the Jesuits even after they were emancipated. Jesuits described many of these glebe slaves as good and faithful Catholics.[6]

The majority of Jesuit slaves worked the land as field hands. One Jesuit described field hands as "a stubborn, dull set of mortals, that do nothing but by driving." Another Jesuit threatened to sell some unproductive workers; at which point, some of these slaves ran away. Too much kindness, at least in the minds of these Jesuits, rendered the slave workforce inefficient. Through the mid-1700s, Jesuit field hands earned roughly 540 sterling per year, which constituted more than three-fourths of the annual income from the Jesuit farms.[7]

Some Jesuits continued to preach on behalf of the good treatment of slaves, with one priest specifically denouncing his congregation (as he evidently could have criticized some fellow Jesuits) for treating their slaves as "inferior species." Another Jesuit warned that "he who takes no care of his domesticks is worse than an infidel and has denied his faith." Regard your slaves as "Brothers in Jesus Christ," admonished this Jesuit.[8] Jesuits usually provided for elderly slaves and also welcomed slave children into the Jesuit slave community.

Into the 1760s, 40 percent of the recorded baptisms at the Jesuit Saint Francis Xavier Church at Newtown were of slaves, even though slaves probably constituted only about 12 percent of that Catholic community. While a portion of these baptisms would have been to persons owned by non-Catholics, Catholic owners across southern Maryland still appeared to be more diligent in baptizing slaves than they were of their own children.

BEGINNINGS OF REVOLT

Like British colonists up and down the Atlantic coast, southern Maryland Catholics grew incensed when the British Parliament passed the Stamp Act of 1765, which taxed just about everything. Maryland colonists were hardly relieved when English authorities repealed the tax, except for that levied on tea. In 1773, wealthy Catholic Charles Carroll of Carrollton publicly challenged parliament's taxation without colonial representation. Eight months after the Boston Tea Party, a number of Catholic Marylanders in August 1774 turned the *Mary and Jane* away from the public landing at Saint Mary's River, refusing to pay the tax on the ship's cargo of tea. 1774?

Charles Carroll of Carrollton

As tensions grew, the international Society of Jesus was suppressed for a variety of unrelated and rather complex reasons. The Maryland Jesuits (or, more accurately now, ex-Jesuits) still maintained some cohesion, and even extended their ministry, largely because they were not deprived of their property, including their slaves.

Charles Carroll swayed Maryland to join the revolt against King George III. On July 4, 1776, Carroll signed the Declaration of Independence, the only Catholic to do so. Later that year, Carroll and his cousin, the most prominent ex-Jesuit, John Carroll, traveled with Benjamin Franklin to Canada on a diplomatic mission. The mission failed to secure the support of Canada for the American Revolution, but endeared Franklin to him. John Carroll cared for Franklin during the illness Franklin suffered throughout the trip. Carroll subsequently called Franklin "My dear & venerable friend."[9]

Other Catholics, including Philadelphians Thomas Fitzsimons, Stephen Moylan, and John Barry, fought in the revolution alongside countless Maryland minutemen. Catholic women such as Sara McCalla and Mary Wateus of Philadelphia, and Mary Digges Lee of Maryland, cared for wounded soldiers.

In late July, Catholic Colonel Richard Barnes and the Saint Mary's County militia turned away seventy-two British ships trying to take control of the Chesapeake Bay. Throughout the war, individual British sloops regularly raided southern Maryland, pillaging whatever they could find, including property of the Jesuits, "not sparing the church furniture," according to one eyewitness. A British cannonball nearly took off the head of Jesuit Peter Morris.[10]

Catholics across North America supported the Revolution. Out on the California missions, Spaniard Junipero Serra urged fellow priests to pray for American success, and at Kaskaskia, Illinois, French cleric Pierre Gibault encouraged fellow Catholics to help General George Rogers Clark achieve victory in the western theater of the war.

As preliminary peace talks began, John Carroll convened the priests of Maryland and Pennsylvania in late June 1783 at the ex-Jesuit plantation of White Marsh. Out of this and two other meetings, Carroll and six priests were elected as a "Representative Body of the Clergy." These priests asked the pope to grant all American Catholic priests the privilege to select the first American bishop from their ranks. As the pope considered this request, Benjamin Franklin was negotiating a peace treaty in Paris. The pope's representative in Paris asked Franklin about a possible American bishop. Franklin recommended his old friend, John Carroll.

THE NEW UNITED STATES

As the Continental Congress organized around principles of democracy and freedom, John Carroll beamed, "With the overthrow of British rule a great change came about. Everywhere freedom of religion was established, and in some states Catholics do not differ from others as regards legal rights and general conditions." On behalf of priests and lay people, alike, John and Charles Carroll congratulated George Washington, expressing "joy, and unbounded confidence in [his] being called, by an Unanimous Vote, to the first station" of the United States.[11]

As confirmed in the Bill of Rights, the United States would have no established religion, which distinguished the United States from many Europeans countries by this time. Northern Germany was largely Lutheran;

Switzerland was Calvinist; England was Anglican; and France, Spain, and Italy were Catholic. In the United States, citizens could exercise the religion of their choice.

Rome meanwhile granted a one-time exception to the rule that the pope alone chose bishops. Twenty-six priests, mostly former Jesuits, assembled at White Marsh and almost unanimously chose John Carroll as the first bishop of Baltimore. English Bishop Charles Walmesley consecrated Carroll at Lulworth Castle in Dorset, England, on the Feast of the Assumption, August 15, 1790. Carroll's newly formed diocese encompassed the entire United States, from the Atlantic Ocean to the Mississippi River, from Florida's northern border to the Great Lakes.

Carroll initially embraced distinctively democratic principles, advocating that priests, for instance, elect bishops as well as celebrate Mass in the language of the people (and not in Latin, as was more common at that time). After a series of challenges, however, Carroll grew leery over too much democracy within the Church.

Some sixteen thousand Catholics, including about 3,200 slaves and nineteen mostly elderly priests, composed less than 1 percent of the entire population of the brand-new United States. The majority of these Catholics still lived in Maryland, mostly in the southern vicinity of Saint Mary's County.

Yet Philadelphia also boasted a small, thriving community that included publisher Matthew Carey. Carey printed the first Catholic version of the Bible to be released in the United States (later known as the "Carey Bible"). Maybe seven thousand Catholics with just five priests lived spread out across Pennsylvania.

Another 1,500 Catholics resided elsewhere, including about two hundred in New York City. Irish Franciscan Charles Whelan had laid the cornerstone for Saint Peter's Church, the first of New York, but then resigned amidst controversy with the Catholic trustees who oversaw construction of Saint Peter's. Whelan moved to frontier Kentucky. Another Irish priest, Charles Nugent, completed the church. Nugent, however, resigned four years later in 1790, leaving the fledgling New York community on its own.

Other religious leaders displayed greater staying power. Marylander Anne Matthews joined a European contemplative religious order, professing

Sister Bernardina, as rendered by
artist Mother Mary Joseph, O.C.D.

vows as Sister Bernardina with the Discalced Carmelites at Hoogstraet in Holland. Back in Maryland, her younger brother, a priest named Ignatius Matthews, next instructed Bernardina, "Now is the time to found in this country, for peace is declared and religion is free." In 1790, Bernardina led three nuns from Holland to Port Tobacco, Maryland. In the vacated home of Bernardina's Uncle Charles Neale, she established the first community of nuns, a branch of the Discalced Carmelites, in the United States. [12]

In 1791, a group of French diocesan priests, the Society of Saint Sulpice, or Sulpicians, fled the extreme anti-clericalism of the French Revolution and landed in Baltimore. There they opened the first school for the education of priests in the country, Saint Mary's Seminary on Paca Street. (Sulpicians later established Mount Saint Mary's College at Emmitsburg, Maryland.) In the seminary chapel the Sulpicians instructed free blacks escaping another revolution going on in Haiti, or Saint-Domingue as the island was called under French rule.

The Establishment of Georgetown

As part of a financial agreement with Bishop Carroll, the ex-Jesuits lent their 1,500-acre plantation at Bohemia (northeast of Georgetown) to the Sulpicians so that they could use plantation proceeds to sustain the seminary. The Sulpicians soon sold eight Bohemia slaves, including a mother who was separated in the sale from her three-year-old daughter. The ex-Jesuits were enraged and eventually reclaimed Bohemia, but the slaves were lost.

Carroll had previously purchased one acre overlooking the Potomac River outside the village of George-Town, hoping that local Catholics, along with some European benefactors, would assist in raising an American Catholic college on this site. But rich Maryland Catholics reportedly believed the ex-Jesuits, who, with extensive tracts of land (or plantations, as they were then called), appeared to be wealthy and did not need any help.

Some outsiders claimed that the American ex-Jesuits had grown obsessed with material holdings, sometimes to the neglect of spiritual duties. European Catholics similarly were dissuaded from supporting the proposed school, especially after an Irish ex-Jesuit, who had spent a winter in Maryland, reported that the American ex-Jesuit plantations were worked by "a prodigious number of negroes" who were "whipped, and almost flayed alive."[13]

Raised in one of the largest slave holding families of Maryland, John Carroll did not deny that ex-Jesuits whipped their slaves, yet he explained that "the instances are rare indeed, and almost unknown, of corporal punishment being inflicted on any of them who are come to the age of manhood." Carroll claimed that the slaves owned by the ex-Jesuits were, in general, treated better than European peasants and more humanely than most other Maryland slaves. To be owned by the ex-Jesuits and thus to be called a "priest's negro," was, according to Carroll, "proverbial for one, who is allowed to act without control," that is, a worker who essentially was free.[14]

With little local or European support, Carroll used proceeds from the ex-Jesuit plantations to open Georgetown College on January 2, 1792. Two years later a new building (now called Old North) was planned with construction costs coming at least initially from the plantations. Seven years after that, the Sisters of the Visitation established the first Catholic school for girls in what was the original United States, Georgetown Academy for Young Ladies (now Georgetown Visitation Preparatory School).

To meet ongoing financial burdens at Georgetown College, the ex-Jesuits cut some costs (such as the president's salary), and raised money elsewhere (including through tuition), but the primary burden of financing the school still fell on slave labor at the plantations, supplemented in part by slaves who worked right at the school. "Old Rachael" and "Old Ginny" were moved north from the plantations to Georgetown, where they worked as cooks. Instead of paying tuition, several parents also supplied slaves for the college's use.

Slaves similarly contributed to the broader Catholic experience, with slaves constituting about 20 percent of the overall Catholic population of Maryland at this time. In Saint Mary's County at the end of the century, about 60 percent of the households owned slaves, averaging seven slaves per household. The more assets Catholics held, the more likely they were to own slaves. And Catholics tended to be more prosperous and thus larger slave-holders than their neighbors, especially in Saint Mary's County.

Catholics evidently did not entertain the moral objections to slavery professed by Quakers and others at this time. Catholics simply let economic forces determine slaveholding practices. In short, Catholics who could afford slaves owned slaves, some pretty many. Dr. Richard J. Edelen may have been the most prosperous individual Catholic in southern Maryland in the late 1700s. At Society Hill Manor House, which enjoyed a panoramic view of Breton's Bay, Edelen reportedly "raised his family in grand style" drinking a lot of tea. Edelen owned about thirty slaves.[15]

John Carroll, like many non-Catholic ministers of his day, viewed the dawn of the United States as an "excellent opportunity" for advancing religion. No more than 10 percent of the country were members of any particular church at that time, while significant groups of unevangelized Native Americans remained within the limits of the United States.[16]

GROWTH IN THE U.S. CATHOLIC PRESENCE

In 1792 Carroll sent French priest Gabriel Richard to the Northwest Territories. Richard eventually opened a school in Detroit, but it soon burned to the ground in the fire that leveled the entire city. Amidst the ruins, Richard coined what became Detroit's motto, *Speramus meliora; resurget cineribus*, "We hope for better things; it will arise from the ashes."

Richard was elected a nonvoting delegate of the Michigan Territory to the U.S. House of Representatives, the first Catholic priest to serve that body. Richard also cofounded the Catholepistemiad of Michigania (which became the University of Michigan). He moreover evangelized some Native Americans and even won the admiration of Shawnee chief Tecumseh, who otherwise detested Americans.

Gabriel Richard

A New England contemporary of Richard was far less successful. After converting to Catholicism while on a trip to Europe during the Revolutionary War, and after being ordained a priest in Paris, Boston-born John Thayer informed Pope Pius VI that he intended to convert all of New England to Catholicism. Boston Catholics comprised at that time less than one hundred persons out of a total population of eighteen thousand.

Thayer antagonized the only other priest in Boston, French exile Louis de Rousselet, disgraced fellow Catholics with some kind of lewd behavior, sparred with local Protestant ministers, and lambasted several non-Catholic yet reportedly "honest people" by telling them they were bound for hell for having attended Protestant services.[17]

Carroll longed for a priest who might don more "amiable, conciliatory manners."[18] His prayers were answered when Francis Anthony Matignon arrived the summer of 1792. Matignon soothed tensions within the local Catholic community, and with the help of his priest friend, John Louis Lefebvre Cheverus, eventually created a conciliatory climate for Catholicism in New England. Thayer meanwhile bounced from one place to the next for several years, causing trouble wherever he went.

In 1795 Carroll ordained Russian Prince Dimitri Gallitzin. Having studied at Saint Mary's Seminary, Gallitzin was the first priest to achieve all of his seminary training in the United States. Carroll sent Gallitzin to several congregations in Maryland and Pennsylvania, where Catholics repeatedly complained of Gallitzin's overzealous nature and aristocratic manners. "Try to win the affection of [the] congregation," Carroll advised, "with a mild temper, occasionally overlooking things that were not as they should be, correcting by gentle persuasion instead of carrying...authority to extremes."[19]

Gallitzin asked Carroll to be transferred to Maguire's Settlement, which housed about a dozen persons, the first English-speaking Roman Catholic congregation west of the Allegheny Front (in Western Pennsylvania at what is now Loretto, near Pittsburgh). Revolutionary War veteran Michael Maguire had donated land to Carroll with hope that a church and resident priest would be established there.

Gallitzin used his extensive inheritance to help thousands of Catholics move to the settlement. In 1799 he built Saint Michael's Church out of white pine logs, but then Russian authorities cut off the flow of money from his inheritance. He quickly fell into debt. Because of Gallitzin's financial woes, and because of his relentless zeal, Carroll did not support the subsequent occasions when Gallitzin was nominated to become a bishop. Moreover, some parishioners grew increasingly uncomfortable with Gallitzin's energy. Others followers revered Gallitzin, particularly after his death in 1840. By that time, Gallitzin's congregation had exploded to an estimated ten thousand mostly German immigrant Catholics.

In 1872 a Pennsylvania town was named after Gallitzin, and in 1899 the president of U.S. Steel, Charles M. Schwab donated $150,000 to build atop Gallitzin's tomb the Romanesque Revival Saint Michael the Archangel Church, adjacent to the original church site. Schwab had grown up attending Mass at Saint Michael Church.

With the rise of various immigrant groups, the American Catholic Church had certainly moved beyond Maryland. For almost two hundred years, that is, from the landing of the *Ark* and the *Dove* until the early nineteenth century, Maryland Catholicism was essentially all that had existed of the Catholic Church in the United States. Summarizing early American Catholic history, in 1879 the great-great-great-great-grandson of the indentured servant Thomas Spalding, Bishop John Lancaster Spalding of Peoria, Illinois, spoke at the Great Hall at Cooper Union in New York City, where American Presidents from Abraham Lincoln to Barack Obama have given addresses. "How did the Catholic Church begin in the United States?"

John Carroll statue at Georgetown University

Spalding asked. After a dramatic pause, Spalding rightly answered, "It began with a little colony down in Maryland."[20]

But by the end of the century, Maryland's dominance in the American Catholic Church had begun to fade, as Spalding and subsequent historians would recognize. In 1884 American Catholicism's first fully professional historian, layman John Gilmary Shea, organized the U.S. Catholic Historical Society. Georgetown University dedicated in 1912 an impressive bronze statue of Bishop John Carroll inside the university's front gates. Seven years later, priest-professor Peter Guilday at the Catholic University of America formed the American Catholic Historical Association. Catholics were beginning to celebrate their past, as well as gain a better understanding of where they had come from.

Into the 1940s, historian and longtime Notre Dame archivist, Holy Cross Father Thomas McAvoy argued that the Maryland tradition had helped create a distinctive American flavor in the Catholic Church of the United States. Yet another Notre Dame historian thirty years later downplayed the role of Maryland. With the wave of nineteenth-century immigrants, Jay Dolan argued that "The Anglo-American predominance had faded into the background, and the church became a decidedly immigrant community with a heavy Irish flavor." Poor immigrant Catholics replaced polished, polite gentlemen from Maryland, Dolan noted.[21]

Other historians, including Jesuit James Hennesey, less willingly gave up on the ongoing influence of Maryland. Xaverian Brother Thomas Spalding carefully traced the repeated rise and fall of the Maryland tradition. Concerning Vatican II in the 1960s, for example, Spalding described a "successful restoration" of the Maryland tradition, at least in Baltimore.[22]

By this time the Prince Gallitzin State Park had opened some thirty miles from Gallitzin's tomb. In 1996 Pope John Paul II elevated Saint Michael Church to the status of a minor basilica, and in 2005 the pope named Gallitzin a "Servant of God," the first step toward sainthood.

CHAPTER FIVE

Kentucky Sinners
and Saints

*A*s the population of Maryland grew throughout the late 1700s, nonstop farming had depleted most Maryland fields. A series of droughts and floods had worn out older farmers. Young Catholic Marylanders began to look beyond Maryland. Five hundred miles to the west, Shawnee and Cherokee peoples had agreed not to live on their traditional hunting grounds. Too many warriors had lost their lives attempting to claim for their tribe this sacred land, what some natives called the "Dark and Bloody Ground," Kentucky.

In early 1783 a bankrupt gambler named Raphael Lancaster led a scouting party from southern Maryland to central Kentucky (to the vicinity of today's Bardstown). Lancaster's son, John Lancaster, reported back favorably to Maryland. A Pennsylvania surveyor, John Filson, published a small book that similarly praised *The Discovery, Settlement and Present State of Kentucke*. Filson's work touted the heroics of Daniel Boone and included a map.

About sixty southern Maryland Catholic families formed a "league" pledging to migrate to Kentucky. The first group left in early 1785. Over the next twenty-five years, more than 25 percent of the white inhabitants of southern Maryland emigrated to various places, especially Kentucky. The majority of Kentucky pioneers who claimed any religious affiliation tended to be Baptist, Presbyterian, or Methodist, thus leaving these first Kentucky Catholics still in the minority.

In late March of 1787, a band of warriors on Eighteen Mile Island just above the Falls of the Ohio (at present-day Louisville) fired upon a flatboat of Maryland Catholics. An ounce ball ripped through both thighs of Catholic Thomas Hill, while another bullet took the life of the steersman, a slave named Hall. Hall's body fell upon and thus protected from further attack, Hill's seven-year-old son, Clement.

Clement Hill eventually fathered seventeen children who bore countless descendants. Other Kentucky Catholics, including some slaves, similarly descended from the Hill caravan. Some survivors of the initial assault bought farms on Pottinger's Creek in central Kentucky. After Thomas Hill recovered from his wounds, he purchased sixty-three acres adjoining the property of another Catholic, Henry Cambron, on nearby Cartwright's Creek. At Hill's home, a score of Catholic families gathered for prayer. Hill was the largest slaveholder of these immigrants, about a quarter of whom owned slaves.

The high demands of frontier Kentucky encouraged cooperation between master and slave, while the openness and isolation of the area rendered scrutiny of slave activity nearly impossible. There were, as one pioneer noted, "few drones" on the frontier. Male and female, black and white, young and old worked together. Most Catholics probably followed the practice of another early pioneer who reportedly "was just as exacting of service at the hands of her children as she was at the hands of her colored slaves."[1]

Yet slaves more acutely felt the isolation of the frontier. Free persons often emigrated with families, sometimes relocating entire Maryland neighborhoods in Kentucky. Individual slaves, on the other hand, were chosen for the frontier with little concern for family and social ties. With only about fifty white Catholic families congregating along various creeks in central Kentucky in 1787, then maybe three hundred households six years later, slaves owned by Catholics had few chances for communication with other slaves.

ADVENTURES TO THE NORTH

In April 1788, John Lancaster and three companions again descended the Ohio River from Fort Pitt (now Pittsburgh). To the north, Lancaster

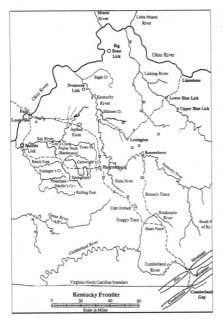

Early Kentucky Settlements

saw no inhabitants, except at Marietta, which had been established that same month as the first permanent nonnative settlement north of the Ohio River (in what would become the state of Ohio). Lancaster floated past more settlements to the south, including past Limestone (now Maysville, Kentucky). For a measly sixty-six and two-thirds cents per acre, prospectors could buy land on both sides of this stretch of the Ohio River (near what is now Cincinnati).

On May 8 an odd current sucked Lancaster's boat out of the river into the mouth of the Great Miami River (near the present Ohio/Indiana border), at which point some warriors emerged from the banks. Shawnee Jim stood up in his canoe to demand that Lancaster surrender, but Shawnee Jim lost his balance and fell into the water. Lancaster jumped in to save Shawnee Jim, hoping to merit some favor with the Shawnees. Shawnees pillaged Lancaster's flatboat and tied Lancaster and his companions spread eagle to the ground. Enraged that outsiders were desecrating their sacred hunting grounds, the Shawnee threatened to torture and murder Lancaster's party.

But the next morning, Shawnee Jim announced that according to Shawnee custom he would adopt Lancaster to replace Shawnee Jim's son, who some time before had been killed fighting other nonnatives. Shawnee Jim renamed Lancaster as Kiohba, which means "fast running deer." He separated Lancaster from his companions (who may have then been executed) and marched Lancaster north to a Shawnee settlement, probably near present-day Chillicothe, Ohio. The Shawnee treated Lancaster well, but after a month or so, Shawnee Jim's daughter advised Lancaster to run.

John Lancaster

Shawnee Jim had just taken the girl's mother into the woods to beat her and probably would whip Lancaster next.

Lancaster ran in an indirect, southerly route, eating only wild turkey eggs over six days before finding the Ohio River. Lancaster tied together driftwood, hurled his body aboard the makeshift raft, and passed out. Lancaster floated down the river, landed on the Kentucky side just above the Falls of the Ohio, and awakened to the sound of a rooster, which told him that his people were nearby. (Native Americans did not cultivate chickens.) Rescuers delivered Lancaster to Pottinger's Creek. Fellow pioneers celebrated Lancaster as a local hero.

Margaret and Robert Abell meanwhile led another band of Maryland Catholics westward, eventually landing south of Pottinger's Creek on the banks of the Rolling Fork River. In the spring of 1791 Robert Abell's sister, Alethaire, and her husband, Benedict Spalding Jr. (grandson to William and Ann Spalding of Maryland) joined the Rolling Fork settlement. Along with many other pioneer Kentucky Catholic women, Alethaire Spalding was an independent lady who reportedly "had a brilliant mind and was remarkable for her amiability and other personal attractions." Her living room served as the local station where Catholics gathered for prayer. One of her descendants claimed that Alethaire Spalding was remembered by Protestants and Catholics as a saint.[2]

Pioneer Kentucky Catholics begged for priests, but generally were disappointed. After causing trouble in New York, Charles Whelan had escaped to Kentucky, but three years later, he left in the spring of 1790 amidst further accusations of slander. William de Rohan emigrated in 1791 with a group

Stephen Theodore Badin

of settlers from North Carolina, but he also proved unsatisfactory, probably because of alcoholism. After three years, de Rohan abandoned Kentucky.

FATHER BADIN COMES TO KENTUCKY

In 1792 Kentucky became a state, the first beyond the east coast, and in 1793 the first priest ordained in the United States, Stephen Theodore Badin, walked from Baltimore to Fort Pitt before descending down the Ohio River to Kentucky.

Badin complained about deplorable frontier conditions. "[T]he priests have done more harm to the Church [in Kentucky]," Badin asserted, "than [have] its declared enemies." Much to his regret, Kentucky Catholics entertained many vices, including dancing, their "amusement par excellence." Like many French-speaking priests who would land in the United States during the French Revolution, he fostered a strict moral code.[3]

Badin established a base near the Elkhorn Creek (not far from Lexington in Scott County), where Catholic settlers had built a log chapel and a small adjoining cabin. Badin visited various households or stations, spending much of his time reintroducing proper Catholic piety. After Anthony Wayne's 1794 victory over the Shawnee at Fallen Timbers, threats from native inhabitants in the Ohio River valley lessened, and more easterners moved westward. By 1803, a thousand Catholic families clustered in various communities across central Kentucky.

Badin lived on horseback, with little rest, animated, as one report put it, by "the awful responsibility of his charge." He occasionally purchased land, yet he did not build a single church in Kentucky. He focused instead on improving the religious character of his congregations. Upon reaching a station, he heard confessions all morning long, and said Mass in the afternoon. Catholics could not receive the sacraments from him unless they proved unfaltering adherence to his strict moral code.[4]

A so-called "lady of distinction," who lived at Cartwright's Creek, cherished her Catholic faith but also entertained "an uncommon stock of worldly pride." Her possessions included a fine piece of land, the largest home in the area, and an unusual collection of English silver. One afternoon, this lady held a dinner for Badin. Upon plunging his fork into the food placed before him, Badin asked the hostess, "When was this fowl killed?" Badin had unusual eating habits, generally demanding, for instance, that any poultry be killed the day before he ate it. "Last night," the hostess replied. Not believing her, he asked a slave the same question, and the slave gave the same answer. Badin then looked straight at the hostess and proclaimed, "The mistress tells an untruth, and the maid swears to it." The hostess confessed, "Indeed, Father, I ordered the fowls to be killed last night, but the servants were kept busy till a late hour, and they deferred the job till morning. I hope you will be able to make out your dinner on roast lamb." This he did, but not before ordering the hostess to say twelve rosaries.[5]

Badin routinely reminded free adult pioneers that they were morally responsible for children and slaves. "I make the Fathers and Mothers, Masters and Mistresses," he explained, "accountable for such neglect in their children and servants.… From the same principle I oblige them to catechize frequently their dependents, and forbid the traffick of their slaves with Infidels, &c."[6]

Independent-minded pioneers often dismissed Badin as a strange speaking Frenchman with unrealistic high moral standards. One parent complained to Bishop Carroll that Badin had ordered her child to hold a hot ember in the child's hand in order to feel what hell was like.

Badin focused on children and on slaves and trained select persons, usually free women, as catechists. "Mind this," he instructed his helpers, "no morning prayer, no breakfast; no evening prayer, no supper…be good, and you will never be sorry for it." Some children mastered their lessons, and many slaves learned to read.[7]

One Catholic remembered that "On Sundays in the absence of their pastor, the greater parts of the congregations were wont to repair to the nearest church, or station, and there engage in exercises of piety. Often on such occasions, in lieu of a sermon, one of the catechists would read a chapter from some work of Catholic piety; and thus were formed in all habits of punctuality in the performance of religious duty." Badin praised many of his catechists.[8]

Like most Catholics at that time, Badin believed that a priest had to extend the sacrament of extreme unction, or last rites, (now the anointing of the sick) to every dying Catholic in order to ensure the dying soul a place in heaven. As a result, he ran at the beck and call of his community and generally overlooked such things as the source of his next meal and the maintenance of his property.

Bishop Carroll ordered Kentucky Catholics to pay their priests, and many parishioners agreed to support Badin, but few actually came through. His clothing was homespun, the cheapest material available, and all that he could afford. For a while he ground corn in a hand mill. Out on the circuit, he endured many dangers. More than once he was taken for dead.

A Scott County Catholic, Joseph Fenwick, eventually offered Badin an old Fenwick home, along with a young slave boy. In this fashion, perhaps as early as the spring of 1794, Badin became a slaveholder. He had been in Kentucky for about a year. Over the next couple of decades, he would own ten slaves.

An "old and faithful family servant" named Harry probably had moved with Catholic Marylanders to Kentucky as part of the first wave of immigrants. According to the people who knew Harry, "When any one of his fellow-servants was sick…[Harry] was always called for; and on these occasions, he did everything in his power to console and instruct the sick person, by the bedside of whom he was wont to recite his beads, and to say all the prayers he knew." Just like Badin, Harry readied souls for their final reward.[9]

After Harry was sold to a non-Catholic, Harry induced Badin to purchase him, all the while promising that his labor would more than cover the purchase price. A year or two later, Badin found Harry dejected in the fields. When he asked Harry what was the matter, Harry explained that he was afraid he might die before he could repay Badin his just due. Badin told him not to worry, and Harry's spirits were restored.

In June 1795, Badin moved to Pottinger's Creek. There, he resided at Holy Cross on property that was owned by one of the leading Catholic pioneers in the area, Basil Hayden, Sr. Local Catholics could not quite get around to completing a formal rectory as they had promised, so Badin lodged in a small cabin on the property. He christened the structure Saint Stephen's in honor of his patron saint. Most Catholics called his house Priestland.

Basil Hayden had promised Badin the services of the few slaves that Hayden had purchased for Holy Cross's founder, William De Rohan, but Hayden failed to deliver these workers. Other parishioners reneged on their promise to cultivate the surrounding two hundred acres at Priestland. Badin was reduced to a beggar. With a drought the following summer, he figured, "Divine Providence has the design perhaps to punish…[the parishioners] for their indolence." With the drought, he thought the people got what they deserved.[10]

CHANGES IN THE CATHOLIC LANDSCAPE

In 1796 French priest Michael J.C. Fournier made the Rolling Fork settlement his home. Seven years later, when working on his farm, Fournier burst a blood vessel and died. Catholics on the Rolling Fork were left without a resident minister.

A French classmate of Fournier's, Anthony Salmon, arrived at Priestland on January 31, 1799. Salmon soon grew devoted to the slaves. While at the house of Thomas Gwynn near Bardstown, Salmon quizzed the slaves on their catechism, asking a sixteen-year-old girl, "Which is the last sacrament you would wish to receive were you at the point of death?" Looking down to the last on the list before her, she said, "Matrimony." Salmon's ministry appeared promising until less than a year after his arrival, Salmon was thrown from his horse. A slave spotted the injured priest, but he was kept from seeking aid by his bigoted Protestant overseer. Eventually Salmon was taken to Thomas Gwynn's house, where Salmon died on November 10, 1799.[11]

The troublesome, wandering, wealthy Boston priest, John Thayer, arrived in Scott County, Kentucky, the year Salmon died. Thayer came with grandiose plans, including a vague proposal to eliminate slavery and a promise to establish a convent in Kentucky. Kentucky Catholics did not like Thayer. One of the most revered lay Catholics on the frontier, Eleanor Bradford

Lancaster, informed Badin of Thayer's frequent sexual abuse of women who had sought his absolution in the confessional. After various women delivered sworn testimony against Thayer, Thayer admitted to his misbehavior, but added, "Is there any thing but kisses & embraces? & who can judge my intention?"[12]

Charging that Thayer had committed offenses much more serious than kisses and embraces, Badin "heartily despise[d]" Thayer." Trustees at Scott County asserted that no money could make up for Thayer's crimes, and Protestants blamed the Catholic Church for hiding a bad man as a priest. Bishop Carroll moaned when word of Thayer's exploits spread to the east coast.[13]

After a tumultuous five years, Thayer left Kentucky exclaiming from the port of New Orleans that he should have never been ordained. But then, Thayer resumed his priestly ministry in England and Ireland, where he gained a following of women. Thayer most likely continued his sexual indiscretions. After his death, the executor of Thayer's will followed Thayer's wishes and built an Ursuline convent near Boston with Thayer's inheritance. Several years later, an angry mob burnt the convent to the ground after hearing unsubstantiated rumors that priests had sexually abused the nuns living there.

Evangelical Protestantism took off after the Kentucky Cane Ridge Revival of 1801, which spurred the Second Great Awakening. In 1803 President Thomas Jefferson purchased from France the vast Louisiana territory (out of which all or portions of fifteen states would be carved). The United States doubled in size.

The newly acquired city of New Orleans was dominated by the controversial Spanish Capuchin pastor of the Church of Saint Louis, Fray Antonio Moreno Arze, more commonly known as Père Antoine. Because of Père Antoine's ongoing dominance of New Orleans, nine years later, when Louis Valentin Dubourg was consecrated the first administrator (and later bishop) of Louisiana and the Floridas, Dubourg resided not in the diocesan seat, New Orleans, but in St. Louis.

With few reliable priest coworkers on the Kentucky frontier, Badin endorsed certain prayer books that he thought might promote uniformity of religious practice. Maryland Jesuits published the most popular religious book in Kentucky, the *Pious Guide to Prayer and Devotion*. This work promoted the ability of each person to participate in the mystery of salvation. It also downplayed the role of the hierarchical Church, the saints, and priests.

Badin preferred the work of another early Kentucky missionary. Fellow Frenchman John Baptist David's *True Piety* encouraged Catholics to perform every religious act with care and diligence. Catholics should carry crosses, examine their conscience, read spiritual works, give alms, visit the sick, poor, and incarcerated, and withdraw from worldly things. Pleasures and amusements must be minimized. In sharp contrast to the *Pious Guide*, *True Piety* exaggerated the corruption of human nature, and the inability of humans to do any good without God's grace.

Fun-loving Kentucky pioneers did not like *True Piety*, and did not like the priests who promoted it, including Badin and the Belgian, Charles Nerinckx. Arriving in Kentucky in 1805, Nerinckx built ten churches. Like Badin, Nerinckx tirelessly road the circuit. Upon arriving early in the morning to hear confessions, Nerinckx was once asked by local Catholics where he had spent the night. "With Captain Dogwood," Nerinckx said, meaning that he had slept under the trees.[14]

Some Kentucky Catholics grew to revere the physical and spiritual stamina of Nerinckx and Badin; many did not. Representing the Rolling Fork and Pottinger's Creek communities, Robert Abell and John Lancaster refused to pay Badin the sixty pounds that he requested as annual salary. Badin likened Abell and Lancaster to Jacobins who had recently plundered the Catholic Church during the French Revolution.

Another French priest, Michael Barrière, had granted Lancaster power of attorney over the church at Holy Cross. Lancaster had built this church during Barrière's short, four-month stay in Kentucky. But Lancaster did not maintain the structure according to Badin's standards. After birds had defiled the altar with dung, Badin threatened to close the building. Lay women continued to perform rituals in the church, but no priest celebrated Mass at Holy Cross for ten months.

In 1805 twenty French priests and brothers of the Order of Cistercians of the Strict Observance, more commonly called Trappists, landed in

Kentucky not far from Holy Cross. The land where these Trappists resided was infested with eight hundred snakes. The Trappists soon left Kentucky (but another group returned forty-three years later to establish at a different central Kentucky location the current Abbey of Gethsemanie).

Also in 1805 John Lancaster persuaded Dominican Fathers, led by Maryland-born Edward Dominic Fenwick, to pick Kentucky over Georgia as the place to establish the first permanent Dominican home in the United States. Dominicans opened Saint Rose Priory near Cartwright's Creek just outside the town of Springfield, Kentucky. Of English origin, the Dominicans proved more sensitive than their French counterparts to frontier customs. Three years after establishing themselves in Kentucky, the Dominicans opened the college of Saint Thomas Aquinas, which produced the first native Kentucky priests (and also educated Jefferson Davis, the future President of the Confederacy).

Nerinckx and Badin finally returned to Holy Cross about the time John Lancaster ran for U.S. Congress in the summer of 1806. Badin favored Lancaster's opponent. While Nerinckx conducted services inside the church, Badin slipped outside to confront a crowd of men gathered in the church-yard. "Gentlemen, I am sorry to find you here, at the time of benediction," he said. Addressing the leader of the group, "Mr. Lancaster," Badin asked, "would you rather electioneer than receive the benediction of the Holy Sacrament?" The men fell silent, and Badin walked away, at which point Lancaster laughed.[15]

Badin turned around. "What is the matter, Mr. Lancaster?" "I say, sir, you are mistaken," Lancaster explained, "I am not electioneering." "But you are not [attending Mass]," Badin insisted, "and it is a bad example given to children and negroes; it would be better to stay at home." Lancaster replied, "I have as much right to be here as you." "Mr. Lancaster," Badin said, "you are acting improperly." Lancaster then cut a twig with a knife and approached him. Badin moved toward Lancaster. Lancaster declared, "Sir, I wish you to know that, if you will drive others, you will not drive me." "If I drive others," Badin shot back, "I will drive you with them." Badin walked away, unable to hear Lancaster mutter, "You are not in France, we are in a free country, Sir."[16]

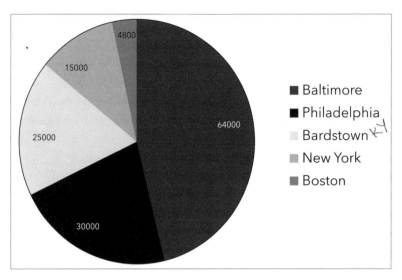

Rough Estimate of U.S. Catholic population (1808)

Badin next reminded the congregation inside Holy Cross to revere the church, the sacraments, and the priest. He also demanded public penance from Lancaster. In subsequent days Badin repeatedly wrote to Bishop Carroll to detail the confrontation with Lancaster (who lost the election but never showed remorse to Badin). Badin also informed Carroll that Kentucky law did not permit trustees to hold church property. As a result, Carroll allowed Badin to seize control of Holy Cross from Lancaster, and to put all other assets of the church of Kentucky in Badin's name.[17]

THE CREATION OF THE DIOCESE OF BARDSTOWN

Carroll next contemplated a bishop for Kentucky. Many Catholics feared that Badin would be chosen. The vast majority of Kentucky Catholics opposed his rigidity, exacting discipline, contentious nature, and relentless opposition to dancing. Badin recognized his incompatibility and in 1807 went to Baltimore to recommend another candidate, French Sulpician Benedict Joseph Flaget.

In 1808 Pope Pius VII raised Baltimore to the level of an archdiocese that oversaw four new dioceses, Boston, New York, Philadelphia, and Bardstown. Bardstown probably had about half as many Catholics as Baltimore, and about the same Catholic population as Philadelphia. Yet Bardstown by far encompassed the largest territory of the now five Catholic areas. The diocese of Bardstown extended from the Great Lakes to the Deep South, from the Appalachian Mountains to the Mississippi River (including most of Kentucky, Tennessee, Missouri, Illinois, Indiana, Ohio and Michigan).

Out of the diocese of Bardstown would come thirty-six other dioceses, including Cincinnati, Vincennes, Nashville, Detroit, and Chicago. In just thirty years, eight Bardstown priests became bishops. Countless other ordained and unordained women and men from Kentucky served the larger American Catholic community.

Badin was not pleased with the institutional growth of Bardstown, especially since he had to surrender his leadership. After a lengthy dispute with Bardstown Bishop Benedict Joseph Flaget (the man whom he had recommended for the position), Badin handed over legal rights to most of his Kentucky Catholic Church assets. Yet believing that Flaget had mistreated slaves in his ambitious building campaign, Badin arranged that his slaves not be given to Flaget but be taken care of by their white baptismal sponsors. Badin then fled to France in 1819.

In 1828 Badin returned to the United States, but not to Kentucky. With help from Miss Campau, a missionary woman who had spent many years "for the honor of religion" among Native Americans near Detroit, he devoted his remaining days to Potawatomi and other indigenous peoples. He once visited some Ottawas near Fort Wayne. After hunters boiled a catch of pigeons, feathers and all, he readily dug in. When one of Badin's nonnative companions named Colerick hesitated, Badin scolded him, "Do not irritate and insult the red men; we might suffer from it. Strip the feathers from the legs and you will find them eatable."[18]

In northern Indiana, Badin purchased and then donated the land on which Holy Cross priest Edward Sorin built the University of Notre Dame in 1842. Bishop Flaget was at that time in the process of moving the diocesan seat from Bardstown to Louisville. A dramatic increase in the number of Catholic immigrants had warranted such a change. About the time Flaget passed away in 1849, Badin retired from missionary work. He spent his

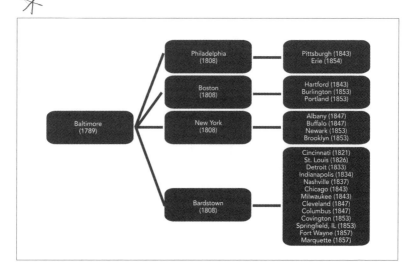

U.S. Dioceses before Civil War
Other dioceses were added with and after the 1803 Louisiana Purchase (New Orleans, 1793; Mobile, 1829; Little Rock, 1843), with further split of Baltimore (Charleston and Richmond, 1820; Savannah and Wheeling, 1850; Alexandria, 1853), and with westward expansion (Dubuque, 1837; Los Angeles, 1840; Portland, OR, 1846; Galveston, 1847; Minnesota, Sante Fe, and Seattle, 1850; San Francisco, 1853)

remaining days in Cincinnati, though restlessness occasionally took him back to missionary territory.

In his early eighties, Badin returned to Fort Wayne, where his host, fellow French priest J. Benoit, heard an odd knocking sound coming from the church belfry. Upon further investigation Benoit discovered Badin using a hatchet to knock away the painted lattice work around the church bell. "What are you doing there, Father Badin?" shouted Benoit. "Don't you want your bell to be heard?" asked Badin.

Badin died in Cincinnati on April 19, 1853. His remains were eventually placed in a log chapel replica of his missionary headquarters, built on the site where his original 1831 cabin stood. The chapel now overlooks Saint Mary's Lake at the University of Notre Dame.[19]

Central Kentucky Catholics seemed to forget about Badin but revered Flaget, along with many other early contributors to the Kentucky Catholic Church. Through many generations, Kentucky Catholics named offspring after ancestors and relatives who had built the Church there. Residents of the Bardstown area to this day refer to this part of the state as "an American holy land." The landscape still includes the memory, if not the structures, of numerous Catholic churches, schools, convents, seminaries, and cemeteries that grew out of the early diocesan period.

In 1793 after Bishop Carroll made Badin the first priest ordained in the United States, he gave him a three-volume edition of the Douay-Rheims version of the Bible. Badin carried this Bible throughout his quarter century in Kentucky and evidently donated it to the Sisters of Loretto in Nerinx before he left the state in 1819. Almost two hundred years later, on July 14, 2014, the Sisters of Loretto sold Badin's Bible to the University of Notre Dame. Observers can still read Carroll's inscription in the Bible to Badin.

↑ photo

CHAPTER SIX

Leading Women
and Men

*E*lizabeth Ann "Betty" Seton was raised in a New York Episcopalian family, sang Methodist hymns, and admired the Quaker lifestyle. Her mother died before she was three. Her father remarried but divorced his second wife, and then he died when Seton was in her twenties. And Seton's husband declared bankruptcy and died before she turned thirty. Left alone with five small children, and wearing black the rest of her days, Seton was drawn to the solemnity of the Catholic Church. Family and friends mocked Seton for joining what they called the church of the poor. Seton responded by proclaiming that the Catholic Church was "the only ark in the world" outside which there was no salvation.[1]

In 1808 (the same year Pius VII carved four new dioceses out of Baltimore) Seton moved to Baltimore, professed vows as a religious sister, and organized the first American order of nuns at the former Fleming house (commonly called the Stone House) in rural Emmitsburg. Seton modeled her order after the Daughters of Charity of Saint Vincent de Paul and called the group the Sisters of Charity of Saint Joseph. By 1810 the sisters had moved into a more suitable log structure called Saint Joseph's House (now called the White House). Seton's sisters pledged to perform "works of piety, charity and usefulness and especially for the care of the sick, the succor of the aged and infirm and necessitious persons, and the education of young females." In Saint Joseph's House, the Sisters of Charity founded the first free U.S. Catholic school for girls, called Saint Joseph's School.[2] Other

Elizabeth Ann Seton

religious orders similarly formed at this time.

Seton meanwhile contracted tuberculosis and suffered with it the rest of her days. She buried two daughters and two young sisters-in-law at Emmitsburg. Maintaining faith in God, Seton nonetheless professed that "the black clouds I foresee may pass by harmless." Shortly before she died, Seton told a friend, "Mind not my health. Death grins broader in the pot every morning, and I grin at him and show him his master." The sisters buried her under an old oak tree in the convent's cemetery that she called "God's Little Acre." (The tree stood until 1984.) [3]

Beyond Baltimore

As early religious orders formed, the broader American Catholic community likewise organized. Bishop Carroll consecrated three new bishops over a few days in the fall of 1810. He had suggested all these candidates to Rome. But installation of new Church leadership did not always go smoothly.

Philadelphia Catholics included many good and faithful women and men, but serious problems had plagued that community from the beginning. In November 1810, Carroll consecrated the sickly Irish Franciscan Michael Egan as Bishop of Philadelphia. Eleven priests ministered to about thirty thousand Catholics spread over Pennsylvania and Delaware and the western and southern parts of New Jersey. Egan died four years later, eaten up by conflicts with trustees of Philadelphia's Saint Mary's Church.

Chaos ruled the six years that followed, during which time the priest left in charge of Philadelphia, Frenchman Adolph Louis de Barth, lived mostly in western Pennsylvania. During de Barth's absence, Irish priest William Hogan took charge of Saint Mary's Church in Philadelphia. Charismatic,

William Hogan

popular, and courageous, yet also aristocratic, arrogant, and head-strong, Hogan lacked proper training as a priest, disdained authority, and acted impulsively. Hogan often committed questionable acts goaded on by trustees who did not get along with other clerical leaders.

The elderly second bishop of Philadelphia, Irishman William Conwell, excommunicated Hogan twice, after which time Hogan associated with the notorious ex-nun, Maria Monk. Like Monk, Hogan published anti-Catholic tracts. Yet Rome also eventually ordered Conwell to resign due to his ineptitude during the Hogan affair. De Barth, Hogan, and Conwell, along with a slew of other Philadelphia priests, were charged with various sexual crimes. Hogan and Conwell faced legal proceedings (and both were exonerated).

Some twenty years after the diocese of Philadelphia was created, Pope Pius VIII raised Irishman Francis Patrick Kenrick from priest-professor in Kentucky to Coadjutor of Philadelphia with full powers of administration. Kenrick finally brought peace to Philadelphia by firmly asserting his authority.

Catholics in New England experienced much less trouble. On November 1, 1810, Carroll consecrated Frenchman Jean Lefebvre de Cheverus as Bishop of Boston. With help from Cheverus's friend and priest coworker, Abbé François Matignon, Cheverus ministered to about 4,600 Catholics, including 750 persons in the Maine Indian missions.

During many years of ministry both before and after the establishment of the Boston diocese, Cheverus and Matignon had lived among natives and had mastered their dialect. Both men also visited other scattered Catholics. They nursed the sick and buried the dead especially during two yellow fever epidemics. Cheverus and Matignon also collected funds to build the first cathedral of the Holy Cross, all the way earning the respect of many non-Catholics, including President John Adams, who headed the list of Protestant contributors to the cathedral building fund.

Carroll had not offered a candidate for the bishop of New York, which prompted Rome to select Italian Dominican Richard Concanen in 1810, but Concanen died waiting for a ship to the United States. Over the next five years, an Alsatian Jesuit, Anthony Kohlmann, served as Vicar General over the New York diocese. At that time, the diocese included the state of New York and northern New Jersey. Kohlmann opened the first Catholic school for boys in New York, the New York Literary Institution, and planned to build a cathedral.

A French woman had meanwhile brought a slave named Pierre to New York from Haiti, and set him free in her last will and testament. Pierre took the last name Toussaint, after Toussaint L'Ouverture, the man who had recently freed Haiti from French rule. Pierre Toussaint married Juliette Noel, a slave twenty years younger than Toussaint. Toussaint had purchased Juliette, and then set her free. The Toussaints were deeply devoted to each other, and also cared for the poor, nursed the sick, and opened their home to wayward youth.

The Toussaints helped Kohlman raise funds to build Saint Patrick's Cathedral (now the Basilica of Saint Patrick's Old Cathedral) in lower Manhattan on Mulberry Street. In an era when blacks were not allowed to ride horses in New York City, Toussaint walked to Saint Patrick's Cathedral every day to attend Mass. The church stood so much on the fringe of the city (today only about twenty blocks from the former World Trade Center) that a fox was captured in the churchyard not long after the church had opened.

Four years into Kohlmann's term as vicar general, Pope Pius VII appointed Bishop Concanen's former student, Irish Dominican John Connolly, as the second bishop of New York. But Connolly's crossing took so long that New York Catholics figured his ship had been lost at sea. Finally arriving about a year after his appointment, Connolly inherited three churches, four priests, and about fifteen thousand mostly poor Irish Catholics.

Despite substantial debt, Connolly built a half dozen churches, ordained five priests, and introduced Elizabeth Seton's Sisters of Charity to New York. The Sisters of Charity opened Saint Patrick's School across the street from

Pierre Toussaint

the cathedral. Ongoing tension with lay trustees and between Irish and French clergymen nonetheless marred the next decade of New York Catholic history. After ten years as bishop, Connolly contracted a disease from two of his priests, Richard Bulger and Michael O'Gorman. The two priests had caught the illness (and subsequently died) while ministering to the sick of the parish. Connolly passed away as well.

BACK IN BARDSTOWN

On November 4, 1810 Carroll consecrated Benedict Joseph Flaget Bishop of Bardstown. Flaget arrived in Kentucky in early June 1811 "without money, without a house, without property, almost without any acquaintance…in the midst of a Diocese two or three times larger than all of France…and myself speaking the language, too, very imperfectly." Somewhere between twenty thousand and thirty thousand Catholics lived under Flaget's vast jurisdiction.[4]

On a farm three miles south of Bardstown, Flaget built a thirty-by-eighteen-foot, two-story log house. Flaget named the structure Saint Thomas in honor of Thomas Howard, the Catholic who had donated the land. Flaget put fellow Frenchman John Baptist David in charge of three seminarians they had brought from France at what was called Saint Thomas's Seminary, located on the same property. Tension between French clergy and native laity continued, and Flaget railed against trusteeism.

But Flaget also welcomed a number of local women who came forward to form three distinct religious orders. With encouragement from Charles Nerinckx, in April 1812 Mary Rhodes, Christina Stuart, and Ann Havern founded the Friends of Mary at the Foot of the Cross. The Sisters of Loretto, as the order was soon renamed, was the first American congregation not directly linked to a European motherhouse. Nerinckx's original rules for the Sisters of Loretto were harsh and contributed to the premature death of some of the sisters. The order nonetheless flourished in their primary ministry, the education of young girls.

Nerinckx also started a black sisterhood devoted to the education of slave children. Three young black women came forth and moved in with the Sisters of Loretto, but Nerinckx died before the new black branch was firmly established.

"Answering the call of John Baptist David to form another religious order dedicated to the education of girls, Teresa Carrico and Elizabeth "Betsey" Wells on December 1, 1812 took up residence at the log house built by Flaget at Saint Thomas. Four other women, including Catherine Spalding, soon joined Carrico and Wells. The group then elected Spalding the first superior of what became the Sisters of Charity of Nazareth. About ten years later, the women moved north of Bardstown and engaged in numerous ministries.

In a small, two-story building behind Saint Louis Church in Louisville, Catherine Spalding opened Presentation Academy for Protestant and Catholic girls, and also reached out to "levee rats," that is, poor children residing near the wharf. After the death of his wife, a Protestant father from Pennsylvania asked Spalding to care for his two girls, one an infant. "I will look upon this child and raise it as it were my own," Spalding replied. The infant slept in Spalding's room. The child wept bitterly when she discovered that "Mumsie," that is, Catherine Spalding, was not her real mother. The "Penn babies," as the girls were called, became the first orphans the Sisters of Charity of Nazareth cared for at Saint Vincent Orphanage (located on the same property as the original school, near Fifth and Walnut where the cathedral, Spalding University, and today's Presentation Academy now stand).[5]

Ten years after the Sisters of Loretto and Sisters of Charity began, Angela Sansbury organized the first Dominican convent in America. Like the

Mother Catherine Spalding

other Kentucky sisters, the first Dominican sisters were poor, barely able to squeeze into the log cabin that Dominican priests had set up for them at Saint Rose near Springfield. The Dominican women nonetheless decorated their home with jonquils, or March lilies, that every spring covered the Cartwright Creek valley in which they resided (and which still bloom around the larger convent and Saint Catharine College that the Dominican Sisters run to this day).

EXPANSION INTO THE WEST AND NORTH

Other female religious orders grew outside Kentucky. A young French girl, Rose Philippine Duchesne, had marveled over stories of American missionary priests. In 1817 the newly consecrated Bishop of Louisiana, William Dubourg (who still resided at St. Louis), visited the Sacred Heart convent that Duchesne had joined in France. She begged Dubourg to take her to the United States. Ursulines, 1727

With four fellow sisters Duchesne arrived at New Orleans in 1818 and traveled up the Mississippi to what she called the "the remotest village in the U.S.," St. Charles, Missouri. Across the river at Florrisant, she established the first community in the United States of the Sisters of the Sacred Heart of Jesus.[6]

Within a decade the Sisters of the Sacred Heart grew to six communities with numerous schools for girls, including one for Potawatomi children in Sugar Creek, Kansas. Countless religious sisters from various congregations would similarly work with Native Americans. Unable to master the native language, Duchesne primarily ministered to the sick at Sugar Creek.

Ursuline Sister

She also spent long periods in prayer, which caused native children to call her *Quahkahkanumad*, which means "Woman Who Prays Always."

Another religious group dreamt of greater success with natives. Upon the invitation of President James Monroe and Bishop Dubourg, Jesuit Charles Van Quickenborne, with seven Belgian seminarians, three Jesuit brothers, and six slaves, left Maryland the morning of April 11, 1823. "To Convert the Indians chiefly did we bid farewell to our Country and our homes," one of the seminarians exclaimed. "To the West they are to be found. Let us go!"[7]

Most travelers hired a pilot to assist them down the Ohio River from Wheeling, Virginia (now West Virginia), but Van Quickenborne saved money and simply purchased a pilot's manual. Twelve frightful days followed. The slaves constantly prayed the rosary. The beleaguered group finally abandoned the river at Louisville, and walked the rest of the way to St. Louis through bug invested fields.

When the Jesuits settled at Florissant, Duchesne predicted greater success in her ministry to Indians, but sadly found out that Van Quickenborne "would have nothing to do with us." Early European clergymen often fought with strong frontier women like Duchesne. Van Quickenborne was an especially contentious man, called "Napoleon" (what later generations might call "Hitler") by the seminarians and slaves he bossed around.[8]

With no assistance from the sisters, Van Quickenborne opened a school for Cherokee boys called Saint Regis Seminary, but Cherokee parents quickly withdrew their sons because these parents were alienated by his insistence that the Cherokee don European ways. Van Quickenborne suspended further outreach to natives.

Dubourg unexpectedly resigned as Bishop of Louisiana in 1826, after which time, Rome divided the diocese in two and appointed Dubourg's assistant, Italian Vincentian Joseph Rosati, the first bishop of St. Louis. Two years after that (about when Rome named another Vincentian, Leo de Neckère, Bishop of New Orleans), Rosati transferred to Van Quickenborne and the Jesuits the nine-year-old Saint Louis College. The Jesuits reestablished the college in a new building on Washington Avenue (now Saint Louis University on Grand Boulevard). Not far away, and during the same year, Elizabeth Seton's Sisters of Charity opened in John Mullanphy's house on St. Louis's Spruce Street the first Catholic hospital in the United States (called the St. Louis Mullanphy Hospital).

Also in 1826 the Irish-born John England put on his formal bishop's attire to address a joint session of the United States Congress. England had been Bishop of Charleston, South Carolina, for six years, had started the first regularly published Catholic newspaper, the *United States Catholic Miscellany*, and had written the *Constitution for the Diocese of Charleston*, which empowered lay people to collaborate with the clergy in the mission of the Church (and which tempered the abuses of trusteeism). For over two hours England lectured Congress on the compatibility of the United States and the Catholic Church.

A few years later, congressmen argued that Native Americans should be placed on reservations, which provoked John England to encourage priests to minister to these displaced peoples. As a result, Jesuit Pierre-Jean De Smet set out from St. Louis for the Bitterroot Valley of western Montana to try again to work with natives. This time De Smet and his fellow Jesuits adopted a less offensive attitude than earlier championed by Van Quickenborne in the failed Cherokee school. De Smet explained,

> In the beginning [of this new encounter]...we [came to realize that we] were very different peoples. We came from totally different worlds, each of which was very old. But we were also alike. We were human beings, occupying a portion of this earth that each of us considered to be the very center. We also shared a belief in a

mysterious power beyond ourselves, that made all life possible. We called it Amótkan or God; Sumeš or Sacrament. It was everything.[9]

For a time, the Salish people trusted De Smet, but when he and fellow Jesuits reached out to enemies to the Salish, the Blackfeet, the mission fell apart. De Smet spent the rest of his career defending Native American rights, famously winning over Lakota holy man, Sitting Bull, who wore a crucifix De Smet gave him. De Smet did not persuade Sitting Bull, however, to trust U.S. Government officials (who eventually killed him).

Recognizing the Holiness of American Catholics

A little before De Smet enjoyed success among the Salish, Slovenian missionary Frederic Irenaeus Baraga picked up the work of missionary Gabriel Richard in Michigan. A talented linguist, Baraga mastered the Ottawa language and won the nickname "the Snowshoe Priest" for tireless marches through harsh winters. (In time, Pope Pius IX named Baraga the first bishop of Sault Sainte Marie, Michigan, now the Diocese of Marquette.)

Dominican Samuel Charles Mazzuchelli also snow-shoed across what would become Iowa and Wisconsin in an "uninterrupted racing," as one account put it, "to points hundreds of miles apart." Mazzuchelli administered the sacraments and preached the word of God to French-Canadian fur traders, American pioneers, and Ojibwe, Ottawa, Menominee, and Winnebago peoples. Mazzuchelli founded over thirty parishes and two colleges, and built more than twenty churches, along with a number of civic structures. As various treaties hurt indigenous folks, Mazzuchelli protested vigorously to Congress about injustices done to natives.[10]

Baltimore had meanwhile grown into a haven for Catholic refugees from the Haitian revolution, rendering Baltimore the "free black capital of America." French-born tax collector James Joubert had fled Haiti during the revolution, eventually landing in Baltimore where he joined the Sulpicians on Paca Street. In 1827 Joubert assumed control of the ministry to Haitian refugees that emanated out of Saint Mary's Seminary. Joubert then approached fellow émigré and free black teacher, Elizabeth Clarisse Lange. In 1828 Joubert and Lange formed the Oblate Sisters of Providence, the first permanent religious community of Catholic women of African heritage in the United States. The Oblate rule declared that the sisters were "a Religious society of Coloured Women…who renounce the world to consecrate themselves to God, and to the Christian education of young girls of color."[11]

In 1841 the Daughters of Charity of Emmitsburg built a new chapel, and in 1846 Elizabeth Seton's son, William, donated $250, a substantial amount for the time, to build a mortuary chapel for his mother's remains. In 1850 the Emmitsburg community merged with the French Daughters of Charity, perhaps realizing some of Seton's original intentions. Before forming the Sisters of Charity, Seton had hoped to join the French Daughters of Charity of Saint Vincent de Paul, but the Napoleonic Wars prevented her from traveling to France and realizing this dream.

After 1850 the Emmitsburg sisters wore the distinctive wide white cornette (a headdress that seems to have wings) of their French counterparts. But the Sisters of Charity in Cincinnati refused to merge, believing that joining the French group entailed abandoning Seton's original charism. The Cincinnati sisters kept wearing the mourning dress of Elizabeth Seton.

On March 17, 1963, Pope John XXIII beatified Seton, recalling that "In a house that was very small, but with ample space for charity, she sowed a seed in America which by Divine Grace grew into a large tree." In 1965 the Daughters of Charity moved Seton's remains to Saint Joseph's Chapel that they had just completed in conjunction with the building of a new Motherhouse. On September 14, 1975, Pope Paul VI canonized Seton, the first native-born citizen of the United States to become a saint. "Elizabeth Ann Seton is a saint," Paul VI proclaimed, "St. Elizabeth Ann Seton is an American…Elizabeth Ann Seton was wholly American! Rejoice for your glorious daughter. Be proud of her. And know how to preserve her fruitful heritage." In 1991, Pope John Paul II designated Saint Joseph's Chapel as a minor basilica.[12]

Three years earlier, John Paul II had canonized the woman who always prays, Rose Philippine Duchesne. Duchesne's remains rest in the Shrine of Saint Philippine Duchesne in St. Charles, Missouri. In 1993 and 1996, respectively, John Paul II also declared Samuel Mazzuchelli and Pierre Toussaint "venerable," a significant step in the process toward sainthood. Toussaint's remains were moved from the cemetery around New York's

Old Saint Patrick's Cathedral to Saint Patrick's Cathedral on Fifth Avenue. Considered the founder of Catholic charitable works in the United States, Toussant is the first layperson buried in that cathedral's crypt. In 2012 Pope Benedict XVI declared venerable the snowshoe priest, Frederic Baraga.

CHAPTER SEVEN

Irish and German
Immigrants

*A*fter a harrowing trip across the Atlantic Ocean in early 1809, twenty-three-year-old John O'Raw informed his parents, "Through the mercy of divine Providence I am still in existence." Many young Catholic men fled Ireland throughout the eighteenth and nineteenth centuries. For a long time Great Britain had prohibited Catholics from owning land, and stripped them of their religious rights. Many Irish Catholics lost their faith. Some sought better opportunities elsewhere. Large numbers died on the so-called coffin ships escaping Ireland. [1]

It is "almost impossible to believe," remarked Baltimore Archbishop Ambrose Maréchal, the number of refugees flocking to the United States. "About two hundred immigrants per day came to our shores [in 1818]," exclaimed Maréchal, and "among these there were very many Catholics." The need for laborers to build the Erie Canal across the northeastern United States prompted further immigration. Small but tight Irish communities developed in Philadelphia, Providence, New York, Baltimore, and Boston. From 1810 to 1830 the American Catholic population doubled. [2]

Some non-Catholic groups feared Catholics were gaining too much ground. In 1830 Presbyterians recruited a popular preacher, Lyman Beecher from Litchfield, Connecticut, to win the West (now called the Midwest) for Protestantism. As president of Cincinnati's Lane Theological Seminary, Beecher delivered fiery addresses that charged, "The Catholic system is adverse to liberty, and the clergy to a great extent are dependent upon foreigners opposed to the principles of our government." (Much to Beecher's chagrin, his daughter, the future author of *Uncle Tom's Cabin*, Harriet Beecher Stowe, befriended Cincinnati Bishop John Purcell.) [3]

As Lyman Beecher raged against Catholics, several Irish women immigrated to the United States, joined the Ursuline sisters, and opened a school for girls at Charlestown just outside Boston. In 1832 a disgruntled student and a convert to Catholicism, Rebecca Reed, denounced the Charlestown convent as a wicked and corrupt place. Two years later the Boston *Mercantile Journal* complained that Sister Mary John Harrison had escaped the convent only to be recaptured and reimprisoned. The following morning, several handbills posted around Charlestown aired further accusations of sexual misbehavior at the convent. Two days later, August 11, 1834 sixty or so Scots-Presbyterians burned the convent to the ground.

Another disgruntled convert named Maria Monk associated with a women's Canadian Catholic order, the Religious Hospitallers of Saint Joseph. Nuns at the convent supposedly forced Monk to "obey the priests in all things," which included living "in the practice of criminal intercourse with them." Monk allegedly conceived a child through a priest, escaped to New York City, and in 1836 published her incredibly popular *Awful Disclosures of the Hôtel Dieu Nunnery of Montreal.*[4]

The Ancient Order of Hibernians immediately organized near New York's Saint James Church. A Catholic fraternal society whose origin dated back to mid-sixteenth century Ireland, the Ancient Order of Hibernians in the United States assisted Irish Catholic immigrants and guarded Catholic churches from anti-Catholic violence. Branches of the Hibernians formed at Pottsville, Pennsylvania, and spread as far as California, but the activities and very existence of the Hibernians were kept secret for a number of years. The trustees of New York's Saint Patrick's Cathedral meanwhile built a wall around the churchyard to protect it from possible attack. And Maria Monk extended her tale in subsequent editions of her book.

A steady, though smaller stream of Germans also moved to the United States. These Germans might more accurately be called Pomeranians or Bavarians or be named after one of the other many independent states that constituted what was at that time a loose German confederation. Germany did not exist as a separate country until the late nineteenth century. The people living in what would become the German nation mostly spoke German, though they used different dialects and different words. German speakers were Lutheran, Jewish, and Roman Catholic. And German speaking people immigrated for a variety of economic, social, religious, and political reasons.

About a hundred miles west of St. Louis, seven families from the Westphalia region of Germany settled in 1835 near the Maries River (in present-day Osage County). The green, rolling hillsides of middle Missouri reminded them of their German homeland. These immigrants were well educated. They hoped to associate with an institution of higher learning. In August 1835 Jesuits from Saint Louis College (now Saint Louis University) visited the Maries River region, celebrated Mass with the immigrants in a log hut, and built a school.

Some German newcomers to middle Missouri still grew disappointed by the primitive conditions of frontier America and returned to Germany. Others flocked to the city of St. Louis, whose population doubled in about five years to around sixteen thousand. Over the next decade, that number increased five times to about eighty thousand persons. About half of the newcomers were Catholic. Other American cities, including western towns like Milwaukee and Cincinnati, saw similar increases from German immigration.

Ferdinand Helias and Francis de Sales Brunner

In 1838 St. Louis Jesuits sent Ferdinand Helias to reside among the Germans still in rural central Missouri. Helias had been born to a wealthy family in French Flanders (now Belgium) in the same house where the Holy Roman Emperor Charles V had been raised some three hundred years before. After Helias joined the Jesuits, his Flemish superiors sent him to America. They deemed Helias too wild and energetic for any European cloister.

Upriver from the hut in which central Missouri immigrants had previously gathered to pray, Helias used his family wealth to erect a new church. He christened the structure Saint Joseph's. Saint Joseph's congregation started to call the area around the church New Westphalia (later shortened

Ferdinand Helias

to Westphalia). Helias returned to St. Louis in 1842 due to some undisclosed trouble with parishioners, but went back to Westphalia six years later and blessed the cornerstone for a new Saint Joseph's Church (still standing). The town that grew up around the church replicated an Old World Village. Jesuits stationed at Saint Joseph's helped preserve the German heritage of the immigrants, and also used Saint Joseph's as a stepping stone for further missionary efforts among Native Americans.

Helias also served as the first Catholic priest to minister to the inmates of Missouri's state prison in Jefferson City, about twenty miles from Westphalia. A Missouri court sentenced to death a young Englishman, Henry Lane, for some heinous crime. Various ministers tried to make an impression on Lane as he prepared for his execution. But Lane rejected their counsel. Then Helias met with Lane. In a few days Lane "walked to the scaffold without handcuffs and with a crucifix in his hand," all the while warning spectators against the ills of drunkenness. The rope broke as the hangman put the noose around Lane's neck, but Lane was not phased. "He preserved to the end in his pious sentiments," onlookers observed, "the sacred names of Jesus and Mary rising to his lips in the brief spell of agony that preceded death."[5]

About the same time that central Missouri was settled, other Catholic immigrants from the German provinces of Westphalia and Oldenburg cleared dense forests and uncovered productive farmland about a hundred miles north of Cincinnati (in what is now Mercer County). These Catholic immigrants helped build two canals that connected Lake Erie to the Ohio River, and that ran just to the east and west of the immigrants' newly cleared land. German immigrant farmers sent produce north and south along the canal, and worked secondary jobs in the many manufacturing plants that popped up in the area. This hybrid rural-manufacturing economy enabled Catholic immigrants to weather the cyclical challenges of farm life. The region grew prosperous.

Francis de Sales Brunner encouraged these immigrants to organize around the Catholic Church. Born in Switzerland, Brunner had been ordained a priest at the Swiss Benedictine Mariastein "Mary of the Rock" Abbey, but political turmoil in Europe provoked him to abandon Europe and head to the United States. When crossing the English Channel, he survived a storm supposedly due to the fact that he was carrying a painting depicting the Miraculous Madonna of Mariastein. Brunner had saved some sacred objects, including this painting and a number of relics, mostly bones of saints, from vandals threatening his Benedictine Abbey.

In the United States, Brunner founded several monasteries and mission stations, including in 1843 what he called Maria Stein, set up to serve the German immigrant community north of Cincinnati. Brunner donated the sacred objects he had saved from Europe to the Sisters of the Precious Blood who settled at Maria Stein. German immigrant craftsmen subsequently built many churches in this area with steeples, each topped with a cross. Local Catholics began to refer to their new American homeland as the land of the Cross-Tipped Churches.

Continuous strife in parts of Europe, especially in Italy, provoked European Catholic leaders to send more relics to the United States in order to preserve them. Ohio's Maria Stein sisters began to maintain perpetual adoration, that is, praying around the clock before their growing collection of sacred objects. In the late nineteenth century, Suitbert Mollinger, the pastor of the Most Holy Name of Jesus Parish in Pittsburgh's Troy Hill neighborhood, built Saint Anthony's Chapel to house an even larger collection of relics. (Today Saint Anthony's houses the largest collection of relics outside the Vatican, between four and five thousand items. Maria Stein houses the second largest collection in the United States, about eleven hundred relics.)

Back in Ohio on November 9, 1843, former President John Quincy Adams laid the cornerstone for the Cincinnati Observatory. Cincinnatians named the hill on which the observatory stood Mount Adams in honor of the President. Adams supposedly praised the observatory "as a beacon of true science that should never be obscured by the dark shadows of superstition and intolerance symbolized by the Popish Cross" (that is, by the Catholic Church). Upon hearing these words, Cincinnati Bishop John Purcell purportedly prayed that the observatory would fail. Whether Adams actually spoke these words is unclear (and Purcell's response is just as uncertain), though the ideas attributed to Adams (and to Purcell) definitely captured some anti-Catholic (and pro-Catholic) sentiment of the time.[6]

Anti-Catholic violence surfaced elsewhere. In the summer of 1844, some native-born residents of Philadelphia claimed that the new Irish Catholics in town wished to remove the Bible from schools. Philadelphia Catholics actually only asked that Catholic children be allowed to read the Douay-Rheims, or Catholic, version of the Bible as part of the mandated daily biblical readings. In a series of riots from May 6 to July 7, 1844, Irish Catholics and native-born residents of Philadelphia clashed. Two Catholic churches were destroyed, and twenty-nine people, some from each side, were killed.

EFFECTS OF IRELAND'S POTATO FAMINE

In October 1845, blight devastated the main crop of Irish farmers. "It is the most dreadful the state the potatoes are in in Ireland," wrote Hannah Curtis to her brother John Curtis. He had immigrated to the United States some time before. "We are greatly afraid there will be a famine this year if the Lord does not do something," Hannah added. Six months later, Hannah's uncle, William Dunne reported, "There is neither Employment nor food [in Ireland], the people…in a starving state and dying in hundreds."[7]

As the "Great Hunger" continued through 1852, at least one million Irish women and men died. "Every one that can go to America is going," Hannah Curtis reported, "as there is no prospect of any thing here but poverty and sickness." Please send money so that I can join you in the United States, Hannah begged her brother. "Send…for me now."[8]

From 1845 to 1855, 1.8 million mostly poor, illiterate, Gaelic-speaking, Irish Catholic farmers and laborers left Ireland for Canada and the United States. Most of these immigrants could not afford to move beyond the east coast. Even those who could head west tended to favor large cities, where they soon constituted the country's first urban poor. Irish immigrants escaped starvation in Ireland only to find grim circumstances in America.

Irish neighborhoods, such as Five Points in lower Manhattan, festered as disease-ridden, crime-infested slums where corrupt landlords ruled. Taverns such as Manhattan's McSorley's Old Ale House grew as popular places for Irishmen to forget bad times, and to hope for a better life. (Following the motto "Good Ale, Raw Onions and No Ladies," McSorley's did not admit women until legally forced to do so in 1970).

Many Catholic bishops offered spiritual and material aid. John Hughes of New York and Peter Kenrick of St. Louis, both Irish immigrants, organized national congregations, that is, communities where people with similar backgrounds speaking the same language worshipped under the same roof. Known as "Dagger John" and the "Lion" for their aggressive styles, Hughes and Kenrick, respectively, reintroduced immigrants to the Catholic faith. Hughes also created one of the country's first independent Catholic school systems. Many bishops followed suit.

Hughes, Kenrick, and other bishops also opened lending institutions, commonly called the "Bishop's Bank." Immigrants struggled to secure loans at reasonable rates from secular banks but readily trusted the church with their money. The church, in turn, gained resources to build the institutions necessary to meet immigrant needs. Kenrick's bank was so successful that during a major economic crisis that affected the entire country, Kenrick lent money to the city of St. Louis. Purcell's bank in Cincinnati, on the other hand, failed under the lackadaisical bookkeeping of his brother, Father Edward Purcell.

Young Irish immigrant men took whatever jobs they could find, including manual labor that slaveholders considered too risky for slaves. Irish women found occupations that were less available in their homeland, including domestic work, nursing, and teaching. Many Irish women later took on factory jobs. The number of female Irish immigrants eventually outnumbered male Irish immigrants (though Hannah Curtis probably never made it to the United States).

Following the directives of the Catholic Church, Irish women married, bore many children, and carried the brunt of family responsibility. Yet the most successful female Irish immigrants may have been those who remained single. Irish women far exceeded all other immigrants groups who joined American religious orders.

Irish immigrants gained political power through association with New York's Tammany Society. Founded at the time of the American Revolution and named for Tamanend, a Native American leader of the Lenape Native American people, the Tammany Society served as a major hub of the Democratic Party throughout the 1800s. The Tammany Society assisted Irish immigrants in many constructive ways.

The Tammany Society also built a massive hall on East Fourteenth Street, out of which William "Boss" Tweed ran an efficient and horribly corrupt political machine. Tweed developed much of Manhattan, including the Brooklyn Bridge, but also stole as much as two hundred million dollars from the City of New York. Convicted of theft, he died in the Ludlow Street jail. Obituaries reported that he had been raised a Quaker, though he showed no obvious religious affiliation during his lifetime.

German Influence in the Mid-1800s

Attempts to unite the German nation states under one king prompted more democratically minded Germans to consider moving to the United States. After the 1848 revolt against the German aristocracy failed, middle class, educated, and skilled German Forty-Eighters, as they were called, came to the United States. In many cities Forty-Eighters organized musical societies, art and theater groups, and other cultural institutions, including Turner Halls, where German immigrants exercised their bodies and engaged their minds. Milwaukee became known as the "German Athens of America."

German immigrants often came as families. Most Germans headed west to the so-called German Triangle between Cincinnati, St. Louis, and Milwaukee. "You will…ask: is it really good in America," posed J.K. Meidenbauer from Milwaukee, "and I can give you the answer, from my full conviction…. Yes, it is really good here." "I thank the Lord that I am here," wrote another German immigrant, "and regret that I did not come sooner."[9]

"Stay German, German!" advised one philanthropist who sent some German school sisters to America. In countless retreats given to German

Milwaukee's Turner Hall, 1869

immigrants, Jesuit Francis Wenninger similarly encouraged German pride, often proclaiming that, "Language Saves Faith!" The German language so dominated certain areas of Milwaukee that some shopkeepers hung signs to assure non-German patrons that they could find "English Spoken Here."[10]

In 1846 German Benedictine Boniface Wimmer founded the first Benedictine monastery in the United States, Saint Vincent Archabbey, forty miles southeast of Pittsburgh. At the Archabbey, Wimmer trained priests who could speak German. As was customary in Germany, Wimmer also ran a brewery, that is, until Irish Bishop Michael O'Connor of Pittsburgh, an ardent opponent of alcohol, registered his complaint.

While visiting some strong and independent yet unpretentious German Catholics at Jasper in south central Indiana, pioneer Bishop Simon Bruté of Vincennes "saw several of the people shed tears because…there was no one to break the Bread of Salvation for them." In the summer of 1852 the first missionary priest in the area, Josef Kundek, asked for help from Swiss Benedictine monks.[11]

Benedictine priest, Ulrich Christen soon reported that "the inhabitants of Indiana are a good people, simple and open in their disposition; corruption has not yet penetrated into their morals." Two years later, the Benedictines

John Nepomucene Neumann opened Saint Meinrad Priory to secure the faith of German speaking Catholics. Two well-known German mission societies, the *Leopoldinen Stiftung* in Austria and the *Ludwig Missionsverein* in Bavaria, supported such missionary activities all across North America.[12]

John Nepomucene Neumann was a sickly, unattractive, subdued, and stubby German-speaking man from Bohemia (now the Czech Republic). Neumann's German Bishop rejected him as a candidate for the priesthood. But the Vicar General of Cincinnati, Frederic Résé, then recruited him for America. Neumann joined the Redemptorist priests at Pittsburgh. The Redemptorists had organized to serve German immigrants. Although people laughed at Neumann when he rode a horse—his feet did not touch the stirrups—he enjoyed some success in his early missionary efforts.

In 1852 Pope Pius IX appointed Neumann Bishop of Philadelphia, the first German-speaking priest to assume control of an eastern diocese. Neumann opened an incredible number of parishes, about one a month during his eight years as bishop. He also organized the country's first diocesan school system. Schools attached to church parishes (or parochial schools) jumped from one single school to over two hundred schools across his diocese. Philadelphia Catholics admired his frugality. He always wore the same pair of boots, and donated clothes given to him to others more in need.

CONTINUANCE OF LONG-STANDING TRADITIONS

Neumann encouraged the forty hours Eucharistic devotion, a sacred practice some three hundred years old. Immigrants of all sorts brought a strong devotional life to the American Catholic Church. Rosaries, novenas, processions,

→ St. Pius - Holy - Name - Society →

Catholic women ran the earliest devotional societies. Men tended to lead mutual-aid and charitable organizations. But by the end of the nineteenth century, men also formed devotional groups. Holy Name Societies grew extremely popular among immigrant Catholics. Holy Name Societies discouraged men from using profanity, indecency, and vulgarity in speech, all the while honoring the holy name of Jesus. In Cincinnati, Holy Name Societies sponsored an annual march which on October 11, 1914 (pictured here), involved twelve thousand men from diverse ethnic and racial backgrounds. The group ended the march with Mass at Redland Field, the home of the Cincinnati Reds professional baseball team.

scapulars, religious medals, devotion to the saints, and veneration of relics grew hugely popular. The carefully staged Tridentine Latin Mass celebrated transcendent mystery and introduced reassuring sameness to immigrants struggling to adjust to the many uncertainties of a new country.

Benedictine missionary Bede O'Connor reported that German Catholic immigrants along the Ohio River valley "are very exact in the reception of the sacraments and seldom…fail to attend Mass on Sundays and to send… children to school on weekdays." Irish immigrants were similarly devoted. During the sprinkling of holy water before Sunday High Mass, "the hands of these good [Irish] people," O'Connor reported, "are…far above their heads in order to get a drop of holy water…while all the rest of his body makes a deep reverence and the thumb of the right hand makes three large crosses on the forehead, the mouth, and the heart."[13]

Germans formed neat and productive neighborhoods. In Cincinnati, many Germans lived north of a canal that immigrants called the Rhine. They christened the surrounding neighborhood "Over the Rhine." German woman gathered at Over the Rhine's Findlay Market, opened in 1852 (and still in business). Men congregated in numerous beer gardens. In the twenty blocks from Over the Rhine to the Ohio River, mid-nineteenth-century Cincinnati boasted 113 mostly German-run saloons. Especially at Cincinnati's Mecklenburg Gardens (also still open), immigrants learned to avoid "Green horn's peril," that is, get rich quick schemes.

With the influx of western European immigrants, the number of American Catholics jumped from less than 2 percent to about 20, maybe 25, percent of the total U.S. population by mid-century. Members of a short-lived and loosely organized American Party feared that German and especially Irish Catholic immigrants were overwhelming the country. Such immigrants were hostile to republican values and governed by a foreign pope, the American Party claimed. When asked for more detail about the activities of the American Party, members responded, "I know nothing."

In St. Louis in the summer of 1854, some Know-Nothings, as the group was normally called, denied several Irish Americans the right to vote. A scuffle broke out. An Irishman stabbed a boy. Anti-Irish mobs retaliated and attacked Irish neighborhoods. The mob then moved toward Saint Louis College. The president of the school, Jesuit John Baptist Druyts, walked back and forth across the front of Saint Francis Xavier Church calmly reading the psalms. The mob turned away. The following summer, on another election day, hoodlums again attacked Irish Catholic neighborhoods in Louisville. On what became known as Bloody Monday, more than twenty people were killed.

Up the Ohio River from Louisville, a different kind of violence helped build the immigrant church. During a severe storm in the Atlantic Ocean in 1859, Archbishop Purcell of Cincinnati vowed to Mary, the Mother of God, that if he survived he would build Mary a shrine. Before the year was over Purcell laid a cornerstone in Mount Adams two blocks from the Cincinnati Observatory. Purcell then erected a cross on the construction site, asked Catholics to pray for the success of the project, and built wooden steps to assist pilgrims climbing the hill. (To this day Catholics still climb the steps, now on Good Friday.)

On the feast of the Immaculate Conception, December 9, 1860, Purcell celebrated the first Mass at the Church of the Immaculate Conception, or Immaculata, as Purcell liked to call the church. (Pope Pius IX had proclaimed the Dogma of the Immaculate Conception five years before.) Immaculata was the eighth church built for Catholic German immigrants in Cincinnati. Purcell occasionally wrestled with Germans over who ran the church of Cincinnati, but more often admired German faith, steadiness, patience, and frugality. At the same time, Purcell denounced fellow Irishmen as disorderly and intemperate. Purcell especially tried to discourage Irish wakes.

The Cincinnati Observatory housed the world's second largest telescope that nonetheless could not peer through the billowing clouds of pollution from downtown Cincinnati. Less than twenty years after the observatory opened, the University of Cincinnati moved the telescope from Mount Adams further out of town to Mount Lookout (where it still stands). The following year, the Passionate Order of Priests purchased the vacated observatory at Mount Adams and converted the building into a monastery. With Purcell's blessing, the Passionists next built for Irish Catholics Holy Cross Church adjoining the monastery. As was true in Mount Adams, in many American cities, Irish and German Catholic churches often stood but blocks away.

A SHIFT IN THE GERMAN PRESENCE

After the Homestead Act of 1862 made land available at cheap prices, German immigration increased. A German merchant, Simon Peter Paul Cahensly, became the leading advocate for German immigrants coming to America. Many of these immigrants passed through Castle Clinton (sometimes called Castle Garden) on the tip of Manhattan. Castle Clinton had been established to help immigrants safely transition to America. Officials at Castle Clinton helped immigrants find jobs through the labor exchange located next door.

Then the unification of the separate states into one German empire in 1871 disfavored certain German citizens, while the May laws of 1873 (part

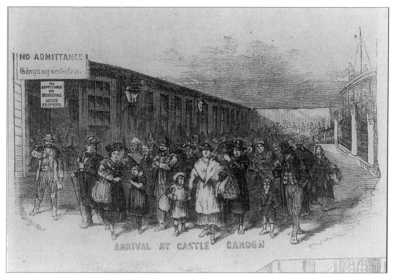

Arrival at Castle Garden, 1866

of the religious persecution called *Kulturkampf*) assaulted Catholics by undermining the pope's authority, abolishing religious orders, and punishing bishops who protested. German Catholics soon surpassed the number of Irish Catholics arriving each year in the United States.

Such growth spurred a new wave of anti-Catholicism. In 1887 the American Protective Association formed to drive Catholicism from the United States, but after a brief period of contention faded from the American scene. The number of German and Irish immigrants also began to decline. By 1890 southern and eastern Europeans, especially Italians, outnumbered Irish and German immigrants.

At the end of the nineteenth century, the Ancient Order of Hibernians, along with its female counterpart, the Daughters of Erin, included nearly two hundred thousand members. The Hibernians entertained some dubious associations, including with the Molly Maguires, a rather elusive and probably corrupt organization in the anthracite coal fields of Pennsylvania. The Ancient Order of Hibernians exerted more positive influence through numerous dances, concerts, picnics, excursions, and sports programs that promoted Irish culture and identity. Almost every American Catholic parish with Irish connections had branches, called divisions, of the Ancient Order of Hibernians.

Germans formed countless social and religious associations. The Turner movement alone sported some sixty-five thousand members in the late nineteenth century. Open celebration of German heritage nonetheless dropped out of sight after the United States joined Allied Forces against Germany in World War I. German American immigrants hid their roots, with Milwaukee's "German Club" renamed the "Wisconsin Club," and the "German-English Academy" renamed the "Milwaukee University School."

In 1917 half of Cincinnati's population could speak German. Many Cincinnatians only spoke German. But with the rising anti-German sentiment of World War I across the country, including in Cincinnati, states closed German-language schools, dismissed German teachers, and banned German-language classes. Cincinnati's Public Library withdrew all German books from its shelves, and many German Americans anglicized their names. Schmidt became Smith, for example. In Cincinnati's Over the Rhine, Bremen Street became Republic Street, and Hanover Street became Yukon Street.

After the war, new versions of old German associations emerged. In various cities branches of Kolping Societies, for instance, opened with the spirit of their mid-nineteenth century German founder, Father Adolph Kolping. Kolping offered "Help for self-help" as a means of uplifting all German peoples. After the rise of Hitler and the outbreak of World War II, German heritage groups again went into hiding.[14]

Appreciation of German and Irish roots eventually reemerged. In 1970 when Cincinnati's Irish Holy Cross Church merged with the German Immaculata Church in Mount Adams, the Ancient Order of Hibernians marched Holy Cross's statue of Saint Patrick to Immaculata in order to make Irish Catholics feel more at home. For years thereafter the Hibernians "stole" the statue so that it might lead Cincinnati's annual Saint Patrick's Day parade.

In 1976 a block party held near Cincinnati's downtown Fountain Square celebrated the city's German heritage. The following year Pope Paul VI canonized Bishop John Neumann. Cincinnati's German block party was repeated and has since grown to become America's largest Oktoberfest, attracting more than half a million visitors each year. German Catholic heritage is celebrated year round in many rural communities. In the farmland surrounding the cross-tipped churches of Maria Stein, some Catholic families still speak German.

CHAPTER EIGHT

Abolitionists and
Angels of Mercy

*T*he Catholic signer of the Declaration of Independence, Charles Carroll of Carrollton, planned to free his 316 slaves. But releasing such a large number of persons who were, as Carroll put it, "incapable of providing for themselves" only spelled disaster. He consequently educated his slaves in religious matters and with practical skills.[1]

In 1797 Carroll introduced a bill before the Maryland State Senate for the gradual abolition of slavery. Carroll proposed that the state buy all female slave children, educate them, and free them at twenty-eight years of age. These educated women would then prepare enslaved men for freedom. The bill did not pass.

Many Catholics from Maryland to Kentucky (and eventually from Missouri to South Carolina) nonetheless continued to educate and even empower some slaves. On July 9, 1812, a day that President James Madison had proclaimed a National Day of Public Humiliation and Prayer, a Protestant spied one of Father Badin's slaves, Jared, working in a Kentucky field. "To whom do you belong?" asked the Protestant. "To priest Badin," answered Jared. Knowing that Badin was out and about, the Protestant asked, "Well, why is not your master at church, praying for the government? Does he not know that this is the day named in the proclamation?" Jared replied, "Massa prays for the government every Sunday and even every day: we Catholics do not pray by proclamation only. But, massa, why are not *you* at church, praying for the government?" Taken aback by such a confident slave, the Protestant rode on.[2]

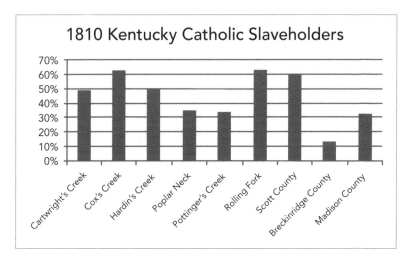

Badin instructed Catholics to be good to their slaves and also denounced some Kentucky Baptists who "treat[ed slaves] almost like animals…without giving them either instruction or compensation…feed[ing them] with coarse food and dress[ing them] meagerly." Such treatment provoked a few Baptists to join an anti-slavery congregation in Ohio. Other Baptist, Methodist, and Presbyterians similarly advocated immediate abolition, that is, the instant end to slavery.[3]

By 1810 about half of Kentucky Catholic households included slaves. The majority of the first Maryland immigrants to Kentucky may have been poor, but, as one observer noted, "they [soon] make a fortune and then enjoy luxury and grandeur," including slaves. Only 40 percent of Presbyterian and Methodist, and 30 percent of the Baptist homes included slaves in the same area at the same time.[4]

Belonging to a church often coincided with some affluence, with frontier Kentucky Catholics tending to be more prosperous, holding about five slaves per household. Protestants held four, and the non-churched less. In southern Maryland, Catholics similarly outpaced non-Catholic slaveholders, with a slightly higher percentage of southern Maryland Catholics owning a somewhat higher number of slaves.

Bishop Flaget of Bardstown held as many as twenty-five slaves, most of whom he sent to Catholic institutions as the need for labor arose. Flaget considered slaves "different from other human beings," and preferred free to slave labor, but he simply could not afford hired hands at that time. Flaget's slaves raised the giant columns and finished the breastwork of Bardstown's Saint Joseph's Cathedral, opened in 1819. Free workers considered the job too dangerous to undertake. [5]

A DIFFERENCE IN OPINION AND APPROACH

Upon arriving in the United States in December 1820, newly consecrated Irish Bishop John England of Charleston grew devoted to the poor Catholics scattered across his diocese (which included South Carolina, North Carolina, and Georgia). Bishop England was poor, himself, walking the streets of Charleston barefoot. He routinely addressed sophisticated and educated audiences yet cherished the morning liturgies he celebrated for poor blacks in the cathedral every Sunday. Not "friendly to the existence or continuation of slavery," as England put it, he brought to Charleston in 1830 the Sisters of Our Lady of Mercy to teach black children how to be free.[6]

In the wake of the 1831 slave revolt in Southampton, Virginia, when Nat Turner and seventy fellow blacks killed somewhere between fifty-five and sixty-five whites, a Charleston mob accused Bishop England of favoring immediate abolition. As a result, England closed the school for black children. Other Catholic leaders, including some Virginia priests similarly tried to dissociate Catholicism from abolitionism. After Southampton, slaveholders equated abolitionism with violent rebellion.

At this time the priest in charge of the worldwide organization of Jesuits, the Superior General Jan Roothaan from Rome asked an Irish Jesuit, Peter Kenney, to investigate the "corruption and immorality" associated with slaveholding in the United States. The large number of slaves found on the deteriorating Jesuit properties in Maryland lived together like animals, or so Roothaan had heard. Should the plantations along with their slaves be sold with "the revenue [used] for other things," Roothaan wondered?[7]

Many younger Jesuits said yes, hoping to open new, more urban ministries. Older Jesuits tended to say "no," explaining that slaves on the Jesuit plantations were "children whose care and well-being has been given to us by God." Still other Jesuits responded more abstractly, contending that dark skin was not a mark of God's punishment, as some scripture scholars had claimed, but was the consequence of the climate in which people lived, as science had demonstrated. No fundamental difference existed between free and enslaved persons, therefore. Slavery was rooted in tyranny and greed.[8]

By 1835 Georgetown College had fallen nearly fifty thousand dollars in debt. On October 27, 1836, Roothaan approved the sale of all Maryland Jesuit slaves. The Jesuit in charge of Saint Inigoes, Joseph Carbery, lamented Roothaan's decision and reportedly "prayed and he prayed and he pleaded with the Fathers and begged that such a dreadful thing might not happen."[9]

Sometime before, Carbery had divided up Saint Inigoes into small farms, placing individual slave families in charge of each tract. Each family paid a modest annual rent. Carbery claimed that this experiment was successful, but it had not alleviated the Jesuit debt.

The nationwide financial panic of 1837 delayed the sale until June 19, 1838, when the Jesuit in charge of Maryland, the Provincial Thomas Mulledy sold 272 Jesuit slaves for $115,000 to two Louisiana planters, Jesse Batey and the former Governor of Louisiana, Henry Johnson. The average price per slave was $422, a typical sum for that time.

Sheriffs descended upon the Jesuit plantations and "dragged [slaves] off by force to the ship," as reported by Thomas Lilly, a Jesuit manager of one of the farms. Another Jesuit, Peter Havermans, charged, "No one does this sort of thing except evil persons, such as slave traders who care about nothing but money, or those who by necessity are so pressed by debts that they are forced into such a sale." Other Catholics and non-Catholics similarly protested. Archbishop Samuel Eccleston of Baltimore specifically complained that families had been split up.[10]

Roothaan had stipulated that proceeds from the sale should not be used to pay debts, but on July 9, 1838, Mulledy paid eight thousand dollars to Archbishop Eccleston, and $21,800 to Georgetown College. Both transactions alleviated debt. Upon learning of these payments, Roothaan ordered Mulledy to resign.

In October 1838, Bishop John Purcell of Cincinnati told an audience in his native town of Mallow, Ireland, that he lamented "the fatal contrast," that is, the inconsistency of the Declaration of Independence with slavery.

Purcell blamed England for introducing the "virus" to colonial America, and longed for a truly free United States. But Purcell also contended that such an improvement "however desirable...could not from prudential motives [be] introduce[d] as soon as it [is] wished." Purcell disdained slavery, but back in the United States refused to take a public stand on the matter for quite some time.[11]

About a year later, Pope Gregory XVI issued on December 3, 1839, an apostolic letter "Concerning the Not Carrying on the Trade of Negroes." Gregory did not condemn the institution of slavery yet criticized Christian slaveholders who reduced any people to slavery, or who exercised "that inhuman trade by which negroes, as if they were not men, but mere animals...are...bought, sold, and doomed sometimes to the most severe and exhausting labours." In other words, the pope condemned what the Jesuits had recently done.[12]

Despite earlier advocacy of gradual abolition, Bishop John England of Charleston by this time claimed to have known "many slaves who would not accept their freedom...and some who have refused it." Some people were "naturally fitted" for slavery, England came to believe, and even enjoyed certain advantages, including "food, raiment and dwelling, together with a variety of little comforts."[13]

THE STATUS OF SLAVE FAMILIES

Close quarters on various Catholic farms sometimes bred endearment between master and slave. Black women nursed white babies, white and black children played together, and slaves often knew no home other than that of their master. One black boy raised on Cox's Creek north of Bardstown developed the Celtic brogue of his Irish master, while a crippled slave child named Charles received unceasing care from his owner, Nancy Lancaster. Catherine Spalding of the Sisters of Charity of Nazareth included her slaves as part of the Nazareth "family...blacks and all."[14]

The leading American Catholic theologian of the day, Bishop Francis Patrick Kenrick of Philadelphia, insisted that slaves must "render service to their masters," and that masters must "be just and kind" to their slaves, all for the sake of good order. Moreover, masters should offer slaves the sacraments, through which slaves gain access to heaven. Only in heaven, masters and slaves stood on equal ground, added Kenrick.[15]

Priests certainly baptized many slaves, including Mary at Saint Rose Church in central Kentucky. Thomas Medley owned her father, and the widow Yates owned Mary and her mother. Like Mary's case, 36 percent of the antebellum slave baptisms at this typical southern Catholic Church noted that the slave parents did not live on the same farm. Another 40 percent failed to name the father of the slave child.

Relatively small slave households in Kentucky determined that married couples generally would not be owned by the same person and thus were less likely to live together. Of the eighty slave marriages recorded during two decades after 1840 at Saint Rose, only seven involved slaves owned by the same master. Burial records for free people regularly noted family ties, but gave no such indication for slaves. More typical was one remark which simply noted the interment of "A black child belonging to somebody."[16]

The Catholic newspaper of Kentucky, the *Catholic Advocate*, periodically posted for sale "OATS," "WHEAT," and "LIKELY NEGROES." Three Bardstown Catholics, Joseph Price and brothers William and John Mattingly, sold slaves downriver. Other Catholics occasionally set slaves free, but the vast majority of Catholic slaveholders handed slaves down to future generations. Catholic slaveholder Joseph Carrico willed his slaves to his children yet also informed them that a good horse was more desirable than a good slave.[17]

A slave's family grew important if that slave ran away. A Catholic in Lexington, Kentucky, announced that his slave, Bill, had fled, hoping to make his way to Bardstown, "as his wife was taken to the neighborhood of that place a short time ago." Two other Catholic masters suspected that their runaway, Paul, would not stray far from his native county, "as his family are there [and] we think he would leave it very reluctantly." And after "a bright mulatto boy" named Tom disappeared, his Catholic owner (probably his father) suspected that he may have fled south to Hart County, where he had been raised.[18]

The appearance of mulatto (meaning "mixed") slaves most likely indicated somewhere in the person's lineage a black slave mother and a white free father. Toward the end of legalized slavery in the United States, nearly a quarter of the slaves in one Kentucky county where many Catholics congregated were designated mulatto. Bishop Augustin Verot of Saint Augustine, Florida considered slavery to be sanctioned by God, but still denounced the abuse of slave women that was implied in the rise of mulattos.

"Unruly" bondsmen or women were whipped. Judge Elisha Metcalf of Saint Michael's Catholic Church in central Kentucky baptized all his slaves, and, just as routinely, beat them. "It was no uncommon thing," Metcalf's slave, Harry Smith, recalled, "for Massa to have forty or fifty slaves tied and whipped a day for…trifling affairs." Neighbors regularly paid Metcalf twenty-five cents per slave to administer a beating, thus making the judge a "whipping master."[19]

The fourth time that Edward McLean began to whip Maria of Richard Beall, she pulled out a knife and stabbed him twice. McLean died later that day and was buried at Saint Rose. A Catholic jury convicted Maria of murder, and Judge C.C. Kelly sentenced her to death by hanging. But before the order could be carried out, Kentucky Governor Thomas Metcalfe surprisingly intervened. Metcalfe judged that Maria's action was not altogether unjustifiable and thus granted her a free and full pardon.

JOHN MATTINGLY

Irish Catholic Richard "Dick" Yeager raised his four children in remote central Kentucky before some "new comers" made fun of him for treating the mother of the children, a slave named Jane, as his wife. As a result, Yeager put his entire family on the auction block. "We children knew something terrible was being done," recalled Isaac, "but we were not old enough to fully understand." For three thousand dollars, the auctioneer divided five slaves among five owners, with Isaac becoming the property of Bardstown slave trader, Catholic John Mattingly.[20]

When Mattingly traveled to Mississippi to sell 170 slaves, his wife gathered the remaining Mattingly slaves, including Isaac, every morning in her dining room, where she distributed prayer books, taught young ones to read, and instructed all on how to pray. Upon John Mattingly's return to Kentucky, he screamed at his wife, "If you teach them to pray and read they may think they are human beings."[21]

The following Sunday, Mattingly preached to his slaves, "You must under-stand you are just the same as the ox, horse, or mule, made for the use of the Whiteman and for no other purpose.... If you don't do what is right by me, why, my duty is to kill you." After Mattingly discovered that one of his slaves, Bob the Canadian, planned to run away, Mattingly whipped Bob, laid hot coals on his back, and slit his throat, "taking care not to cut the jugular," as Isaac testified, "but cutting just enough so he would die gradu-ally in torture." [22]

Years later, Isaac concluded that slavery had dragged slaveholders down "to a condition lower than their slaves, making them human demons." Isaac abhorred the white blood in his veins. Anyone who dared to "color the Institution to make it appear as though the old days of American slavery were patriarchical days to be desired" was sorely misinformed, concluded Isaac. [23]

Some slaves nonetheless clung to the Catholic Church. During a mission, or Catholic revival, held at Maryland's Saint Thomas's Church in the 1850s, bad weather turned many Catholics away. "The exception" according to one observer, "were the negroes who from the first day flocked to the exer-cises and the sacraments." Other free Catholics on other occasions simi-larly praised enslaved blacks for their piety. One Jesuit lamented that white Catholics "do not by the same token continually demonstrate better fruit or greater devotion." [24]

An unusually high percentage of black women and men, both free and enslaved, joined Baltimore's Catholic confraternities, or volunteer pious organizations. Black Catholics also organized antebellum mutual aid soci-eties. More than sixty years after the end of slavery, former Maryland slave Charles Coles declared, "I am still a Catholic and will always be." "You might say that the masters were reserving themselves this earth," one Jesuit concluded, "while their slaves were laying claim on heaven." [25]

Slavery fueled the cotton industry of the Deep South, but into the 1840s and 1850s, it had become an inefficient and costly system in the upper South with Irish and German immigrants beginning to take on work formerly performed by slaves. As the percentage of Catholic slaveholders in southern Maryland declined, Catholic slaveholders across the country sent excess workers to cities to learn trades, and some Catholic religious orders abandoned slave territories. In part because of slavery, some Jesuits left Kentucky to take over Cincinnati's Athenaeum College (now Xavier University). Other Kentucky Jesuits transferred to Saint John's College at Rose Hill (now Fordham University in New York City).

About the only Kentuckian with any Catholic connection who openly opposed slavery in the antebellum period was Irish-born E. J. "Patrick" Doyle. When Doyle was arrested in 1846 in Louisville for attempting to sell free blacks into slavery, then was apprehended in Lexington in the summer of 1848 for leading a slave insurrection, some Catholics blamed his inconsistent behavior on his Presbyterian connection.

The American Catholic bishops who gathered at the 1852 First Plenary Council of Baltimore did not discuss slavery, focusing instead on the waves of German and Irish immigrants. Some priests nonetheless increased their ministry to slaves and to former slaves. In 1858, Jesuit Peter Koning, for example, set up a chapel for free blacks in the upper gallery of the Saint Louis College Church. A handful of Jesuits still in Kentucky similarly offered catechetical instruction to free and enslaved blacks in the neighborhood. But only about a dozen showed up, that is, until the Jesuits introduced music to the classes. "Singing…seems to encourage them and stirs them to pious rivalry," noted one Jesuit.[26]

Many Catholics charged that recent splits in the Presbyterian, Baptist, and Methodist churches had unduly incensed the national debate over slavery. The Catholic Church stood as the only major denomination that had not been severed. The Catholic Church had never split over anything, one of Flaget's assistant bishops, Kentucky-born Martin John Spalding claimed, while the root problem to the brewing national crisis was Protestant dissent, not slavery.

THE CIVIL WAR BEGINS

Jefferson Davis became president of the Confederate States of America on February 18, 1861. Two weeks later Abraham Lincoln took charge of the much diminished United States. At 4:30 in the morning of April 12, 1861, Confederate troops began to bombard Union forces at South Carolina's Fort Sumter. The Civil War had begun.

Two days later, Charleston Bishop Patrick Lynch sang a hymn of praise, the *Te Deum*, to celebrate Sumter's surrender to the Confederacy. New York Archbishop John Hughes, on the other hand, flew a Union flag and encouraged Catholics to serve the North. St. Louis Archbishop Peter Richard Kenrick said nothing about the war, ever, and even refused to preach at all during the first two years of the conflict. "I have decided to stay out of these troubles as much as possible," Kenrick informed his older brother, Francis Kenrick, then Archbishop of Baltimore.[27]

On April 15, Lincoln called for seventy-five thousand soldiers. Cincinnati Archbishop John Purcell told Catholics, "The President has spoken and it is our duty to obey him as the head of the nation." Purcell then flew a huge, ninety-foot-long Union flag from the spire of Cincinnati's Saint Peter in Chains Cathedral. Virginia priest William Barry meanwhile proclaimed, "With my whole heart and soul I am with the *South and the Right*, now and forever." Catholic men enlisted on both sides, and seventy Catholic chaplains, whom soldiers called "Holy Joes," split fairly evenly in service to the North and to the South.[28]

Some chaplains served impartially, but all the Catholic sisters "day ain't for de Noff nuh de Souf," as one slave explained, "dey's for God." Six hundred ninety-three mostly Irish women from twenty-two religious congregations volunteered to help as nurses. Most other persons who served in this capacity were well-intentioned yet untrained women who typically ran at the sight of blood. Catholic sisters were the only truly qualified nurses of the Civil War. Military officials from the North and South begged them to serve.[29]

Archbishop Purcell "gladly consented" when military men asked for help from Cincinnati sisters, but Archbishop Hughes issued "very strong objections," rightly fearing for the safety of the sisters of New York. Bishop John McGill of Richmond opposed sisters helping anywhere but in the Catholic hospital of Richmond. Richmond sisters then begged him to serve wherever the need arose, explaining that such service constituted their mission. McGill relented. Across the country sisters closed schools and suspended whatever ministry they were engaged in as the thunder of war approached.[30]

Sister Anthony O'Connell

Union and Confederate forces first clashed in July 1861 near Manassas, Virginia (at what Union soldiers called the First Battle of Bull Run), where Euphemia Blenkinsop, a Daughter of Charity from nearby Emmitsburg, reported "we were for two long days in the very midst of the sounds of war...our poor sisters, though the shells were flying around them, did not even interrupt their duties." At hospitals to the north in Washington, D.C., and to the south in Richmond, Virginia, sisters cared for hundreds of wounded men, paying no attention to uniforms, only recognizing, "There is so much suffering and so much to be done."[31]

Anthony O'Connell of the Sisters of Charity of Cincinnati had organized the hospital at Camp Dennison fifteen miles outside of town, but was on her way to another Union stronghold in western Maryland when she received an urgent telegram. "Return at once," Archbishop Purcell ordered. "Two boat loads of wounded soldiers from Pittsburgh Landing [at Shiloh, Tennessee] to be cared for!"[32]

Instead of returning to Cincinnati, O'Connell headed straight down the Tennessee River to Shiloh where she tended to the wounded laid out on "floating hospitals." "More than four or five hundred sick and wounded lay heaped on one another [in these river boats]," reported a witness. The boats periodically moved upriver due to, as O'Connell recalled, "the terrific stench from the bodies of the dead on the battlefield." "Amidst this sea of blood," recalled a Shiloh man, "[O'Connell] performed the most revolting duties for these poor soldiers." Both sides christened her the "Florence Nightingale of America."[33]

On many other battlefields from Antietam to Gettysburg, and in numerous military hospitals across the country sisters felt the brutality of war. Rats invaded their makeshift living quarters, while an awful smell once kept a group of sisters awake all night long. The next morning they discovered two amputated legs mistakenly left in the room next door.

Some soldiers spat upon sisters just because these men had been taught to despise Catholics. Because of the sisters' unusual dress and their vow to never marry, a few onlookers wondered "whether they were human beings or not." One soldier shot at an enemy recovering in the same hospital, with the bullet missing the target but piercing the distinctive headdress of a sister, her wide white cornette.[34]

Through such challenges, sisters offered heroic, holistic healthcare, routinely dressing wounds, occasionally performing surgery, and always caring for a man's spiritual well-being. A soldier "who had been taught to believe badly of Sisters" changed his ways after a Sister of Mercy sat with him around the clock with a thumb pressed on the hole caused by a bullet that had severed an artery in his neck.[35]

A doctor told a Civil War amputee that he would not live through the night. "I have a great favor to ask," the soldier told an attending sister. "I have a mother…" "I understand," the sister said. "You want me to write to her." "Yes," the soldier cried. "Say that her child is dead, but do not tell her how I have suffered. That would break her heart."[36]

The War Draws to an End

On September 1, 1862 Archbishop Purcell publicly proclaimed that such horrors could have been avoided if only the South would have agreed to abolish slavery "after a given period, say fifty, seventy, or a hundred years…

and in the meantime, as Northern states had done, fit her slaves, by education, to be men." The war had rendered compromise no longer possible, and Purcell thus advocated the emancipation of slaves within three months.[37]

John Baptist Purcell

Three weeks after Purcell's address, Lincoln issued the Emancipation Proclamation, scheduled to take effect three months later on January 1, 1863. Purcell's paper,

Martin John Spalding

the *Catholic Telegraph*, soon became the leading Catholic voice in favor of emancipation. Some other Catholic and secular newspapers denounced Purcell as an abolitionist, while Archbishop Martin Spalding of Louisville called Lincoln's Emancipation Proclamation "atrocious."[38]

"It is…generally admitted by all good and moderate men," Spalding explained, "that slavery is a great social evil." But how can the United States free itself from this wrong, he wondered, "without ruining the country and causing injury to the poor slaves themselves?" This was the real problem according to Spalding. And a practical solution was not easy.[39]

Spalding contended that Catholics consistently had promoted gradual emancipation through diligent preparation of the slaves (and their masters) for emancipation. But after abolitionists began their violent crusade, no sensible human being dared to entertain in public any plan for liberation lest that person be dubbed an abolitionist. Many Catholics nevertheless continued to educate blacks and, thus, ready them for autonomous living.

The war intensified on the battlefield and spread to the streets as Irish Catholics rioted against the Conscription Act of March 3, 1863, which forced poor citizens to serve as Union soldiers. In and near Gramercy Park in New York City, at least four hundred, and maybe as many as 1,500, rioters were killed. Jefferson Davis meanwhile thanked the Catholic sisters for their ongoing service. Lincoln called them "veritable angels of mercy."[40]

As soon as the war ended, American bishops reached out to former slaves, with Purcell and Spalding (who became Archbishop of Baltimore in the summer of 1864) starting churches and schools specifically aimed to assist African Americans. Many former Catholic slaves nonetheless left the church.

POSTWAR EFFECTS ON BLACK CATHOLICS

Augustus Tolton had been born a slave and was baptized at Saint Peter's Catholic Church in Brush Creek, Missouri. During the Civil War his father fought for the Union, and his mother dramatically crossed the Mississippi River with three small children, including Augustus, to freedom at Quincy, Illinois. In 1880 Franciscan priests from Illinois sent Tolton to Rome because no American seminary would accept him. In 1886 Tolton was ordained at Saint John Lateran Basilica in Rome, the first black Catholic priest from the United States.

Tolton ministered for about a decade in Quincy and Chicago, serving black and white Catholics, a reconciling figure through a difficult period of time. Just before noon on an incredibly hot Chicago summer in 1897 Tolton collapsed while on his way to make several calls in the parish. He died later that day. The *Chicago Tribune* praised Tolton as "one of the foremost clergymen of the Catholic Church in this part of the country...[who] was remarkably popular."[41]

An elderly black woman named Louisa Mason claimed to be a slave long after slavery had been legally abolished. "With great bitterness" Mason remembered that two decades before the Civil War, the Jesuits had sold many of Mason's friends and relatives to the Deep South. Most of these slaves died outside the Catholic Church. Mason had run away to escape being shipped to Louisiana, rejoined the Jesuits, and for the rest of her life preferred to remain a slave to the Jesuits than to risk her salvation owned by someone else or on her own as a free woman. In 1910 the Jesuits gave Mason the "most elaborate funeral" ever held in the old Saint Ignatius Church of southern Maryland.[42]

The year before Mason's death the Jesuits began a weekly magazine, called *America*, which articulated, among other things, "an authoritative statement of the position of the Church in the thought and activity of modern life." Jesuit superiors meanwhile advised a young Jesuit named John LaFarge that it was "better to be a live jackass than a dead lion" and thus released him from the scholarly pursuits that were wearing him out.[43]

Freed from school, LaFarge ministered to the most forsaken, including prisoners at New York's Blackwell (now Roosevelt) Island and black Catholics of southern Maryland. *The Race Question and the Negro* (the title of one of his books) grew to be his primary concern. And for LaFarge, education offered the solution to the problem of race.

While serving as associate editor of *America*, LaFarge gained a reputation as the "Negro expert," but some confident black Catholics, including Constance Daniel, the director of LaFarge's vocational school, the Cardinal Gibbons Institute of southern Maryland, charged him with racism. According to Daniel, LaFarge had failed to treat African Americans as equal partners in the conversation about race.[44]

To the dismay of Thomas Wyatt Turner, a Howard University professor and founder of the Federated Colored Catholics, LaFarge and the Catholic Church had supported segregated Catholic schools. LaFarge and fellow Jesuit William Markoe of St. Louis eventually denounced Turner as having "a little of Black Muslim in him," ousted him as president of the Federated Colored Catholics, and renamed the organization by the softer title, the National Catholic Federation for the Promotion of Better Race Relations.[45]

Unaware of the dispute between these white Jesuits and some black intellectuals, two women who had descended from Jesuit slaves simply claimed that before the Civil War, "[free and enslaved] people got along better; they had more money and more things. They made better crops. People did not have to work so hard. Nobody was stuck up over the others." After emancipation, things changed. "Now if you ain't got plenty of money," reported the two women, "you ain't got nothing."[46]

In 1924 the Ladies Auxiliary of the Ancient Order of Hibernians erected a monument in Washington, D.C., to honor the mostly Irish nuns who had served as Civil War nurses. "They comforted the dying," the monument recalls, "nursed the wounded, carried hope to the imprisoned, gave in his name a drink of water to the thirsty." A decade or so after the monument was erected, a young girl named Paulinus Oakes attended a school run by the Sisters of Mercy in Vicksburg, Mississippi. The school had been occupied by General Ulysses S. Grant's forces during the Civil War. "There was an aura about the buildings themselves, the school and convent," Oakes remembered, "a sacred history so to speak."[47]

In about 1930 a destitute old black man named Washington knocked on the front door of the rectory of Saint Elizabeth Catholic Church in

Brother Pete, a man once owned by the Jesuits at Florissant

downtown St. Louis. The Jesuits had organized Saint Elizabeth's nearly sixty years before as the first Black Catholic parish in Missouri. The housekeeper led Washington to the parlor. He was nearly blind. When the pastor, William Markoe entered the room, Washington extended both hands exclaiming, "Father, I am one of your boys." Markoe explained that all of his parishioners were his children, to which Washington replied, "But Father, I was one of your boys at Florissant."

Though never actually owned by Markoe (who was born after the Civil War), Washington indeed had been born a slave at what was called the "priests' farm," that is, Saint Stanislaus Jesuit Novitiate, a place for training young Jesuits located outside St. Louis in the village of Florissant. Once Washington made clear his history, Markoe wondered "how much restitution the Society of Jesus owed him, not only because of his unrequited labors as a child, but because of the contribution of his parents who also were Jesuit slaves at Florissant."[48]

Restitution perhaps requires many forms. When Francis Cardinal George of Chicago opened the case of the first black Catholic priest, Augustus Tolton, for canonization in March 2010, George prayed that "the Lord send us many more priests [like Tolton]." In the spring of 2012, the Vatican Congregation for the Causes of Saints named Tolton a "servant of God," thus raising him one step closer to sainthood.[49]

CHAPTER NINE

Millionaires
and Laborers

Williiam Shakespeare Caldwell managed theaters in his younger days and later amassed a fortune through various gas work projects. On December 28, 1853, Caldwell married Kentucky blue blood Mary Eliza Breckenridge. Though raised Presbyterian, she had graduated from the Catholic school run by the Sisters of Charity of Nazareth at Bardstown. Soon after the wedding, Louisville Bishop Martin Spalding baptized the new bride.

During the Civil War, the Caldwells moved to Cincinnati where Mary Eliza gave birth to two girls, Mary and Eliza, or Mamie and Lina, as their mother called them. The family next moved to New York City where Martin Spalding, who had been elevated to Archbishop of Baltimore in 1864, baptized the children.

Frequent travel and high lifestyle exhausted Mary Eliza Caldwell. She fell ill on January 6, 1867, and suddenly died. Stricken with grief, William Shakespeare Caldwell moved to Richmond, Virginia, where he sought consolation in the Catholic Church. Though from a Catholic family, Caldwell had not been baptized until now at the hands of Richmond Bishop John McGill. Caldwell next erected Saints Mary and Elizabeth Hospital in Louisville. He placed the institution under the direction of the Sisters of Charity of Nazareth.

Before the turn of the nineteenth century, the United States boasted over four thousand millionaires, including many Catholics. Catholic philanthropists donated to Catholic organizations in cities where they

MISS MARY GWENDOLEN CALDWELL.

Mary Gwendolen Caldwell entertained personal or business interests, oftentimes to meet the needs of Catholic immigrants. In every major American city where Catholics resided, Catholics built new, bigger, and better churches (during what historians call the brick and mortar era of American Catholicism).

In 1868 seventeen-year-old Thomas Ryan fled Virginia's war-torn Piedmont region in search of better economic opportunities. While on the train to Baltimore, the conductor convinced him to convert to Catholicism. He subsequently grew wealthy through investments in street-cars and railroads.

Ryan's wife, Ida Barry Ryan, donated over twenty million dollars ($210 million in today's money) toward the construction of numerous Catholic institutions, including Saint Jean-Baptiste Church in New York's Upper East Side, a gymnasium and dormitory at Georgetown University, and the Cathedral of the Sacred Heart in Richmond (the first American cathedral built by one family). Pope Leo XIII proclaimed Ida Ryan a countess of the Catholic Church, a title rarely given, and sanctioned her remodeling of a railroad car into a chapel for private devotions. Ida Ryan christened this chapel the "Pere Marquette" after the seventeenth-century Jesuit explorer Jacques Marquette.

Frances Fisher grew up in a prominent North Carolina family but her father, Confederate Colonel Charles Fisher, died at the Battle of Manassas, and the Fishers lost their fortune. She then converted to Catholicism. Under the pen name Christian Reid, Fisher in 1870 published *Valerie Aymer*, the faith-filled story of her family's misfortune. Most of her subsequent forty-one novels explored Catholic themes. Fisher used royalties from her books to reclaim the family estate. She also donated land for the Sacred Heart Catholic Church in her hometown of Salisbury.

The Great Chicago Fire of 1871 consumed both the Cathedral of Saint Mary and the Church of the Holy Name on State Street. Holy Name pastor John McMullen saved the Blessed Sacrament from the flames and then combed the country for donations to rebuild both churches and to aid the homeless. Chicago Catholics worshiped in what they called the shanty cathedral, a boarded-up burnt house on Cass Street before Bishop Thomas Foley in 1875 dedicated the new Cathedral of the Holy Name on the cleared State Street lot.

Years later a little girl gave Bishop Camilius Maes of Covington, Kentucky, a bright new silver dollar, the first money she had ever earned, to help him build an impressive French gothic cathedral. Maes placed the girl's donation in the cornerstone, and used the one hundred thousand dollars from Covington distillers Peter O'Shaughnessy and James Walsh to raise the rest of Saint Mary's Cathedral (now Basilica) of the Assumption.

STRENGTHENING CATHOLIC EDUCATION

As American bishops gathered in Baltimore in late 1884, Bishop John Lancaster Spalding of Peoria (Archbishop Martin Spalding's nephew) revealed big news. Eleven years before, William Shakespeare Caldwell, while on his deathbed, had suggested to his ten-year-old daughter, Mamie, that when she turned twenty-one, she should donate one-third of her inheritance to build a national Catholic University. Spalding announced on October 26, 1884 that twenty-one-year-old Mamie Caldwell would deliver three hundred thousand dollars to fulfill her father's wishes. Workers laid the cornerstone for the Catholic University of America (at Caldwell Hall) four years later.

During a six hour ceremony that began at 10:00 a.m. on Sunday, November 9, 1884, pomp and circumstance opened the Third Plenary Council of Baltimore. The long procession from Archbishop James Gibbons's residence to the cathedral included fourteen archbishops, sixty-two bishops, six abbots, thirty-four religious superiors, eleven seminary rectors, eighty-one theologians, and twelve minor officials. (The first, and at the time, only American Cardinal, John McCloskey, was sick at home in New York.) Though not the most brilliant or energetic church leader, Gibbons was an extremely

In June of 1895, John Lancaster Spalding (standing, center) delivered an address entitled "Hero Worship" at the Golden Jubilee celebration of the University of Notre Dame. The stage behind him was crowded with numerous ecclesiastical dignitaries including Cardinal Gibbons and Archbishop Ireland (sitting left and center, respectively). Spalding spoke against the propensity of young people to worship unworthy characters. Then, as one witness later recalled, Spalding "with a malicious twinkle in his eye and with a slight sweep back of him...exclaimed: "Put a bit of purple on a man and he is a hero." Gibbons was the only man wearing purple. Restlessness swept over the audience until a smile spread across Gibbons's face.

practical man who exuded deep inner calm. He smiled a lot. Over the next month, Gibbons superbly moderated council sessions.

At the end of the first formal day of meetings, November 10, 1884, Archbishop John Ireland of Saint Paul vigorously defended the place of the Catholic Church in American life. "To Americans...who love the republic," he intoned, "I fearlessly say, your hope is in the Catholic Church, because she is the mighty power today to resist unbelief and vice." The Church has always stood for liberty, Ireland claimed, and Catholics readily embraced the American republic, "the government I most cordially cherish." For him, as well as for many Church leaders listening to his address, the bond between the Catholic Church and the United States constituted a marriage made in heaven.[1]

Among the recommendations of the council, the bishops mandated that every parish open a school (called a parochial school) where all Catholics should send their children. Catholic schools began to pop up everywhere. But John Ireland, who lived amidst an extremely successful Minnesota public school system, saw things differently. On a trial basis, he leased some Catholic schools in his archdiocese to two public school districts.

An unidentified Catholic school scene from the early twentieth century, typical of schools across the United States.

The districts maintained the schools, and religious instruction was held outside regular school hours. Some bishops, including Spalding, charged that Ireland's so-called Faribault-Stillwater plan (named for the two public school districts involved) had abandoned Catholic education. But the Vatican allowed Ireland's plan to stand, at least for the time being.

Spalding and Ireland had been good friends. Both men were leading Catholic intellectuals of the day. Admirers described Spalding as a restless "live wire" who marched to the beat of his own drummer. Minnesotans heralded Ireland as "the consecrated blizzard of the northwest," a churchman with high ambition. Spalding liked to tease Ireland, who responded by simply smiling and rubbing his hands, his favorite gesture. But over parochial schools, Spalding and Ireland seriously disagreed.[2]

Following the concise, question-and-answer format created by sixteenth century reformer Martin Luther, American Catholics had produced various catechisms over the years before the bishops at Baltimore selected Italian-born Januarius De Concilio, pastor of Jersey City's Saint Michael's Parish and former Seton Hall philosophy and theology professor, to write a new catechism. De Concilio spent one week completing a draft, which he then revised over a few more weeks with the help of Bishop Spalding.

On April 6, 1885, Archbishop Gibbons approved *A Catechism of Christian Doctrine, Prepared and Enjoined by the Order of the Third Plenary Council of Baltimore*, more commonly called the *Baltimore Catechism*. The seventy-two-page book consisted of 421 questions and answers. Spalding was not satisfied with the work, and other bishops recognized the book's shortcomings. Teachers criticized the catechism's length, monotonous style, incomprehensible language, and number of yes-or-no questions (ninety-one). The *Baltimore Catechism* nonetheless grew as the official text for religious instruction of Catholic children in the United States.

Other publications from this time period supplemented the *Baltimore Catechism* and Catholic education in general. Civil War nurse and Holy Cross sister Angela Gillespie of Saint Mary's College in South Bend, Indiana, edited a series of *Metropolitan Readers* and also managed *Ave Maria*, a magazine that focused on Catholic families. The founder of the University of Notre Dame, Holy Cross Father Edward Sorin, had begun *Ave Maria* right after the Civil War. By the turn of the century *Ave Maria* was the largest English-language Catholic magazine in the world.

Other popular publications included Paulist Father Isaac Hecker's periodical, the *Catholic World*; Archbishop Gibbons' manual of instruction, *The Faith of Our Fathers*; and the Cincinnati Franciscan friars' monthly *St. Anthony Messenger*. From Cincinnati and Detroit, former slave Daniel Rudd published the *American Catholic Tribune*, one of the most successful black newspapers in the country with ten thousand subscribers. Rudd also helped establish the Black Catholic Congresses, which met for the first time in 1889, and which aimed to enrich the lives of African American Catholics.

RENEWED FOCUS ON THE NEEDS OF IMMIGRANTS

In 1890 the Saint Raphael Society, which German merchant Peter Paul Cahensly had founded seven years before, gathered in Lucerne, Switzerland, to discuss the needs of American immigrants. In a document known as the Lucerne Memorial, the Saint Raphael Society recommended separate churches for each immigrant group, priests of the same nationality as parishioners, parochial schools formed along ethnic lines, native languages included as a subject in school curriculum, and representation of each ethnic group in the Church hierarchy.

Bishop Spalding considered the suggestions of the Lucerne Memorial to be prudent. "Anything which makes immigrants more satisfied also makes them better citizens," Spalding explained. Archbishop Ireland, on the other hand, believed that the Lucerne Memorial promoted German nationalism. Ireland linked the Lucerne Memorial to the school question. In both cases Ireland wanted a more distinctively American response. The debate over parochial schools, and how to treat ethnic backgrounds, continued.[3]

After 1890 Italian, Mexican, French Canadian, and Eastern European (especially Polish) Catholics flocked to the United States. The Eastern Europeans included some Eastern Rite Catholics, who brought to North America the distinctive onion-dome steeples, which Archbishop Ireland viewed as un-American.

Teresa Demjanovich was born in Bayonne, New Jersey, the youngest of seven children of Alexander and Johanna Demjanovich, Byzantine-Ruthenian Eastern Rite Catholics from what is now Eastern Slovakia. Teresa graduated from New Jersey's College of Saint Elizabeth in Convent Station. Classmates recalled that Teresa knelt at all hours in the college chapel, constantly praying the rosary. Two years after graduation, Teresa joined the Sisters of Charity of Saint Elizabeth at Convent Station.

While deathly ill, Teresa professed final vows as Sister Miriam Teresa. Six days later, she died of acute appendicitis at twenty-six years of age. Friends next revealed that Teresa had entertained visions of Mary and of Saint Therese. Sisters revered Teresa's memory by cutting locks of her reddish brown hair and chipping off pieces from the granite cross at her grave. Other persons subsequently reported miraculous favors and cures. A New Jersey boy, Michael Mencer, was going blind but completely recovered after invoking Teresa, who was known for her bad eyesight.

Italians most often immigrated to escape overcrowding in southern Italy, and frequently landed in the United States poor and without resources, much like Irish immigrants before them. Italian immigrants took on various jobs, often construction work where employers sometimes posted three rates of payment in descending order: whites, blacks, Italians.

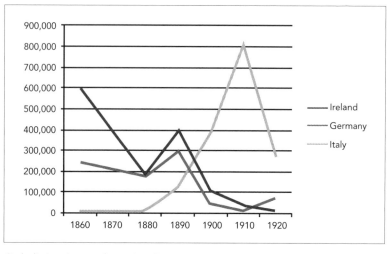

Catholic immigrants, by nationality

With the new flood of immigrants, immigration officials opened Ellis Island. Unlike Castle Clinton from years before, which had aimed to help newcomers, Ellis Island was opened largely to keep out undesirable immigrants. Over sixty-two years of operation, more than a quarter million persons were turned away from Ellis Island.

Frances Xavier Cabrini brought to Manhattan the order she had founded in her native Italy, the Missionary Sisters of the Sacred Heart of Jesus, to help Italian immigrants. Cabrini promoted what she called "education of the heart" as a "feeling for God in an environment of affective relationships in which education becomes an act of love." Cabrini's sisters lovingly cared for orphans, prisoners, the sick, and anyone in need, soon establishing houses across the country.[4]

ATTENDING TO THE LABORERS

Many immigrants eventually found employment in the expanding factory system which converted the United States into a leading industrial nation, as well as an exploiter of the working class. From 1870 to 1890 dissatisfaction in factories, mines, and railroads periodically escalated, including during a rally in Chicago's Haymarket Square where workers begged for an eight-hour work day. When police tried to break up the protest, someone threw a bomb. In the melee that ensued, seven police officers and four workers were killed.

Immigrant laborers subsequently organized in hidden places and with secret handshakes to safeguard activities from hostile and powerful management. Amidst this struggle, Archbishop Gibbons took a stand. "I would rather grasp the soiled hand of the honest artisan," Gibbons proclaimed, "than touch the soft, kid-gloved hand of the dandy."[5]

One secret organization, the Knights of Labor, elected as their president the mayor of Scranton, Catholic Terence Powderly. During the economic depression of the mid-1880s, membership in the Knights of Labor soared to over seventy thousand mostly Catholic workers spread across industrial North America. Alarmed by this growth, Archbishop Elzéar-Alexandre Taschereau of Quebec convinced the pope to outlaw the Knights of Labor in Canada. After Baltimore street car workers went on strike to win a twelve hour work day, Archbishop Gibbons, on the other hand, concluded that any effort like the Knights of Labor that aimed toward the amelioration of unjust working conditions deserved his encouragement.

With explicit support from Archbishop Ireland, Bishop Spalding, Bishop John Keane of Richmond, and Cardinal Manning, Archbishop of Westminster, Gibbons wrote to Rome in support of American workers. In an age when social questions were paramount, Gibbons declared that the Church should no longer deal primarily with parliaments and princes, but with the masses. "To lose the heart of the people would be a misfortune for which the friendship of the few rich and powerful would be no compensation," explained Gibbons.[6]

Rome revoked its ban against the Knights of Labor in Canada, and after Gibbons's memol was leaked to the American press, Gibbons won the reputation as the champion of the working class. The vast majority of American bishops stood with Gibbons on the side of laborers. Throughout the rest of his life Gibbons continued to advocate for workers, in late June 1891 criticizing the rich for neglecting their duty to less fortunate persons. "One sanctimonious millionaire," Gibbons argued, caused more deadly harm to Christianity than a dozen thieves and drunkards.[7]

Clearly affected by such statements, Pope Leo XIII on May 15, 1891, released his most famous social encyclical, *Rerum Novarum* (literally, "Of new things," and commonly called "On the Condition of the Working Person"). Leo made clear that the Church had a right and duty not only to teach principles of justice, but to apply this teaching to the real world. The Church is not "so preoccupied with the spiritual concerns of her children," Leo explained, "as to neglect their temporal and earthly interests." To the delight of Gibbons, Leo defended the right of workers to form labor unions, to earn a just wage, to expect decent working conditions, and to own private property. In this, Catholic social teaching was born.[8]

MATTERS OF JURISDICTION

Other matters remained unresolved. At the invitation of Archbishop Ireland, Italian Archbishop Francesco Satolli arrived in New York City at the end of 1892 to investigate the affairs of the American Catholic Church and to resolve the parochial school question. He endorsed Ireland's plan to lease Catholic schools to public systems. Rumors next spread that the pope would appoint Satolli the first permanent papal delegate to the United States, which prompted Archbishop (and now Cardinal) Gibbons to protest against what he considered the imposition of direct Roman rule over American affairs. Most American bishops did not speak publicly on the matter but apparently agreed with Gibbons. Throwing caution to the wind, Bishop Spalding boldly proclaimed that the appointment of Satolli "would be a disaster for the Church."[9]

After Pope Leo XIII appointed Satolli the first Apostolic Delegate to the United States on January 24, 1893, suspicion against Catholics increased. Henry Bowers had organized the American Protective Association, or APA, a few years before in Clinton, Iowa, largely to protest the bishops' support of parochial schools, which he considered a challenge to public school education. Once the "American Pope," that is Satolli, was appointed, APA membership skyrocketed, rising to about a million members.

According to the APA, Catholic bishops urged congregations to form a Catholic political party. The also claimed that the pope issued some mysterious "Instructions to Catholics" that commanded Catholics to kill all heretics on the feast day of Saint Ignatius Loyola, July 31, 1893. Amidst such claims, APA members secretly pledged to "use my utmost power to strike the shackles and chains of blind obedience to the Roman Catholic church." For a brief period, the APA gained some political influence, particularly in Detroit, Milwaukee, and Kansas City.[10]

Bishop Spalding dismissed the claims of the APA as "ridiculous," yet also lamented that "fresh fuel was thrown upon the fire of bigotry," when Italian Archbishop Satolli, "who though a foreigner, with no intention of becoming a citizen, ignorant alike of our language and our traditions, was supposed to have supreme authority in the church in America." Satolli rebuked Spalding (as well as some other progressive thinkers) and thus instituted a cautious and conservative climate in the American Catholic Church.[11]

In May 1893 Leo XIII ended the debate over parochial education by encouraging separate Catholic schools, yet also left to the discretion of local bishops as to whether some Catholic children might attend public schools. Satolli then returned to Rome, where he was named a cardinal (though the position of Apostolic Delegate to the United States continued, and remains to this day).

Informed by Satolli, in an encyclical named *Testem Benevolentiae*, Leo XIII on January 22, 1899, condemned certain republican principles he called "Religious Americanism." These principles were supposedly championed in a recent French translation of the *Life of Father Hecker*, the founder of the Paulists. The translation included a new, enthusiastic introduction by Archbishop Ireland.[12]

Later that same year, the University of Notre Dame awarded the founder of the Catholic University of America, Mary Gwendolyn Caldwell, the Laetere Medal. First awarded sixteen years before, and announced every year on the fourth Sunday in Lent, or Laetare Sunday, the Laetere Medal honored an American Catholic "for outstanding service to the Church and society." Shortly after receiving the award, Caldwell suffered a stroke and nearly died. She then confessed to a friend that she actually had left the Catholic Church the winter before she had received Laetere Medal. According to one account Caldwell also was estranged from Bishop Spalding by this time.[13]

The next year, Spalding visited Pope Leo XIII in Rome. Leo asked Spalding about Americanism. Spalding claimed that such teachings did not exist and that the Catholic faith in America was the same as that in Rome. "That is what many American bishops have written to me," the pope acknowledged, but "there was that poor Father Hecker." Leo continued. "He taught the guidance of the Holy Spirit without the Sacraments." Spalding responded, "Holy Father, I knew Father Hecker well and intimately, and he was a holy, disinterested, zealous and enlightened priest. I am certain that he never believed or taught what they accuse him of." Despite this exoneration, the pope continued to criticize Hecker until finally an exasperated Spalding interjected, "Holy Father, did you know Hecker?" The pope admitted that he did not. "Well then," Spalding said, "I did and a better Catholic we've never had." Leo never again mentioned Americanism in public.[14]

After Chicago Archbishop Patrick Feehan suffered a fatal stroke the summer of 1902, Catholic and non-Catholic leaders from across the country almost unanimously recommended that the pope name Bishop Spalding as Feehan's successor. "It is absolutely necessary," Spalding's long-time friend, Archbishop Patrick Riordan of San Francisco explained, "that a first class man should be sent to Chicago. Affairs there are in a most deplorable condition and I know of no one who is able to remedy this except Bishop Spalding."[15]

Yet Cardinal Satolli oversaw the selection process. Satolli uncovered vague and unlikely rumors that Spalding had entertained a longtime sexual affair with Mamie Caldwell. Based on this news, Satolli nixed Spalding's promotion to Chicago. Shortly thereafter Spalding suffered a stroke which effectively ended his career.

Moving into a New Century

Mary Jones had fled the Irish potato famine before yellow fever killed her husband and four small children. The Great Chicago Fire then destroyed her dressmaking shop. Jones toiled in obscurity for the next twenty-five years before finally, overcome by loneliness and old age, she reinvented herself as "Mother Jones." Wearing antique black dresses and exaggerating her age, Mother Jones promoted Catholic social teaching like a street preacher, using humor, profanity, and wit. While most women remained home, Mother Jones openly proclaimed, "Pray for the dead, and fight like hell for the living."[16]

In 1902 West Virginia district attorney, Reese Blizzard, described Mother Jones as "the most dangerous woman in America" who only need "crook… her finger" and thousands of discontented miners would lay down their tools in protest. The following year, Mother Jones marched dozens of children crippled by long hours in textile mills from Philadelphia to the summer home of President Theodore Roosevelt in Long Island. Mother Jones made the plight of child laborers, along with many other cases of injustice, front-page news.[17]

Wellesley College graduate and Catholic convert Marion Gurney had established New York City's first Catholic settlement house, which aimed to protect and deepen the faith of Catholic immigrants by teaching Catholic doctrine. In 1902 Gurney brought to New York the Confraternity of Christian Doctrine (or CCD), a Catholic teaching program that had been highly successful in England. Eight years later and with the help of Jesuit priest Francis McCarthy, Gurney established the Sisters of Our Lady of Christian Doctrine. In the spirit of the Incarnation, that is, the belief that God lived on earth in the person of Jesus, these women lived among poor immigrants in New York. The sisters soon spread to other American cities.

In 1905 Pope Pius X praised the *Baltimore Catechism* as "the most effective means for spreading the glory of God and securing the salvation of souls," and he also ordered that every parish establish a CCD program. Catholic education of all kinds subsequently involved mastering (oftentimes memorizing) the catechism, and CCD became the primarily means of educating children (and their parents) who did not attend Catholic schools. (The *Baltimore Catechism* endured for more than fifty years before it was revised. The revised edition carried on for another twenty years, that is, up to the Second Vatican Council).[18]

In 1907 Pope Pius X condemned a broad category of thought called Modernism. Among other things, Modernism promoted the idea that essential teachings of the Church, that is, dogma, evolve over time. Modernism had developed in parts of Europe, but after 1910 Pius X ordered that Catholic bishops, priests, and academics from around the world, including in the United States, take the anti-Modernist oath. The oath professed that "the doctrine of faith was handed down…from the apostles through the orthodox Fathers in exactly the same meaning and always in the same purport." Fifty-seven years later the pope finally rescinded the requirement to take this oath.[19]

By 1946, Pope Pius XII had canonized the "Patroness of Immigrants," Frances Xavier Cabrini, the first United States citizen made a saint. On October 4, 2014, Cardinal Angelo Amato, prefect of the Vatican Congregation for Saints' Causes beatified Sister Miriam Teresa Demjanovich, the first American beatified in the United States. Newark Archbishop John Meyers, Paterson Bishop Arthur Serratelli, and Bishop Kurt Burnette, head of the Byzantine Catholic Eparchy of Passaic, attended the ceremony held at the Cathedral Basilica of the Sacred Heart in Newark.

Over the years the University of Notre Dame bestowed the Laetare Medal nearly every year with one exception. In 2009 Harvard Law professor and former United States Ambassador to the Holy See, Mary Ann Glendon, for the first time in history, refused the award. That year Notre Dame had selected President Barak Obama as its commencement speaker. Because of Obama's pro-choice policies, Glendon protested that Notre Dame had violated the United States Conference of Catholic Bishops' recent instruction that Catholic institutions should not honor persons who act in defiance of fundamental Catholic moral principles.

Numerous other more willing recipients of the Laetere Medal include historians, musicians, authors, artists, activists, politicians, doctors, soldiers, and one United States President, John F. Kennedy. Other awardees include philanthropists John A. Creighton, the founder of Creighton University, and Mary Merrick, the founder of the Christ Child Society, a charitable organization dedicated to serving at-risk children in Washington, D.C.

CHAPTER TEN

War Hawks
and Peace Doves

*I*n 1917 Cardinal James Gibbons of Baltimore feared that American Catholics whose country of origin was at odds with American allies might not endorse U.S. involvement in World War I. Gibbons thus formed the National Catholic War Council to demonstrate Catholic support. Gibbons also enlisted the aid of the Irish-American Knights of Columbus, or "Caseys" as they were commonly called. The Caseys had formed thirty-five years before as an insurance company. During World War I, Caseys used their financial know-how to raise significant Catholic contributions for the war.

One million Catholic soldiers constituted over 20 percent of the United States fighting forces. This percentage exceeded the proportion of Catholics in the overall population at the time. Only four of some four thousand conscientious objectors were Catholic.

Canadian-born New York priest Francis Patrick Duffy served as chaplain to New York's Fighting sixty-ninth, which was composed mostly of first and second generation Irish Catholics. Duffy accompanied medics in recovering the wounded from the battlefield and frequently placed himself in the thick of battle. (He still reigns as the most highly decorated cleric in the history of the United States army. He is commemorated by Duffy Square, located in the northern triangle of Manhattan's Times Square).

Numerous Catholic women's organizations assisted servicemen and their families during the war. In Cincinnati, Catholic Anne Tracy organized the Travelers Aid Society, a non-denominational group formed in mid-nineteenth-century St. Louis to help migrants of all sorts. During World War I, Travelers Aid helped soldiers move from home to war and back again. Unlike most other support groups, Travelers Aid provided services regardless of age, gender, or beliefs. The Caseys displayed signs declaring, "Everyone Welcome, Everything Free," but they tended to serve only Catholic soldiers.[1]

In Cincinnati, Tracy's more inclusive Travelers Aid gained the attention of a local philanthropist. He asked a friend of Tracy's, "What do you think she needs most?" "A bath," the friend responded. "Give Miss Tracy a bath." What Tracy really needed were facilities that transient soldiers could use to clean up. The philanthropist provided funds and continued to assist Tracy throughout the war.[2]

John Ryan

Other Catholics lived out their faith in other ways. Born in Minnesota to Irish immigrants who had fled the potato famine, John Ryan learned of Catholic social teaching while studying at Saint Thomas Seminary in Saint Paul. After Archbishop Ireland ordained Ryan and sent him to the Catholic University in Washington, D.C., priest-professors Thomas Bouquillon and William Kerby convinced Ryan that social questions had to be grounded in real life situations, and not just considered in abstract terms.

Ryan later became a professor at Catholic University, where in 1920 he wrote what the National Catholic Welfare Council published as *The Bishops' Program of Social Reconstruction*. This document served as a guide for solving the problems of social justice on which future peace depended. "The ending of the Great War has brought peace," the document began. "But the only safeguard of peace is social justice and a contented people." The bishops supported a minimum wage; equal pay for women; adequate representation in labor disputes; social insurance for illness, unemployment, and old age; and workers' rights to organize. The bishops essentially declared that they would continue to stand with workers and to care for the needy. More than ever before the bishops also aimed to help to shape a more just and peaceful American society.[3]

Ryan spent the rest of his career exploring the practical implications of Catholic social teaching, with three principles governing his thought. First,

Al Smith, during the 1928 campaign

he advocated the "iron law of wages," that is, compensation that allowed workers to live in accord with basic human dignity. Second, he spoke of the need for better distribution of the world's goods. Third, he endorsed the right and duty of the state to promote the common good.[4]

When accused of being a socialist for this proposed reliance on the state, Ryan repeatedly quoted *Rerum Novarum* which declared, "Whenever the general interest or any particular class suffers, or is threatened with harm, which can in no other way be met or prevented, the public authority must step in to deal with it." Ryan also advocated international peace through disarmament, though he avoided pacifism and endorsed the Catholic just war theory.[5]

Moreover Ryan supported the first Catholic to run for president, Al Smith. Shortly after his father's death, Smith had dropped out of school when fifteen years old. He next received what he called a degree from the Fulton Street Fish Market. Smith was not a theologian, but through four terms as Governor of New York, he fought for many of the reforms championed by Catholic social teaching. For instance, Smith enacted laws that regulated women's working and sanitary conditions, instituted fire and health codes, and improved workers' compensation. Smith supported the working class.

At the 1928 Democratic convention, Franklin Roosevelt nominated Smith the "Happy Warrior," and delegates elected him the party's candidate for president. Smith's campaign literature claimed, "The enormous mass of immigrants rightly look upon [Smith] as their mouthpiece, for he is Catholic, though not the tool of the Church; a man of the people in every fibre."[6]

Smith's mother nonetheless claimed that riches, rum, and Romanism had doomed his campaign from the start. Though admirers called Smith the

"Common Man," critics believed that he had distanced himself from his humble roots. He surely had grown wealthy. Opponents also derided him as a "wet candidate" who supported the repeal of Prohibition. They even claimed that he had a DUI, to which Smith replied that he did not know how to drive and that he had never even tried!

Yet Smith certainly was Catholic. Representing many persons suspicious of Catholic connections to Rome, the president of the New York Anti-Saloon League, Methodist Bishop Adna Leonard declared, "No Governor can kiss the papal ring and get within gunshot of the White House." Smith asked that Americans vote not on religion but "only when in their hearts and consciences they become convinced that [his] election will promote the best interests of our country." The people did not agree. Herbert Hoover won the election with 58 percent of the popular vote, and 84 percent of the electoral college.[7]

CATHOLICISM IN THE 1930S

In the wake of Smith's defeat, many Catholics, including one determined young convert, Dorothy Day, heralded Pope Pius XI's 1931 social encyclical, *Quadragesimo Anno*, commonly called "On Reconstructing the Social Order," released forty years after *Rerum Novarum*. After a chaotic upbringing and a tumultuous early career, which included an abortion followed by the birth of her daughter to a common-law anarchist husband, Dorothy Day embraced the Catholic Church.

"I did not want my child to flounder as I had often floundered," Day explained. "I wanted to believe, and I wanted my child to believe, and if belonging to a Church would give her so inestimable a grace as faith in God, and the companionable love of the Saints, then the thing to do was to have her baptized a Catholic." Catholic piety appealed to Day. "Worship, adoration, thanksgiving, supplication," these things Day considered, "the noblest acts of which we are capable in this life." Day praised Catholicism as "the church of the immigrants, the church of the poor."[8]

Day was received in the Catholic Church, and French peasant and former Christian Brother Peter Maurin next schooled her on Catholic social teaching. Echoing *The Bishops' Program of Social Reconstruction*, Day asked, "Why was

Dorothy Day, 1934

so much done in remedying social evils instead of avoiding them in the first place?… Where were the saints to try to change the social order, not just to minister to the slaves, but to do away with slavery?"[9]

Maurin suggested that Day start a paper to help create a better society "in which it would be easier for men to be good." On May 1, 1933, at Manhattan's Union Square, Day distributed the first copies of *The Catholic Worker*, a monthly newspaper sold for one cent a copy (still the price). Day organized the paper around making known the papal encyclicals on social justice.[10]

By December 1933, one hundred thousand copies of *The Catholic Worker* were printed each month. What became known as the Catholic Worker Movement had even opened houses of hospitality for those in need. In 1936 thirty-three Catholic Worker houses (along with a handful of less-than-successful farming communes) spread out across America. The same year *The Catholic Worker* first criticized Nazi Germany.

John Ryan had since denounced Herbert Hoover for his ineptitude during the Depression. Ryan eventually supported Roosevelt's New Deal. Radio priest Charles Coughlin supported Roosevelt's presidential bid from the start, but after Roosevelt was elected, Roosevelt did not consult with Coughlin as he expected he would do, and Coughlin abandoned Roosevelt and denounced Ryan as the "Right Reverend New Dealer." At a time when radio was in its infancy, Coughlin's program drew as many as a million listeners per week, perhaps making him the most popular American radio personality of the 1930s.[11]

Starting in 1937, Coughlin began to lash out against Jews, whom he claimed had unduly influenced Roosevelt. "When we get through with the Jews in America," Coughlin predicted, "they'll think the treatment

Charles E. Coughlin, c. 1933

they received in Germany was nothing." Like many listeners, Al Smith, who, since his presidential run, had served as president of the Empire State Building Corporation, dismissed Coughlin as a "crackpot." Coughlin's radio broadcasts soon disappeared.[12]

THE CATHOLIC PRESENCE IN WORLD WAR II

After Hitler invaded Poland and World War II began on September 1, 1939, most American Catholics proposed to stay out of the conflict. Catholic leaders, most of whom strongly opposed Communism, opposed Roosevelt's early support of the Soviet Union.

Many of the Catholic-run social agencies active during World War I nonetheless again swung into action. Cincinnati's new train station, the Union Terminal, became a major hub of military movement. Still active in Travelers Aid, Anne Tracy converted a vacant thirty-by-sixty-foot tea room (now an ice-cream parlor) off Union Terminal's main concourse into a waiting room for soldiers. Union Terminal's lounge was the first of what would become ninety-four transit rooms opened for service men and women in train and bus stations across the country.

Tracy managed the lounge with help from Episcopalian Bailey Wright Hickenlooper and a slew of volunteers from various faiths who came together as part of the United Service Organizations, or USO. Formed in April 1941, the USO joined six welfare groups: the National Catholic Community Service, the Jewish Welfare Board, the Salvation Army, the YMCA, the YWCA, and Travelers Aid. "Theoretically the three faiths [Protestants, Catholics and Jews] had cooperated before," one USO official remarked, "but their work in the USO was the first time in the history of the world that Jews, Catholics, and Protestants as religionists had together not only made plans, but budgeted for them, and then carried them out in

Tracy's USO lounge included a nursery where this unknown woman cared for this unknown soldier's child.

the practical day-by-day work." Volunteers initially used their own money to purchase cigarettes, postcards, stationary, and refreshments. "We started with cookies," explained Tracy.[13]

Japan bombed Pearl Harbor on December 7, 1941, and the United States entered the war. An overwhelming majority of American Catholics supported the effort. Radio personality Bishop Fulton Sheen characterized the conflict as a "theological struggle" between good and evil, but Dorothy Day announced that *The Catholic Worker* would maintain its pacifist stand, insisting that a nonviolent way of life stood at the heart of the gospel.[14]

Anne Tracy simply instructed her volunteers not to discuss the war (which was the official advice of the USO). Instead, "there must be an unusual effort put forth to meet whatever needs…[soldiers] may have," Tracy said. As the number of cookies consumed by soldiers exceeded one hundred thousand per month, different women's groups from the Protestant Council of Churches, the Catholic Women's Association, and the Federation of Jewish Women's Clubs rotated baking and distribution responsibilities.[15]

Iowa Catholic Bill Ball was killed at Pearl Harbor, which prompted the five brothers of Ball's girlfriend, Genevieve Sullivan, to join the navy

Joseph, Francis, Albert, Madison, and George Sullivan (left to right) on board the
USS Juneau

to avenge Ball's death. George, Frank, Joe, Matt, and Al Sullivan enlisted
on January 3, 1942. Against navy policy, all five brothers were assigned
according to their request to the same light cruiser, the USS *Juneau.* During
the Battle of Guadalcanal in the Solomon Islands on November 13, 1942,
a Japanese torpedo sunk the *Juneau.* Frank, Joe, and Matt died instantly.
Al drowned the next day. George survived for four or five days before he
slipped off a raft, overcome either by delirium or grief. Amidst the confu-
sion of war and with some lost paperwork, remaining survivors were not
discovered for eight days.

The morning of January 12, 1943, a naval officer approached the boys'
father, Thomas Sullivan as he prepared to leave his home for work. "I have
some news for you about your boys," the officer said. "Which one?" asked
Thomas. "I'm sorry," the officer replied. "All five." President Roosevelt wrote
a letter of condolence, and Pope Pius XII sent a silver religious medal and
rosary with his message of regret. (The brothers' story was filmed as the

1944 movie *The Sullivans* and inspired, at least in part, the 1998 film *Saving Private Ryan*.)[16]

In the same sea where the Sullivan brothers had lost their lives, and at about the same time as the Sullivan accident, Catholic Lieutenant John F. Kennedy skippered a patrol torpedo boat, PT 109, through a starless, moonless night before a Japanese destroyer, the *Amagiri*, cut in half Kennedy's much smaller vessel. Two of Kennedy's men were instantly killed. Kennedy pulled the badly burned Patrick McMahon by his life vest to the section of the boat still afloat, and then led the other nine survivors on a three and a half mile swim to the tiny, deserted Plum Pudding Island. The navy held memorial services for Kennedy's crew, but then local persons working for the nNavy found the men. Kennedy's scouring for coconuts on nearby islands had kept the men alive for six days, while singing "Yes, Jesus Loves Me" helped them pass the time.

Catholic Charles Green was exempt from military service due to his position with the Dupont Chemical Company in Wilmington, Delaware, but his supervisor once missed the deadline to submit the exemption form, and Green was drafted into the navy. He told his wife, Therese, that he did not want to appeal the decision particularly because so many fathers were being called up. Neither Green nor his wife knew that she was pregnant at the time. On June 19, 1944, that is, thirteen days after D-Day, Green's landing ship tank, LST 523, hit a water mine off Utah beach. Like many other Catholic and non-Catholic women, Therese Green received a telegram informing her that her husband was missing in action. Shortly after her son, Charles Jr., was born, the navy conceded that his father was dead. They never found Green's body.

Catholic men constituted between 25 and 35 percent of the total U.S. fighting forces, an impressive increase from the already high numbers of World War I. Three thousand two hundred seventy Catholic chaplains served Catholic servicemen. Thirty-eight chaplains were killed, and ninety were wounded in action.

Catholic women were less represented among soldiers. American Catholic bishops opposed the establishment of the Women's Auxiliary Army Corps (whose members were popularly known as WACs), claiming the admission of women into armed forces would ruin traditional family roles. Bishop John O'Hara, the Apostolic Delegate for U.S. Military Forces, argued that to preserve "the sanctity of the home," male soldiers would "prefer to peel potatoes and darn [their] own socks rather than have women in the army."[17]

Germany surrendered on May 8, 1945, and the United States dropped atomic bombs on Hiroshima and Nagasaki on August 6 and 9 of the same year. Japan surrendered five days later. American bishops said nothing about the atomic bombs, but the Catholic magazine *Commonweal* moaned that "the name of Hiroshima, the name of Nagasaki are names for American guilt and shame." *America* magazine feared for the dawning atomic age, only hoping "that the evil which will come from the atomic bomb may not outweigh the good which our war leaders, rightly or wrongly, hope to achieve by its use."[18]

An estimated three million soldiers, a fifth of all World War II GIs, over the course of the war passed through Anne Tracy's Union Terminal lounge, which finally closed on June 10, 1946. Six days later, Tracy passed away. Obituaries acclaimed her as "Saint Anne," the "railway shepherd."[19]

POSTWAR PEACE EFFORTS

As the people of Hungary suffered brutal persecution and the world moved to the "brink of disaster" in a possible World War III in the late 1950s, American Catholic bishops turned the old axiom, "If you wish peace, prepare for war," into "If you wish peace, prepare for peace." The bishops increasingly linked peace with social justice, proclaiming in 1959, "True peace for nations as well as for individuals comes from justice, from charity, from the faithful observance of the moral law."[20]

An ardent Vietnamese nationalist and devout Catholic, Ngo Dinh Diem, meanwhile met with prominent American Catholics, including Senator John F. Kennedy, to help bolster Diem's efforts to establish democracy in South Vietnam. After Diem was elected the first president of South Vietnam, American Catholics supported his regime—that is, until he turned into a ruthless dictator. With support from President Kennedy, Diem was overthrown and then assassinated in 1963.

American Catholics, including Catholic worker Christopher Kerns, led the subsequent opposition to further American intervention in Vietnam. On November 9, 1965, a young graduate of the Jesuit Le Moyne College, Roger La Porte set himself on fire before New York's United Nations building. "I am a Catholic Worker," La Porte proclaimed. "I am antiwar, all wars. I did this as a religious action." Jesuit Daniel Berrigan praised La Porte's self-sacrifice, but Trappist Monk Thomas Merton, along with many other anti-war activists, did not. The majority of Catholics, including the American Catholic bishops, deemed that American presence in Vietnam was justified.[21]

On May 17, 1968, nine Catholic activists, including Berrigan and his brother, Josephite priest Philip Berrigan, destroyed draft records they had stolen from a draft board in Catonsville, Maryland. The Catonsville Nine, as the protestors were called, represented a tiny yet provocative group of American Catholics who ardently opposed the Vietnam War. In the wake of such protests, many Catholics became more militantly patriotic than ever before. Catholics most likely were once again overrepresented among U.S. troops sent to Vietnam between 1968 and 1973. Atlanta Bishops Paul Hallinan and Joseph Bernardin nonetheless mused, "What are the demands of true patriotism?" and "Is it possible to speak of a 'just war' today as we did in the past?"[22]

In 1983 the United States Conference of Catholic Bishops issued "The Challenge of Peace: God's Promise and Our Response," which applied the just-war theory to the moral problem of nuclear proliferation in the Cold War era. Catholic teaching begins with a presumption against war and for peaceful settlement of disputes, the bishops declared. And while every nation has a right to defend itself, offensive war is never justified. The use of nuclear or conventional weapons to destroy whole cities, and to kill civilians is also never justified. And defensive responses that involve horribly destructive nuclear weapons certainly exceed any sense of proportionality necessary to justify war.

About twenty years later, American bishops acknowledged the horrible repression of Saddam Hussein's dictatorship in Iraq, yet declared in late 2002, "Based on the facts that are known to us, we continue to find it difficult to justify the resort to war against Iraq, lacking clear and adequate evidence of an imminent attack of a grave nature." The Bishops prayed that President George W. Bush would "step back from the brink of war...and work for peace that is just and enduring."[23]

CHAPTER ELEVEN

Celebrities
and Intellectuals

*T*he horror of World War II spurred an American religious revival, a "God boom," so to speak. Protestants flocked to Billy Graham, and Catholics tuned in to Fulton Sheen. A well-educated, charismatic, storytelling priest, Sheen hosted the NBC evening radio broadcast "The Catholic Hour" through the 1930s and 1940s before starring in his own Sunday night television program, *Life is Worth Living*. Sheen also published various addresses in almost one hundred books, a few of which became bestsellers. Others were "absolutely terrible and should never have been published," at least as Sheen described them.[1]

Sheen lined his television set at New York's Adelphi Theatre with books, dressed in flowing robes of a bishop (Sheen served as auxiliary to New York and bishop of Rochester), and used a chalkboard that an angel supposedly erased. Yet Sheen rarely said much about Catholic teaching, and focused instead on general issues relevant to everyone, such as love, ambition, family, and communism. With thirty million Catholic and non-Catholic viewers, Sheen competed straight up with television's first star, comedian Milton Berle.

Catholics Ed Sullivan, Jackie Gleason, and Grace Kelly similarly won over American audiences, but none of these performers wore their faith on their sleeve, and none so obviously helped inspire the Catholic population as did Fulton Sheen. The number of American Catholics—twenty-one million, or about 16 percent of the overall population in 1940—began to rise in the postwar period. Mass attendance soared.

Fulton Sheen at the Adelphi Theatre

At the same time historian John Tracy Ellis lamented that Sheen "[had] consciously abandoned the life of a scholar for that of the preacher." Others openly criticized Sheen's careless scholarship and historical inaccuracies, with one critic concluding that Sheen was "more interested in imparting an effect than [in disseminating good] information." Sheen's charisma and wit nonetheless clothed American Catholicism in a rather attractive package.[2]

The Academy Award for the Best Picture of 1944, *Going My Way* produced more likeable images of the church. After an elder pastor, Father Fitzgibbon (played by Barry Fitzgerald), ordered some ruffians to go to church, the younger, dynamic Father Chuck O'Malley (played by Bing Crosby) claimed that Mass attendance was not enough. O'Malley emphasized that Catholics should also live good moral lives and even sing for the faith. Advancing such positive ideals, the enormously popular sequel, *The Bells of St. Mary's* of 1945 introduced Sister Mary Benedict (played by Ingrid Bergman) beside Father O'Malley (still played by Crosby).

CATHOLIC AUTHORS IN THE MID-1940S

A number of Catholic authors meanwhile produced a series of semi-historical novels that aimed to humanize the church for young readers. Longtime journalist Anne Heagney led this effort with what she called her "story writing." Heagney's books included *The Marylanders*, *The Spaldings of Old Kentucky*, and *Charity Goes to War*, that is, Heagney's heroic accounts of colonial, frontier, and Civil War American Catholicism, respectively.[3]

Foreshadowing more complex reflection on American Catholicism, the G.I. Bill sent countless veterans, including hundreds of thousands of Catholics, to college. Numerous small Catholic colleges, along with many bigger state schools, expanded overnight to meet the need. More and more Catholics thought more deeply about the faith.

Detailing the New England Irish Catholic immigrant experience through the lens of Catholic social teaching, or "the American Catholic social revolution," as he put it, Catholic novelist Joseph Dever aimed in various works to "authentically reflect…something substantial concerning the human side of Catholicism in America." In his bestselling 1947 novel, *No Lasting Home*, Dever "has given us a real book," as one account put it, "not because he has passion for life, but because he has first loved God."[4]

A friend of Ernest Hemmingway, Harry Sylvester, dedicated his 1947 *Moon Gaffney* to "all good Catholic radicals," including Dorothy Day. Day made a cameo appearance in the novel, as did "the only honest politician in New York," Al Smith. One of Sylvester's characters, Bart Schneider, suggested that a well-educated Catholic might understand Catholic teaching better than did the typical parish priest. Overly "attuned to the clerical voice on the radio" (that is, to Fulton Sheen), too many priests had grown so obsessed with preventing premarital sex that they had, according to Schneider, "confused or somehow perverted" Catholic teaching to give the false impression that Catholics believed that all sexual encounters, including marital relations, were "filthy."[5]

Moon Gaffney won critical acclaim and became a staple of Irish American Catholic literature, but conservative Catholics hated it, especially when Sylvester had Schneider proclaim "I like everything about the Church except the people who run it or try to run it." (Revealing lingering disdain for Sylvester, who eventually left the church, a recent Catholic thinker concluded that Sylvester "lacks even the minimal fame of a Wikipedia entry.")[6]

Thomas Merton's 1948 autobiography, *The Seven-Story Mountain*, thoughtfully navigated through the complex makeup of the human person. Merton's journey from a sinful past toward the Catholic Church and the Order of the Cistercians of the Strict Observance, better known as the Trappists, appealed

Flannery O'Connor always loved birds. She spent her last years surrounded by peacocks.

to countless Americans. Within one year, one hundred thousand copies of *The Seven Story Mountain* were in print. *Time Magazine* reported that Merton had "made the concept of saintliness accessible to moderns."[7]

Like many American Catholic and non-Catholic writers, Merton was overawed by his brilliant contemporary, Flannery O'Connor. "I write her name with honor," Merton exclaimed, "for all the truth and all the craft with which she show's humankind's fall and dishonor and—redemption." O'Connor was a deeply committed Catholic and serious intellectual who proclaimed Catholicism as the guiding force behind all her work. O'Connor's fourteen-year struggle with lupus only intensified her faith and refined her perceptions. For O'Connor, God shined brightest through the misfits of this world.[8]

The *New York Sun* reporter Malcolm Johnson's twenty-four part series, *Crime on the Waterfront* won the Pulitzer Prize in 1949. Five years later, the movie based on the series, *On the Waterfront*, won eight Academy Awards, including Best Picture and Best Actor (Marlon Brando). One of the movie's heroes, Father Barry (whose character was based on the real-life New York Jesuit, John "Pete" Corridan, played by Karl Malden), dramatically proclaimed that a saint cannot hide in a church and that "Christ is on the waterfront."

"Disagreement that Precedes Understanding"
With the American Catholic Church so positively portrayed and clearly on the rise, Paul Blanshard, a leader of the recently formed Protestants and Other Americans United for the Separation of Church and State, sounded the alarm in his bestselling book, *American Freedom and Catholic Power.*

Repeating claims from earlier decades, Blanshard charged that America had a "Catholic problem" in that the Catholic Church was an "antidemocratic and an alien system of control."[9]

Sounding a different alarm, the Catholic Senator from Wisconsin, Joseph McCarthy, on February 9, 1950, claimed that two hundred and five Communists had infiltrated the United States federal government. McCarthy quickly reduced his estimate to fifty-seven infiltrators, all of whom should be immediately expelled (as should, McCarthy added, persons with homosexual orientations). The prominent Kennedy clan of Hyannis Port, Massachusetts, along with much of the American Catholic community, despite their overwhelming support of the Democratic Party, backed the Republican McCarthy, especially his anti-Communist stand.

Yet McCarthy's browbeating tactics and freewheeling style soon erased any favor he had enjoyed. After a series of public hearings, in December 1954 the Senate (minus John Kennedy, who was in the hospital recovering from back surgery) censured McCarthy, making him one of the few U.S. politicians ever disciplined in this fashion. (The term *McCarthyism* has since come to mean demagogic, reckless, and unsubstantiated accusations, as well as public attacks on the character or patriotism of political opponents.)

Also in 1954 longtime priest-professor of theology at the Catholic University of America and editor of the *American Ecclesiastical Review*, Joseph Fenton wrote two reports critical of longtime priest-professor of theology at Woodstock College and editor of *Theological Studies*, Jesuit John Courtney Murray. Much to Fenton's chagrin, Murray had criticized the traditional European ideal of a united Catholic state. In a series of dense philosophical arguments Murray argued that Church and state must be separated according to the classic Catholic differentiation between the spiritual and temporal realms and according to the United States Constitution. Rome favored Fenton's position and ordered Murray to quit writing on Church-state relations.

Historian John Tracy Ellis on May 14, 1955, next complained in a widely circulated and much discussed address that many American Catholics had risen economically and politically but lagged behind intellectually. The Catholic Church of the United States had become "big business," Ellis groaned, and Catholic schools, especially Catholic universities, had fallen far short of original expectations. Catholics should pursue higher education not just to get a job but to make the world a better place, according to Ellis. At Catholic University, Ellis routinely inspired students to such higher aims, as well as encouraged them to tell the whole truth, especially in historical work.[10]

After the Los Angeles Democratic National Convention of 1960 nominated John Kennedy for President, many persons questioned whether a Catholic could hold the land's highest office. John Courtney Murray responded with a resounding "yes." Shortly thereafter, Murray appeared on the cover of *Time Magazine* (as did Kennedy, Sheen, and a few other prominent Catholics). *Time* boasted, "If anyone can help U.S. Catholics and their non-Catholic countrymen toward the disagreement that precedes understanding—John Courtney Murray can." Unlike Murray, Kennedy was not a sophisticated Catholic thinker, and did not always enjoy full support of the Catholic community. When the slimmest of margins elected Kennedy president, the optimistic age for Catholics nevertheless seemed to have reached new heights.[11]

Catholics certainly entered the political realm like never before. Over the next generation, more than twenty-five Catholics served on the presidential cabinet, compared to six in the first one hundred and fifty years of the country. Catholics soon became the largest religious group represented in the United States Congress, with over one hundred members. Moreover, the American Catholic population had doubled from 1940 to 1960, extending to about 25 percent of the total population.

Ministering to the Increasing Catholic Population

At the same time, many Catholic leaders, especially Catholic Sisters, had grown overburdened with Church business, especially the work of running Catholic schools. For quite some time, religious sisters had dominated American Catholic education. In the Archdiocese of Cincinnati, which boasted one of the most vibrant Catholic school networks in the country, three-fourths of the parishes in 1960 included a grade school staffed mostly by fourteen religious orders, including the Sisters of Charity of Cincinnati,

Monsignor John Tracy Ellis

the Sisters of Mercy, and the Sisters of Third Order Regular of Saint Francis of Oldenburg, Indiana. Religious women also controlled Cincinnati's fifteen girls' and five coeducational high schools.

Religious men ran Cincinnati's seven boys' high schools with about forty Marianist brothers and forty diocesan priests teaching at Cincinnati's largest boys' high schools, Chaminade and Elder, respectively. (The boys' schools tended to be about twice as large as the girls' schools.) Men constituted most of the faculties at Cincinnati's male universities, Xavier and the University of Dayton, with laymen outnumbering priests and brothers by about three to one.

At the much smaller women's colleges, Our Lady of Cincinnati (eventually renamed Edgecliff College) and the College of Mount Saint Joseph-on-the-Ohio (now Mount Saint Joseph University), the Sisters of Mercy and Sisters of Charity, respectively, made up about half of the faculty. Into the 1960s, religious teachers still held a slim majority over the total number of lay teachers in Cincinnati, but that would soon change. Across the country, the number of sisters and priests teaching in Catholic schools also soon would dramatically decline.

About 150 miles south of Cincinnati, a Sister of Charity of Nazareth, Kentucky, Isabel Green heeded an older nun's advice that "it's better to *wear* out than to *rust* out." Green served at Nazareth College as registrar, treasurer, dean, financial aid advisor, director of admissions, and alumnae and public relations director, all with little-to-no training and oftentimes doing more than one job at a time. Like many religious women of this era, Green had grown consumed with work and had lost touch with her spiritual inspiration.[12]

For many busy Catholics of the 1950s and 1960s the sacraments similarly had lost meaning. The positive energy of the times "formed, nurtured, and inspired us spiritually, intellectually, liturgically, and socially," recalled Catholic priest Richard McBrien, but the celebration of the Mass left Catholics high and dry. With the priest turned from the people speaking in Latin and often in hushed tones, "Those in the pews tended to pursue their own private devotions," McBrien remembered, "like the recitation of the rosary or reading from a favorite prayer book. Others glanced at the parish bulletin or day-dreamed." Due to the requirement that Catholics not eat or drink after midnight before receiving Communion the next day, relatively few persons actually received Communion, especially at later Masses.[13]

Newborns were baptized days after birth with the mother not present and no parental preparation whatsoever. Catholics were taught to experience the sacrament of Penance in quantitative terms. For every sin a person confessed, the priest ordered a corresponding number of prayers. Wedding parties were expected to "receive" the sacrament of Penance the morning after a wedding, presumably due to the sins committed the night before. Catholic schools fostered this legalistic attitude toward religion through the rote memorization of the *Baltimore Catechism*. In short, the Catholicism of this time "was a mixture of good and bad," McBrien concluded.[14]

Reflecting this mixed church experience, Catholic convert Walker Percy of Covington, Louisiana, published in 1961 his first and most famous work, *The Moviegoer*, which won the National Book Award for fiction. While Percy found much of the language of Catholicism empty of meaning, existential questioning, Southern sensibility, and a deep Catholic faith permeated all of Percy's works, including five other highly acclaimed novels. "It has to do not so much with an explicit faith or transmitting an explicit faith in my writings," Percy explained, "as it has to do with a view of man, of a theory of man, man as more than organism, more than consumer, man the wayfarer. Man the pilgrim. Man in transit. On a journey."[15]

In 1962 James Farl Powers published his debut work, *Morte d'Urban*. Throughout the novel, a charming priest, Father Urban of the fictitious Order of Saint Clement of Chicago, gained national attention as a preacher "without much help from radio and television." In the "fast changing world of today," Father Urban showed that "there had to be a new approach" where church leaders were less concerned about more air time, more publications, more schools, and "more activity of the kind that had already overextended their lines." Father Urban was more comfortable on the golf course than before a camera, a humble and exceptional man of faith who led by personal integrity. Beating out literary giants John Updike, Katherine Anne Porter and Vladimir Nabokov, Powers's *Morte d'Urban* won the National Book Award for fiction, thus marking Catholic winners in two successive years.[16]

SIGNS OF THE TIMES

Responding in a different fashion to the busyness of Catholic life, Thomas Merton advised the hordes of overworked Catholic women and men, "There are times…when in order to keep ourselves in existence at all, we simply have to sit back for a while and do nothing." For quite some time, Merton had been exploring the mystical concept of nothingness from various eastern traditions including Buddhism. Merton turned to the east as a source of enrichment for his western Catholic faith, and encouraged others to do the same.[17]

Like Dorothy Day and many other Catholic activists, Merton also pushed Catholicism toward social action. Boycotts in favor of migrant farm workers, Martin Luther King's March on Washington, the War on Poverty, and repeated calls for nuclear disarmament raised new questions for Americans. "By what right do we protest?" Merton asked. Merton gathered thirteen peace advocates at his Trappist monastery in the hills of Kentucky for three days in November 1964. Quaker A.J. Muste, Mennonite John Howard Yoder, Unitarian W.H. Ferry, Methodist Elbert Jean, and Presbyterian John Oliver Nelson were among those who discussed conscientious objection, the challenge of technology, and the basis for protest. "We used our time together both to explore what we were up against and how best to respond," recalled another participant, Catholic Jim Forest.[18]

Many Catholics, including some of Merton's friends, marched in protest of racial injustice and against the Vietnam War. Across the country Catholic dioceses established offices of urban affairs and social action. At the same time a few Catholics pelted with rocks and eggs the nuns and priests who

Cesar Chavez on one of his many college campus visits across this United States

had protested. When urban renewal moved blacks to previously all-white neighborhoods, many Catholics joined in the national flight to the suburbs.

Leading another crusade for justice, Catholic Cesar Chavez organized the United Farm Workers of America around a nationwide boycott of California grapes. Confident that justice would prevail, Chavez proclaimed "*Sí, se puede*," Spanish for "Yes, one can" or, roughly, "Yes, it can be done." Five years after John Kennedy was killed in 1963, his brother, Robert Kennedy while running for President was killed in California, moments after expressing support for Chavez. (Barak Obama adopted Chavez's slogan for the 2008 presidential campaign.)[19]

Further addressing the signs of the times, Catholic bishops from around the world gathered at Rome from 1961 to 1965. The Second Vatican Council, or Vatican II, helped to focus conversations that had started long before. For quite some time Catholics had been talking about social concerns (led by papal pronouncements on Catholic social teaching), had begun to think differently of other religious traditions (spurred on by the reflections of Merton and others), and had started to reconsider the relationship between church and state (inspired by thinkers like John Courtney Murray).

Vatican II advanced these and other discussions. (Vatican II's *Declaration on Religious Liberty*, for which Murray was one of the chief architects, affirmed the very principle of Church and state separation for which Murray had been previously censored.)

Vatican II's liturgical changes impacted the lives of ordinary American Catholics the most. Bishops placed greater emphasis on the Eucharist, turned the priest around to face the people, relied more heavily on scripture, approved the use of the vernacular (that is, not Latin but the local language), and encouraged active participation of the congregation during Mass. Bishops effectively led believers to find God right in their midst.

Some Catholic leaders feared that this emphasis on the community would strip the Mass of its mystery. Others balked at any kind of change. "Most people were furious," recalled Catholic novelist, Mary Gordon. "Most people were confused and angry and outraged. They felt that the rug had been taken out from them, particularly if they grew up, as I did, in a working-class neighborhood." At the same time Gordon came to see, as did many Catholics, that the "answer" was not "to turn the clock back." Gordon tried to find the best of the new emerging American Catholic Church.[20]

Post Vatican II Catholicism

Over the next decade or so, bishops introduced further advances to the liturgy. For the first time in a long while, Catholics were permitted to eat meat on non-Lenten Fridays and to attend Mass on Saturday night to fulfill the Sunday obligation. Unordained lay people began to serve as readers and Eucharistic ministers. Communion was received in the hand and then with the cup. The sacrament of Penance was reframed as the sacrament of Reconciliation with optional face-to-face encounters with the priest and communal penance services. And a more ecumenical approach to interfaith marriages was introduced. Catholics talked with non-Catholic neighbors for the first time, and official interfaith dialogues took place, particularly with Episcopalians, Lutherans, Methodists, Presbyterians, Southern Baptists, Disciples of Christ, and Orthodox believers.

After some musicians rather unsuccessfully attempted to incorporate modern music into the liturgy, a group of young Jesuits at Saint Louis

Saint Louis Jesuits (standing, left to right) Bob Dufford, John Foley, Tim Manion, Robert "Roc" O'Connor (with his tradmark twelve-string guitar) and Dan Shutte at Loyola University of Chicago, 1979.

University more effectively used acoustic guitars and contemporary melodies to set biblical texts to music in the spirit of Vatican II. Religious sisters visiting Saint Louis University took mimeographed tunes of the Jesuits back to their communities, and the Jesuits released recordings, with their second album *Earthen Vessels* selling over one million copies. This release included "Though the Mountains May Fall," "Seek the Lord," and "Be Not Afraid." The Saint Louis Jesuits, as the group eventually called itself, greatly impacted Catholic liturgies in this country and beyond, and also animated many mainline Protestant liturgical celebrations.

More participational models of church governance also revived post–Vatican II American Catholicism. Priests, nuns, and an increasing number of lay people served on diocesan and parish councils, and in religious senates. New groups organized around black ministries, continuing education, due process, ecumenical affairs, evangelization, family relations, finance, lay ministries, liturgy, media, social justice, spirituality, vocations, and youth ministry. The establishment of the permanent diaconate for men, along with a huge influx of lay women ministers, changed the face of the Catholic ministerial work force.

A senior American archbishop at the council, Karl J. Alter of Cincinnati, moved slowly on Vatican II's liturgical changes, but he expedited developments in education, social justice, and Church governance. Alter appointed the first lay person to the archdiocesan Board of Education and supported this group's subsequent recommendation that every parish have its own board of education. He also advised high schools to include equal representation of laity and priests on their boards, in part to better address growing financial concerns. Area Catholic colleges soon added lay people to their trustees, as well. And Alter quickly established a poverty commission and a human relations commission, both of which addressed urban problems and racial tensions. Many bishops followed suit.

American Catholics celebrated Pope Paul VI's one-day visit to New York City on October 4, 1965. As the first reigning pope to come to the United States, Paul VI toured Saint Patrick's Cathedral, met with Cardinal Francis Spellman, talked with President Lyndon Johnson, addressed the General Assembly of the United Nations, celebrated Mass at Yankee Stadium, visited the Vatican Exhibit at the World's Fair, and finally headed back to Rome, all before the day was over. One million people saw Paul VI in person. Another one hundred million viewed him on television.

Religious orders from across the country (and the world) subsequently gathered to rediscover their spiritual roots. Some groups reaffirmed the ministries instituted by their founders. Others embraced new areas of work, often turning their efforts more directly toward the marginalized, including women and the poor. And many religious women and men donned more common clothing in an attempt to proclaim Christ more effectively to the modern world. At the same time, within four years after Vatican II's conclusion some three thousand priests resigned from the priesthood. Over the next two decades, the total number of priests in the United States remained about the same, even though the total population of American Catholics steadily increased some 13 percent.

Popular German theologian and Redemptorist priest Bernard Häring encouraged female orders to set aside specific places devoted to prayer at each convent. On March 12, 1967, two American Sisters, Marie Goldstein and Ruth Caspar, convened a workshop at the University of Notre Dame to discuss the feasibility of Häring's idea. The workshop concluded that what these sisters called "Houses of Prayer" should be opened across the nation to balance the pervasive "thrust towards hyperactivism" with "a corresponding thrust towards radical prayer." Echoing the ecumenical spirit of Vatican II, the workshop added that each house should become a center for the study of mysticism and ascetic theology, including the practice of yoga and Zen. The spirit of poverty and simplicity should reign, with Houses of Prayer providing a source of divine energy and peace, as well as psychological serenity.[21]

SPIRITUAL EMPOWERMENT

About the time of Thomas Merton's untimely death at Bangkok on December 10, 1968, Isabel Green asked the Sisters of Charity of Nazareth for time away from her many responsibilities to pray. Green spent seven weeks studying the "House of Prayer Experience" or HOPE, in a program sponsored by Immaculate Heart of Mary Sisters Margaret Brennan and Ann Chester in Monroe, Michigan. At the program's conclusion, another woman suggested that a priest should be part of each house, to which the program's main speaker, Bernard Häring emphatically answered, "No-o-o. You are too prone to rely on a priest. This House of Prayer is your charism. Use your own ingenuity to develop it."[22]

Isabel Green studied for three months with Brother David Steindl-Räst at Mount Saviour Benedictine Monastery in Elmira, New York. With help from other religious women, a Catholic layman, and a Jewish expert in Hatha Yoga, Green then converted an abandoned New England structure into a House of Prayer. A wealthy family had built this five bedroom building right on the ocean as the servants' quarters next door to their stone mansion that for some time had been used by the Jesuits as a retreat house at Eastern Point in Gloucester, Massachusetts. After some Boston College graduate students helped renovate the building, Green opened the Gloucester House of Prayer.

"Not much 'busy-ness' or 'business' goes on here," Green explained. Freed for a few days to up to a month from hectic jobs, sisters, brothers, priests, and an increasing number of laypersons refound their inner selves at Gloucester. "For the first time in my life, I feel free," one woman exclaimed, "free to be me." Green never charged any fees, limited conversation to the noontime meal, and kept televisions, telephones, and typewriters away from view. "If you're going to talk to God," Green insisted, "then it's easier when you're not talking to someone else at the same time." Every morning, Green drew guests to the chapel to greet the sunrise, bless the water, and invite God into their hearts. Many religious traditions met at Gloucester, which

Isabel Green outfitted the chapel at the House of Prayer—where David Steindl-Räst (third from right) and others gathered—with sea shells, a portrait of Robert Kennedy, and carpet squares donated from a Gloucester store.

soon inspired other Houses of Prayer across the United States, as well as in Canada, Chile, and Ireland.[23]

At the same time, some Catholics longed for the pre-Vatican II church. In 1970 French Archbishop Marcel François Marie Joseph Lefebvre founded the Society of Saint Pius X with the approval of the Pope Paul VI, but the pope subsequently criticized Lefebvre for refusing to celebrate Mass according to the rite approved by Vatican II. Lefebvre not only insisted on continuing to use Latin, but rejected new theological statements in the Mass such as the declaration that "This blood will be shed for you and *for all men.*" Lefebvre preferred the older, no longer approved, "This blood will be shed for you and *for many.*"[24]

The Society of Saint Pius X expanded to the United States, but Lefebvre remained broiled in controversy with fellow local bishops and with popes for the rest of his life. Writer Mary Gordon visited the Society's house on Long Island hoping to find a vibrant Catholic spirituality, but she concluded that the group (and others like it) longed "not [for] the Middle Ages but the 1950s, not Thomas Aquinas but Bishop Sheen, not Philip the Good but Joe McCarthy."[25]

Other American Catholic scholars feared that secularization and modernism had so influenced the American Catholic Church that the

American Catholic community had become "first and foremost American, rather than Catholic, in its outlook." In 1977 a number of priest scholars from around the country met in St. Louis to embrace "a more friendly approach to the teaching authority of the church." Capuchin Franciscan Ronald Lawler of the Catholic University of America served as president of what soon organized as the Fellowship of Catholic Scholars.[26]

According to the Fellowship's Statement of Purpose, these scholars "wholeheartedly accept[ed] and support[ed] the renewal of the Church of Christ undertaken by Pope John XXIII, shaped by Vatican II, and carried on by succeeding pontiffs." The scholars also recognized that "the questions raised by contemporary thought must be considered with courage and dealt with in honesty." And the scholars pledged to do this "faithful to the truth always guarded in the church by the Holy Spirit."[27]

The following year, cardinals elected Pope John Paul II, which caused many, including the Fellowship of Catholic Scholars, to hope that the new pope would slow down Church developments. Over the next twenty-six years, John Paul II visited the United States seven times, and appointed many more traditional American bishops.

Many other Catholics found other ways to rekindle their spiritual lives. With encouragement from Isabel Green, lay theologian Rosemary Haughton opened Wellspring House for homeless men in Gloucester. Catholic Worker Houses of Hospitality spread across the country, as did many other Catholic social agencies. Retreat centers flourished, and new initiatives such as the Charismatic Renewal, started at Pittsburgh's Duquesne University, run by the Congregation of the Holy Spirit, recharged Catholic parish life. Cursillo, Marriage Encounter, and RENEW movements also flourished. After 1981, the Eternal Word Television Network fostered more traditional Catholic piety with popular host Mother Angelica Rizzo. Thousands of American Catholics flew to Yugoslavia to venerate reputed Marian apparitions at Medjugorje.

After spending nine months in prayer and solitude in a hermitage in Illinois, English-born Catholic Edwina Gateley in 1983 founded Genesis House, a house of hospitality for Chicago women involved in prostitution. In direct response to Vatican II's call for full and active engagement in the Church's life and mission, Gateley also established the Volunteer Missionary Movement to recruit persons to accompany the poor around the world. "We who have received the gift of faith, calling us to personal conversion and transformation," Gateley explained, "are also impelled to share that love." CBS's *60 Minutes* and *48 Hours* featured Gateley's work, while Cardinal Joseph Bernardin of Chicago and President Bill Clinton commended Gateley's efforts.[28]

CHAPTER TWELVE

People of Hope

*I*n the summer of 1965, a Catholic teenager named John Linder spoke for his generation when he proclaimed "[I want] to make the world better." Reflecting this optimistic attitude, Catholics began to herald volunteer work as the premier "high-light" of Catholic education. In addition to chronicling the traditional academic, artistic, and athletic accomplishments, Catholic newspapers praised Catholic students for reaching out to the "poor, handi-capped, [and] neglected."[1]

At the same time, "Young People Need[ed] Help," at least as one Catholic newspaper put it. New challenges had raised a new series of questions. Was television a "Babysitter?" or an "Educator?" American Catholics wanted to know. And how should the Church deal with rampant drug abuse? And what about the "New Morality," a somewhat vague term that suggested the loosening of sexual prohibitions? Conversations about these and other social problems animated the American Catholic community of the 1960s.[2]

Stimulating more discussion, Pope Paul VI convened the Papal Birth Control Commission to investigate whether or not the use of the pill and other forms of birth control violated natural law, that is, the philosophical and theological basis for the Catholic prohibition of unnatural means of birth control. Patty and Pat Crowley of Wilmette, Illinois, readily accepted Paul VI's invitation to serve on the Commission, even though they also lamented that they had "been blessed with only 5 children," a number below what many Catholics at that time believed a good Catholic family should raise.[3]

In service to the Commission, the Crowleys gathered data from thousands of Catholic couples in the Christian Family Movement, an international Catholic organization that the Crowleys had founded fifteen years before. Articulating what became the majority report of the Commission, the Crowleys announced in 1965 that "Most [Catholic couples] say they think there must be a change in the teaching on birth control." A few couples were "horrified" that the church might approve the pill, but the majority were strongly opposed to the rhythm method, which many described as unnatural and contrary to the intimacy, love, and unity of married life.[4]

Fearful that support of traditional Catholic teaching was fading, members of the philosophy department at the Catholic University of Dayton charged a few philosophers and theologians at the school with advocating positions contrary to the teaching of the Catholic Church. Similar accusations popped up at other Catholic universities during this era. After investigating the matter at Dayton, university officials concluded that the accused professors were disrespectful but not unorthodox. Throughout the affair, the archbishop in whose jurisdiction Dayton fell, Karl Alter of Cincinnati, steered clear of the investigation, explaining that a Catholic university was an independent organization that had no legal responsibility to pay "attention to any of the authorities in the Church."[5]

Twice in 1967, Theodore Hesburgh, Holy Cross priest and president of the University of Notre Dame, called presidents from various American Catholic universities, including Georgetown, Seton Hall, Boston College, Fordham, St. Louis, and the Pontifical Catholic University of Puerto Rico to Notre Dame to discuss Catholic higher education in light of the Second Vatican Council. At Notre Dame's retreat in Land O'Lakes, Wisconsin, these leading educators crafted a statement.

The Land O'Lakes statement began by proclaiming that "the Catholic university today must be a university in the full modern sense of the word, with a strong commitment to and concern for academic excellence." Attempting to address the pressing problems of the day, Catholic universities must expose students to non-Catholic, even non-Christian thought. No boundaries should be placed on what is taught, and no books excluded. Advancing Vatican II's assertion that theologians serve as ministers to the

Church, the Land O'Lakes statement concluded that the Catholic university must serve as "the critical reflective intelligence" of society and of the Church.[6]

The Land O'Lakes statement stimulated many conversations, especially at the country's three hundred Catholic colleges and universities. Supporters heralded the statement as a long overdue affirmation of the basic tenets of American higher education, including academic freedom. Critics complained that the statement divorced the Catholic university from the life of faith and thus jeopardized the Catholic identity of American Catholic schools.

ORGANIZING FOR HUMAN RIGHTS

Still in 1967, a diocesan priest who had marched with Martin Luther King from Selma to Montgomery, Alabama, John Egan, also of the University of Notre Dame, called together at Chicago sixteen priests active in urban ministries. These men formed the Catholic Committee on Community Organization (soon renamed the Catholic Committee on Urban Ministry). Housed at Notre Dame, this committee served for many years as a national network for Catholics involved in some aspect of social and pastoral ministry, a virtual "ministry to the ministers."[7]

American Catholic bishops next endorsed Pope Paul VI's 1968 encyclical *Humanae Vitae*, which broke new ground in honoring marital love and acknowledged the changing status of women and the problems of population growth yet also maintained the traditional ban on artificial contraception. "There were many positive things in that encyclical," noted one priest, Bernard Marthaler, though the positives were largely ignored due to the negative prohibition of birth control, the only piece of the encyclical that grabbed the headlines.[8]

Many Catholics openly criticized the encyclical, and in time Rome criticized some theologians, including priest-professor Charles Curran who was removed from his position at the Catholic University of America because he had questioned traditional teaching on birth control (as well as the church's views on homosexuality and the indissolubility of marriage). A sizable majority of married Catholics simply ignored the ban on birth control.

After this poor reception of *Humanae Vitae,* a former highly successful New York stock broker and Catholic convert, H. Lyman Stebbins, founded in 1968 Catholics United for the Faith, or CUF. We live "in a time of crisis," Stebbins surmised, where "there has been a serious weakening of the faith in the hearts of Catholics at every level in the Church." "One of the basic reasons for the existence of CUF," Stebins explained, "[was] to be a little alarm clock to wake people up, and then a center around which they can rally, and act in a way befitting members of Christ's true church." Through subsequent decades CUF remained a small but loud voice in the church. (In 1988, one year before Stebbins passed away, Pope John Paul II conferred on Stebbins a Knighthood of the Order of Saint Gregory the Great.) [9]

At the beginning of 1969, twenty mostly white priests from the Archdiocese of Newark signed a much publicized statement that criticized the archdiocese and the archbishop, Thomas Boland, for having made "no significant contribution to relieving the deplorable agony of the 500,000 black people in the inner-cities of the Archdiocese." One of the few black Catholic pastors in the country, Lawrence Lucas of Resurrection Parish in Harlem, in an angry testimony, *Black Priest/White Church* similarly declared that racism was "the white man's problem," and that the American Catholic Church is a "white racist institution."[10]

The following year, the National Conference of Catholic Bishops endorsed the formation of the National Office for Black Catholics in Washington, D.C. This office served as an umbrella group for other recently organized national groups for black priests, sisters, and lay people. The mission of the office was "to make the Church relevant to the needs of the black community; to assist generally in the black liberation movement; to assist black Catholics in their efforts to become self-determining and to become an effective voice in the whole of Church government." Black Catholics, such as Thea Bowman, a Franciscan Sister of Perpetual Adoration from Yazoo, Mississippi, eventually celebrated, even sang, the joys of the Black Catholic experience. Charges of racism nonetheless continued to plague the American Catholic Church.[11]

In 1969 the American Catholic bishops also started the National Catholic Crusade Against Poverty (now the Catholic Campaign for Human Development) "with the primary goal to carry out the Gospel of Jesus

Thea Bowman

Christ *to bring good news to the poor, liberty to captives, new sight to the blind and set the downtrodden free*…(Luke 4.18)." This "domestic anti-poverty program…works to break the cycle of poverty by helping low income people participate in decisions that affect their lives, families and communities." As the bishops emphasized, this effort is "a hand up, not a hand out." Bishops instituted an annual collection in American Catholic parishes to support this effort.[12]

In December 1971, forty-seven Catholic Sisters from across the United States involved in education, healthcare, and other direct service activities gathered at Trinity College in Washington, D.C. They formed the organization called NETWORK that fostered a new type of justice ministry especially attuned to political realities. Five years later, Catholics celebrated the American bishops' bicentennial theme, "Liberty and Justice for All" when they gathered at Detroit in the first Call to Action conference. Subsequent Call to Action conferences held in various American cities attempted to identify justice-related priorities for both the Church and nation.[13]

American Catholic bishops condemned the 1973 *Roe v. Wade* Supreme Court decision permitting abortion. "Whatever is opposed to life is a *violation* of man's inherent rights," the bishops adamantly and consistently maintained. After the subsequent Supreme Court decision *Webster v. Reproductive Health Services* returned some discretion to the states in abortion issues, Catholic voters carefully scrutinized Catholic political leaders, particularly those who distinguished personal beliefs from public support of abortion.[14]

The Decline of Catholic Life

Catholic schools, which had flourished the previous decade, began to struggle through the 1970s. World War II baby boomers had turned into teenagers (and smaller subsequent generations could not fill the grade schools built for

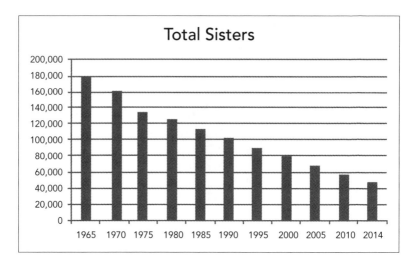

boomers), Catholics had migrated away from the city (where most Catholic schools were located), and the number of lay teachers grew (demanding more of a salary than celibate women and men). The population of religious women in most American dioceses had peaked in about 1960 and then fell nationwide 25 percent from 1965 to 1975.

The presence of Sisters in Catholic schools even more dramatically and more noticeably fell. Whereas roughly half of the Sisters in the Archdiocese of Cincinnati, for example, had typically worked in schools, by 1975 that percentage had dropped to a third, ten years later to a quarter, and then virtually disappeared. The number of priests in Cincinnati, as well as across the country did not start to decline for a couple of decades, but the number of priests in Catholic schools nationwide consistently and significantly fell. Like religious sisters, priests soon nearly disappeared from most American Catholic school systems.

To make matters worse, an increasing number of Catholics across the nation had grown dissatisfied with the church. Overall Mass attendance had been dropping since the late 1960s, probably at an exceptionally high rate among young people. Ninety percent of University of Dayton students reported having been raised Catholic, but only 62 percent still considered themselves members of the Church. National surveys revealed worse numbers with only half of all Catholic students reportedly attending Mass

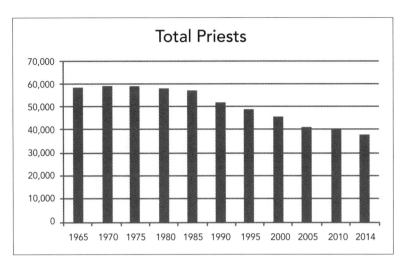

through the mid-1970s.[15]

Priest and sociologist Andrew Greeley tried to identify the cause of the decline in Catholic devotion. Greeley later became the most published priest in American Catholic history, producing more than seventy scholarly works and fifty bestselling novels, but his earliest investigations may have been his most insightful contribution. After careful research, Greeley and his team of researchers concluded that *Humanae Vitae* "marked a turning point in the attitudes of many Catholics, clergy, and laity toward the church." "Strong and converging evidence" demonstrated that *Humanae Vitae* was "both a failure and an organizational and religious disaster."[16]

Humanae Vitae did not turn around eroding support of Catholic teaching against birth control and only increased growing disrespect for church leaders. "Far from reasserting the teaching authority of the church and the credibility of the pope," Greeley's research noted that "[*Humanae Vitae*] has led to a deterioration among American Catholics of respect for both." One of the significant pieces of good news from Greeley's study was that "the positive dynamics released by the [Second Vatican] Council prevented the loss from being worse." At the same time children who did attend Catholic grade and high schools were twice as likely to be "people of hope."[17]

Trying to create more positive experiences within the church, many Catholics sought new approaches to Catholic education. Various teachers

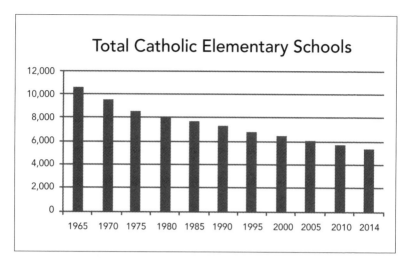

and a number of schools experimented with all kinds of teaching techniques. The president of the National Conference of Catholic Bishops, Cincinnati Archbishop Joseph Bernardin, suggested that "What is needed is...the best of the 'old' approach with the best of the 'new.'" Many archdioceses opened offices of religious education, established clearer qualifications for religion teachers, and organized media centers. Some efforts were quite successful; others not. Catholics United for the Faith seemed displeased with any new developments.[18]

Financial troubles also continued to plague many American Catholic school districts. Over two thousand Catholic elementary schools closed, and some entire Catholic school systems, eventually including most of the Archdiocese of Boston (which did not have a strong Catholic school system to begin with), virtually disappeared.

Other Catholic systems tapped new sources of revenue, such as annual fundraising walks. In time, the Vicar of Education in Cincinnati (where the Catholic school system remained fairly strong), Auxiliary Bishop Daniel E. Pilarczyk, claimed that the earlier "uproar and turmoil" over the possible demise of Catholic education had begun "to simmer down a bit."[19]

WOMEN VOICE THEIR CONCERNS

Some American Catholic women were nonetheless boiling. Despite the fact that experts of the Pontifical Biblical Commission concluded in 1976

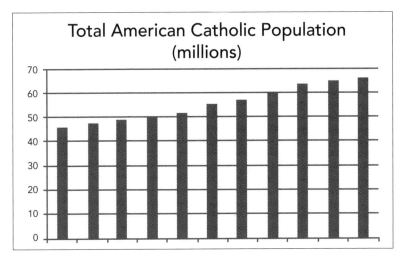

Total American Catholic Population (millions)

that there were no scriptural reasons to prevent women's ordination, the more authoritative Congregation for the Doctrine of Faith declared that women could not be ordained. Jesus "deliberately and courageously broke with" Roman and Jewish customs of the day that had discriminated against women, but "Jesus did not call any women to become part of the Twelve," the Congregation pointed out. And down through history the Church consistently followed Jesus's directive. "By calling only men to the priestly Order and ministry in its true sense, the Church intends to remain faithful to the type of ordained ministry willed by the Lord Jesus Christ and carefully maintained by the Apostles."[20]

Many women, including religious sisters belonging to the Leadership Conference of Women Religious, an organization founded some twenty years before, publicly disagreed with this teaching. The Women's Ordination Conference soon formed as "A Voice for Women's Equality in the Church." After television cameras captured members of the Women's Ordination Conference dramatically interrupting the 1978 annual bishop's meeting in Washington, D.C., the bishops talked to the women, but one participant, Catholic theologian Rosemary Radford Reuther, described these and subsequent conversations with bishops as "a non-meeting of the minds." After a particularly frustrating encounter, another leader, Dominican Sister Margorie Tuite, lamented, "They don't want us, they never wanted us, they are never going to want us."[21]

When Pope John Paul II visited the United States in 1979, the Women's Ordination Conference encouraged many Catholic women and men to wear blue armbands wherever the pope appeared to protest sexism in the church. After holding an all-night vigil at the Washington, D.C., hotel where the pope spent the night, the national coordinator of the Women's Ordination Conference, Ruth Fitzpatrick, held her candle high and greeted the pope with the words "Ordain Women!" John Paul II smiled and shook his head "no." Other Catholics protested in other ways during the pope's visit.[22]

After that time, a number of subgroups to the Women's Ordination Conference formed, including the Women-Church movement, which began in 1983. For the next nine years, Women-Church explored broader questions of women's religious empowerment. In time, the Young Feminist Network also organized.

Pope John Paul II meanwhile reiterated that while women are not "of lesser dignity," they simply were not part of Jesus's "plan" for priestly ordination. "I declare," John Paul II wrote, "that the Church has no authority whatsoever to confer priestly ordination on women and that this judgment is to be definitively held by all the Church's faithful." Cardinal Joseph Ratzinger (who later succeeded John Paul II as Pope Benedict XVI) added that this teaching required "definitive assent," for it "has been set forth infallibly" by John Paul II. But John Paul II never used the word infallible and did not invoke this principle. John Paul II did however next appear to threaten with excommunication anyone who did not uphold the belief that Jesus willed only men to be ordained. The exact nature of John Paul II's warning was nevertheless not altogether clear.[23]

American Catholics were confused. Notre Dame theologian Richard McBrien moaned, "It is utterly irresponsible for the Vatican to say something that doesn't quite mean what it seems to mean." McBrien went on to wonder, "If the Pope wants us to believe that the prohibition against ordination of women is a matter of divine law and divine faith such that the denial of this teaching is a heresy, then that puts everyone who disagrees outside the church. Is that what is being said?" The newly elected president of the National Conference of Catholic Bishops, Anthony M. Pilla of Cleveland, simply asked American Catholics "to allow the Holy Spirit to fill you with the wisdom and understanding that will enable you to accept [the church's teaching against women's ordination]."[24]

Some members of the Women's Ordination Conference eventually conceded that ordination of women would result in nothing but subordination within a patriarchal system and thus looked for new ways to carry on the Catholic faith. One Rochester, New York, parish, Corpus Christi, separated from the local Catholic diocese to form its own faith community, renamed Spiritus Christi. The diocese soon declared that the new community had excommunicated itself, but after a woman was ordained at Spiritus Christi (as were a handful of other women around the world) members of the Women's Ordination Conference offered their support.

The Quality of a Catholic Education

Into the 1980s some young Catholic women reported much more positive encounters with the Church. Betty Wall of Cincinnati's Our Lady of Angels High School beamed that, "A Catholic education means more than reading, writing, and arithmetic. It means developing a mature attitude toward life and religion." Schoolmate Lisa Lohman added that "the cost of a Catholic education is high, yet the value of that education is even greater because I have an understanding of myself and others learned through my religion classes. No price can be put upon this understanding which I value greatly beyond the technical skills learned through other classes."[25]

Many female and male Catholic students from across the country were inspired at that time by the Charismatic Renewal movement, and others routinely trekked to Washington, D.C., for the Annual March for Life, which called for the reversal of the law permitting abortion. The percentage of Catholic children receiving religious instruction, either in Catholic schools or CCD programs, generally rose across the country, and the total Catholic population also increased. But the total number of Catholic children in Catholic education still continued to fall through the 1980s largely due to the low birth rate of the previous decade.

The quality of Catholic education varied from one school to the next, as did the commitment of Catholic parents to Catholic schools. Whereas Catholics through the period of Vatican II almost always sent their children

Dorothy Stang

to Catholic schools, by the 1980s, "things aren't as clear-cut," as one parent, Robert Regis Hyle, put it. Hyle suggested that it depended on the quality of the parent's Catholic education. His own positive experience at Cincinnati's LaSalle High School had convinced him to send his children to Catholic schools, but "it doesn't make me a better parent," he conceded, "and it may not make my kids better students. I think it will make them better people, though, and that is good enough for me."[26]

An increasing number of non-Catholic parents agreed. A Jewish father, Rich Lisner, reportedly sent his son to a Catholic high school because of the school's strong discipline, good sports program, and "a philosophy he appreciated." Andrew Islam, a non-Catholic fourth grader at Saint Rita's in Dayton, Ohio, put it another way: "My dad says the teachers do not get very much money so they must really love their job. They love letting us do fun stuff like math games. Most times they act as if they really like us. Even when they get mad they have a special look on their face. Their care is fun and nice."[27]

New Issues Arise

Through the 1980s, American Catholic bishops took courageous stands on abortion, capital punishment, and the nuclear arms race and on economic justice, federally supported low-income housing, handgun control, a Palestinian state, and aid to developing nations. Joseph Bernardin (then Cardinal Archbishop of Chicago) grouped this wide range of concerns under the category of a "consistent life ethic."

The potential cost for pursuing such a strong ethic became shockingly clear after five soldiers in the National Guard of El Salvador on December 2, 1980, captured, raped, and murdered Maryknoll Sisters Maura Clarke and Ita Ford, Ursuline Sister Dorothy Kazel, and lay missionary Jean Donovan, all American Catholic women working for justice in war-torn El Salvador.

Twenty-five years later, the American Catholic community again grieved news of Sister of Notre Dame de Namur Dorothy "Dot" Stang of Dayton, Ohio. Since the 1970s, Stang had fought for peasants and the environment in the Amazon basin of Brazil, where a soldier fired six rounds into her body, taking her life.

Initiating different kinds of trouble, in 1983 police arrested Louisiana priest Gilbert Gauthe. Some priest sexual abuse had occurred in the American Catholic Church at least since the time of the American Revolution, and a few early cases caused scandal, though for the most part, Church officials kept accusations hidden, burning evidence or burying records in secret files. Such policies began to change in the mid-1980s as more charges saw the light of day. Gauthe was convicted of sexually abusing dozens of altar boys in what became one of the first cases of a pedophile priest to gain national attention. (Gauthe was released from prison in 2002.)

After numerous other cases of priest sex abuse surfaced, in 1992 the United States Conference of Catholic Bishops issued non-binding guidelines for dioceses with regard to abuse cases and charges.

In November 1993, Steven Cook accused Cardinal Bernardin of sexually abusing him some twenty years before. Three months after filing the charges, Cook withdrew the lawsuit saying that he was 95 percent sure his memory of the abuse, which surfaced when he was under hypnosis, was unreliable. Bernardin next met with Cook. To be 100 percent sure that the abuse did not occur, Cook said to Bernardin, "I need for you to look me in the eye and tell me you didn't do it." Cook said Bernardin did this, "And I believed him." Yet Bernardin also seemed to recognize that Cook had been abused by another Cincinnati priest, Ellis Harsham, who had since left the priesthood. The Archdiocese of Cincinnati reached an out-of-court settlement with Cook over charges against Harsham.[28]

In January 2002 a small group of Catholics first met in the basement of Saint John the Evangelist Church in Wellesley, Massachusetts, "to speak of their heartbreak and outrage over revelations that priest sex abusers had preyed upon [their] children and that members of the Church hierarchy had—through both actions and inactions—enabled and covered up those crimes." The *Boston Globe* had just released details of sexual abuse by John

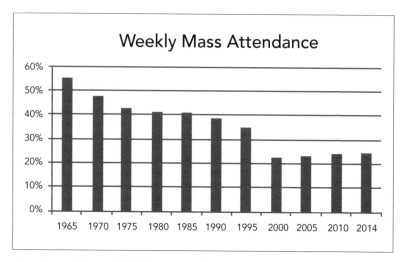

Geoghan, a former Catholic priest. The Saint John the Evangelist basement group quickly grew to over seven hundred Catholics.[29]

A judge sentenced Geoghan to ten years in prison, where a fellow inmate murdered him one year later. A national avalanche of accusations followed, some thirty years old, against numerous American priests. Nationwide Mass attendance hit an all-time low, and many adult Catholics left the church.

Catholics meeting in the basement of Saint John the Evangelist Church then organized as the Voice of the Faithful. Vowing never to be silent again, the group pledged "to provide a prayerful voice, attentive to the Spirit, through which the faithful can actively participate in the governance and guidance of the Catholic Church." (The Voice of the Faithful still aims to support survivors of clergy sexual abuse, support priests of integrity, and shape structural change within the Catholic Church. Membership has grown to over thirty thousand Catholics worldwide.)[30]

In the spring of 2002, Pope John Paul II summoned United States cardinals and other Church leaders to Rome to discuss the priest sex abuse crisis. Later that summer, American bishops met in Dallas, Texas, where they approved the Charter for the Protection of Children and Young People. Schools across the country began to implement new policies and procedures, and sex abuse prevention became a staple part of American Catholic education.

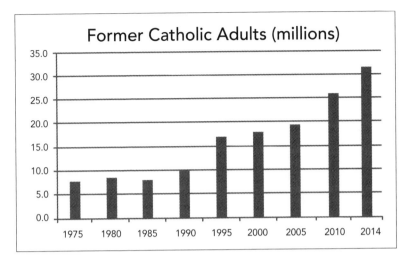

According to figures made public by the United States Conference of Catholic Bishops, from 1950 to 2014, 6,427 bishops, priests, deacons, and seminarians, or about 6 percent of clergy active in the United States during this time, abused 17,259 minors. Many Church officials, including Cardinal Ratzinger when he served as Vatican official overseeing all cases of priest abuse, claimed the numbers were much less. The actual numbers were most likely higher. In the figures the bishops released, they did not include the year after Geoghan's indictment when the controversy was at its peak.[31]

Amidst huge legal settlements against the Church, costing billions of dollars, some bishops resigned, most notably Cardinal Bernard Law of Boston. Law had known of Geoghan's sexual exploits for eight years before police finally put Geoghan in jail.

Another former president of the National Conference of Catholic Bishops, Archbishop Daniel Pilarczyk of Cincinnati, reflected the experience of many church leaders when he confessed that the clergy sex abuse scandal was "without any doubt" the greatest challenge of his twenty-seven years as archbishop. It was a "dangerous time," Pilarczyk recalled, with the health of Catholicism at stake. When asked if the church of the past had protected priests at the expense of victims, Pilarczyk claimed that the original intention had been to protect both sides.[32]

But then an inadequate understanding of the psychology of abuse got in the way. "The problem," Pilarczyk explained, "was we didn't understand the depth and virulence of what was in the psyche of the perpetrator," and thus hoped that moving an offending individual would prevent future acts of abuse. In time, Church leaders came to realize that this was not an effective and appropriate response.[33]

Addressing Catholic Tradition

During this crisis, other significant developments occurred within the American Catholic Church. After years of discussion, on August 15, 1990, Pope John Paul II issued *Ex Corde Ecclesia*, "From the Heart of the Church," to strengthen Catholic higher education. Many Catholic educators welcomed the encyclical's continued support of academic freedom and institutional autonomy.

Six years after *Ex Corde Ecclesia*, American Catholic bishops overwhelmingly approved a plan to implement the encyclical's recommendations, but Vatican officials called for a more legalistic approach, especially regarding *Ex Corde's* statement that "Catholic theologians, aware that they fulfil a mandate received from the Church, are to be faithful to the Magisterium of the Church as the authentic interpreter of Sacred Scripture and Sacred Tradition." Three years later the Vatican approved the bishops' revised plan.[34]

This revision required that all Catholics who teach Catholic theology in a Catholic university receive from the local bishop a *mandatum* (a new articulation of the "mandate" of *Ex Corde*) that confirms the professor "is teaching within the full communion of the Catholic Church." Four years later, the first implementation of the *mandatum* took effect, though bishops had no means of actually enforcing reception of the *mandatum*. In most cases bishops considered the *mandatum* a matter of personal conscience and dealt with it quietly and peacefully.[35]

More than 160,000 young people, the majority from the United States, attended the eighth international World Youth Day held in August 1993 in Denver, Colorado. Pope John Paul II concluded the four-day event with a public Mass at Cherry Creek State Park attended by 350,000 people. "Offer your youthful energies to building a civilization of Christian love," John Paul II intoned. "Be witness of God's love for the innocent and the weak, for the poor and oppressed."[36]

Seventy-three percent of American Catholics polled at that time approved of the pope's handling of his office, but 79 percent also said they followed their own conscience over church teaching on difficult moral issues. Eighty-four percent disagreed with papal pronouncements on birth control, 76 percent favored married priests, and 63 percent favored the ordination of women. The pope responded to such figures saying that "America needs much prayer lest it lose its soul."[37]

American Catholic bishops subsequently voiced stronger stands against abortion, embryonic stem-cell research, and same-sex marriages. Eight American cardinals wrote to President Bill Clinton challenging his veto of the "partial birth" abortion ban. The Catholic Health Association and other Catholic voices similarly criticized a decision by the Ninth United States Circuit Court on end-of-life issues.

Longtime Georgetown University Law professor, Jesuit Robert Drinan, who had served for over a decade as a Democratic United States Representative from Massachusetts, continued his long-standing support of abortion rights, and even praised President Clinton for his veto of the partial birth abortion ban. New York Cardinal John O'Connor sharply denounced Drinan. "You could have raised your voice for life," O'Connor scolded, "you raised it for death. Hardly the role of a lawyer. Surely not the role of a priest."[38]

At about the same time, the American bishops issued "Always Our Children," which reiterated Catholic teaching on homosexuality, but with greater pastoral sensitivity than ever before. The following year, nine bishops and a number of Catholic organizations and individuals signed a full-page ad that appeared in the *New York Times* and that deplored anti-gay violence in the United States.

Acknowledging that the American Catholic community still remained divided on a number of key issues, Cardinal Bernardin helped launch the Common Ground initiative to foster dialogue across the polarities in the Church. All quarters, including some of Bernardin's fellow cardinals, did not receive the initiative well. After two archbishops, Raymond Burke of St. Louis and Sean O'Malley of Boston, later denied Communion to presidential candidate, Catholic Senator John Kerry of Massachusetts, because of Kerry's policies, especially regarding a woman's right to choose, the American Catholic community galvanized, if not polarized, around such issues.

In 1993 Louisiana Sister of Saint Joseph Helen Prejean released *Dead Man Walking*, in which Prejean described the final days of her spiritual advisee, death row inmate Elmo Patrick Sonnier. Director Tim Robbins transformed the book into a movie starring Sean Penn and Susan Sarandon (who won an Academy Award for her portrayal of Prejean). The book also became an opera and a play. Prejean next wrote *The Death of Innocents: An Eyewitness Account of Wrongful Executions*, in which she told the story of two men, Dobie Gillis Williams and Joseph O'Dell, whom Prejean had accompanied to their executions, and whom Prejean believed were both innocent.

When the English version of the *Catechism of the Catholic Church* first reached American bookstores in June 1994, Catholics gobbled it up. "People don't even ask how much it is," reported one bookseller. "They just say, 'Is this the new catechism? I'll have one.'" Within a month, over 1.5 million copies were sold. While not following the question and answer format of the previous *Baltimore Catechism*, the newer 803-page *Catechism of the Catholic Church* was still not light reading. It nonetheless reiterated long-held Church teaching in a more contemporary fashion.[39]

Longing for a more traditional approach to Catholicism, in 1997 long-time conservative host of television's *Firing Line*, Catholic William F. Buckley, released his book, *Nearer, My God*, in which Buckley argued that Christian faith was being replaced by "another God...multiculturalism." Like a minority of American Catholics at the time, Buckley rejected the liturgical reforms following Vatican II, and routinely attended the traditional Latin Mass in his hometown of Stamford, Connecticut.[40]

Later that same year, and about two weeks before he died of pancreatic cancer, Cardinal Bernardin wrote a national bestseller, *The Gift of Peace*, "[a] reflection," Bernardin explained, "intended to help others understand how the good and the bad are always present in our human condition and, that if we 'let go,' if we place ourselves totally in the hands of the Lord, the good will prevail."[41]

THE NEW MILLENNIUM

Upon hearing that the South Tower of the World Trade Center had been hit on September 11, 2001, Mychal Judge, the Franciscan chaplain of the

New York City Fire Department, rushed to the scene. He met along the way Mayor Rudy Giuliani, who asked him to pray for the victims. Judge attended to corpses in the streets before entering the makeshift command post set up in the lobby of the North Tower, where he offered aid and prayers for the rescuers, injured, and dead.

When the South Tower collapsed, debris flew through the North Tower lobby. Police lieutenant Bill Cosgrove found Judge, and, with two firemen, an emergency medical technician, and a civilian bystander, carried his lifeless body out of the North Tower moments before the building collapsed. Photojournalist Shannon Stapleton captured the five men carrying Judge's body on film. The men laid his body before the altar of Saint Peter's Catholic Church, and he was subsequently designated "Victim 0001" the first official victim of the attacks.

Cosgrove credited Judge's death for his life. "I know that sounds weird," Cosgrove explained, "but everybody you see in that picture was saved. And I'm sure had he not been there, I would have been trying to look for other people. And when that North Tower fell, I would have been right in the middle of it, just like the rest of the firemen were, and some of my cops. But nothing was going to happen that day. At least, not to me."[42]

Vatican II had generated a new liturgy with a New Roman Missal that was revised in 1975 and again in 2002. Eight years later, the Roman Congregation for Divine Worship approved a much debated English translation. Among various changes, certain expressions were translated as literally as possible with less concern for the meaning of the texts. The response to the greeting, "The Lord be with you," replaced the familiar "And also with you," with "And with your spirit." In the Nicene Creed "one in being with the Father" became "consubstantial with the Father." And the part of the Eucharistic prayer that previously had proclaimed that Jesus's blood was poured out "for all" was changed to the more literal and more scripturally-based "for many."

American Catholics adjusted to the changes (used for the first time on the first Sunday of Advent, November 27, 2011) even though some prominent Church leaders protested. The scholar whom the bishops had asked to promote the new missal throughout the United States, professor of liturgy and Gregorian chant at Saint John's Abbey in Collegeville, Minnesota, Benedictine Anthony Ruff, openly complained that a small group of bishops had "hijack[ed]" the process of composing the new liturgy and imposed from the "top-down" an "unsatisfactory" text.[43]

After the United States House of Representatives passed the Affordable Care Act (commonly called Obamacare) in late 2009, American Catholic bishops applauded the effort, noting that the Catholic Church had consistently insisted on decent health care as a basic human right. Three years later Congressman and Republican vice-presidential candidate, Paul Ryan of Wisconsin, claimed that his proposed budget reflected the principles of his Catholic faith. But the bishops adamantly disagreed, declaring that Ryan's proposal failed to protect human dignity and to honor the common good and thus adversely affected "the least of these," that is, families living in poverty.[44]

At the same time, American bishops also charged that the Affordable Care Act's inclusion of contraceptive, abortion, and sterilization coverage (the Health and Human Services, or HHS Mandate) violated individual rights. Government should not force anyone to pay into a system that supported moral positions against his or her will, the bishops contended. The Affordable Care Act did allow exemptions for Church and Church-type entities, but some religious groups, including the Little Sisters of the Poor, had to file lawsuits to attempt to gain this exemption.

THE AMERICAN SISTERS

After four years of investigating American Catholic Sisters, in April 2012, the Roman Congregation for the Doctrine of the Faith criticized the Leadership Conference of Women Religious for failing to support key life and family issues. "While there has been a great deal of work on the part of LCWR promoting issues of social justice in harmony with the Church's social doctrine," the Congregation for the Doctrine of the Faith pointed out in its report, "[the Leadership Conference of Women Religious] is silent on the right to life from conception to natural death.... Further, issues of crucial importance to the life of Church and society, such as the Church's biblical view of family life and human sexuality, are not part of the LCWR agenda in a way that promotes Church teaching." Much to the chagrin of the Congregation for the Doctrine of Faith, the Leadership Conference of Women Religious had never corrected its refusal to support priestly ordination only of men.[45]

The president of the Leadership Conference of Women Religious, Franciscan Pat Farrell, responded to the Doctrine of Faith's report by acknowledging the "creative tension" that had existed throughout much history between women religious and church hierarchy. Farrell called for open dialogue between the two groups, as well as invited womens' religious communities to deeper contemplation, prophecy, solidarity with the marginalized, community, nonviolence, and joyful hope.[46]

For fourteen days from June 21 to July 4, 2012 (and every year since), the American Catholic Bishops have organized a Fortnight of Freedom, calling Catholics to reaffirm religious liberty as a fundamental American principle and to work toward the insertion of a "conscience clause" into the HHS Mandate to more clearly free persons of faith from being forced to support something against their will. Critics of the Fortnight of Freedom described the event as an anti-Obama campaign and a Republican Party prayer meeting.

During the first Fortnight for Freedom, a group of American Sisters, with the support of the Catholic social justice organization NETWORK and the Leadership Conference of Women Religious, took to the road. Calling themselves Nuns on the Bus, these women traveled 2,700 miles across nine states to call attention to the needs of the poor, and in particular to challenge Paul Ryan's assertion that his budget reflected Catholic teaching.

Two months later, on September 5, 2012, one of the nuns on the bus, Social Service Sister Simone Campbell, the Executive Director of NETWORK, addressed the Democratic National Convention meeting in Charlotte, North Carolina. The Affordable Care Act will cover struggling American families, Campbell contended. "We all share responsibility to ensure that this vital health care reform law is properly implemented and that all governors expand Medicaid coverage so no more...[people] die from lack of care. This is part of my pro-life stance," Campbell proclaimed, "and the right thing to do."[47]

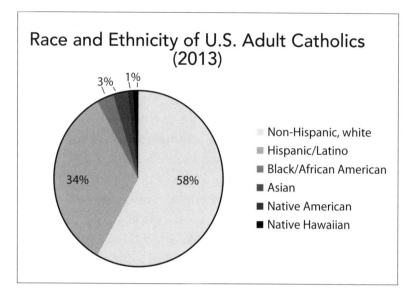

Race and Ethnicity of U.S. Adult Catholics (2013)

3% 1%

34%   58%

- Non-Hispanic, white
- Hispanic/Latino
- Black/African American
- Asian
- Native American
- Native Hawaiian

The summer of 2013 NETWORK sponsored a second "Nuns on the Bus" tour, this time touting immigration reform, an issue over which NETWORK and the American Catholic bishops strongly agreed. The American Catholic community had always included a complex mix of people. The dramatic rise into the new millennium of Hispanic/Latino Catholics, especially of Mexican immigrants, had significantly impacted Catholicism in the United States. The traditional stronghold of the church had shifted from the northeastern quadrant of the United States to the south and west with Hispanic/Latino Catholics responsible for over 80 percent of the new American Catholics over the past twenty-five years. During this time, the percentage of Hispanic/Latino Catholics to the overall American Catholic population rose from 20 percent to 34 percent.

When President Obama issued an executive order in support of some undocumented immigrants, Eusebio Elizondo, the auxiliary bishop of Seattle and chairman of the United States Conference of Catholic Bishops Committee on Migration, rejoiced. "We have a long history of welcoming and aiding the poor, the outcast, the immigrant, and the disadvantaged," Elizondo explained.[48]

When Cardinals the spring of 2013 elected Jesuit Jorge Mario Bergoglio of Argentina as the new pope, most American Catholics cheered. Pope Francis quickly won over many observers by his openness, informality, and choice to live in a modest guest house instead of in the palatial papal apartments. But Francis also alienated some conservatives. Francis warned against an "obsessive" concern with abortion and gay marriage, and encouraged discussion of Church teachings on contraception and divorce.

When asked about gay persons who professed the faith, Francis responded, "If someone is gay and he searches for the Lord and has good will, who am I to judge?" Throughout the first year of Francis's papacy, American Catholics regularly gave Francis extremely high approval ratings. In September 2015, fifty years after a pope first visited the United States, Francis returned.[49]

Catholic Holiness

While writing this book, I restored and hung the antique French doors that I had found in that old salvage shop. I lost three loved ones, Dickie, Lib, and Marguerite (seventy-nine, ninety-five, and one hundred years old, respectively). And Ned came down with cancer. "Everything is different now," Ned explained to me the day he received the diagnosis. He was worried. So was I. Doctors had given Ned's brother similar news a couple years ago, and he died ten days later.

A month into Ned's chemotherapy I drove two hours to Ned's house. We talked over lunch. When Ned napped, I returned to the salvage shop where I had bought the French doors. I hoped to find some doorknobs I might use, but was disappointed. I returned to Ned's. We talked again.

Ned recalled how his brother had received last rites (more properly called the anointing of the sick) just before he had died. Ned asked me if I thought this anointing had helped his brother get to heaven. In an earlier era, I probably would have answered without hesitation "yes." Fr. Badin and many others Catholic leaders certainly were convinced of the power of this sacrament. I was not exactly sure. The anointing certainly had given Ned's sister-in-law some comfort. But did it get her husband into heaven?

From 1492 to 2014 many American Catholics have died. Way too many were killed by the horrible violence of war, disease, and poverty. I suspect that for every death, someone grieved. "Your brother was a good man," I told Ned. "His anointing may have given him some comfort. It certainly consoled his wife. But I imagine he was well on his way to heaven long before his last days."

Putnam household of Main Street (where the public library now stands), Lebanon, Kentucky, circa 1900. (Left to right): Mabel (the horse), Joe and Effie (brother and sister), Nathan Henry Putnam, Sr. (father), Mary Jane, Nathan, Jr., Anna Katherine (Katie), Joseph, Charles, Nell (Blydie), and Anna Edward (nannie) Putman (mother).

I stayed for dinner, and Ned and I talked some more. But Ned was tired. He asked me to spend the night. Over the years I have enjoyed many late night talks with Ned and Jean. This night, about all he could do was watch some TV. I hardly slept.

The next morning Jean served breakfast. Ned soon appeared, almost like his old self. I shared with Ned an old family picture that a photography studio recently had enhanced for me. Together Ned and I identified everyone in the photo, including our grandmother, Blydie (who was about ten years old at the time), the family's help (a woman named Effie who had descended from slaves owned by my family), and my great-grandmother's horse, Mabel.

[image goes here] [need caption from author]

The picture was taken in about 1900, four years before my great-grandfather, a dry goods store owner standing in the center of the photograph, suffered a heart attack and died while on a train vacationing through South Dakota. Nathan Henry Putnam had descended from Israel Putnam, a Revolutionary War General and close friend of George Washington. Putnam served with distinction at Bunker Hill. Subsequent legends celebrated the many exploits of "Old Put," as he was popularly called.

"Blydie was a Daughter of the American Revolution," declared Ned, "Wasn't she?" I told what I knew, namely, that Blydie was a Daughter of the Confederacy. I have the certificate to prove that. But she was not a Daughter of the American Revolution. I had inherited from Blydie a biography of Israel Putnam. Inside the book Blydie had tucked instructions on how to join the DAR, but she never submitted an application. She probably did not have the time and resources to trace her lineage back to the Revolutionary War, as the DAR requires.

Ned suggested that I do the work. I just love talking about this kind of stuff. And Ned is the only one in my family who gets history the way I do. But Ned soon tired, and the conversation was over. I announced that I was driving to Bardstown to see what I could find in the local library about Nathan Putnam. "I'll call you on my way back home to let you know what I find," I told Ned.

Left on Shelbyville Road, right on Hurstborne Parkway, and left on Bardstown Road. I have driven from Louisville to Bardstown more times than I can recall. For over two hundred years, my ancestors have beaten the same path. This journey is a sacred pilgrimage for me. Two new Walmarts now anchor the beginning and the end of this stretch, with just about every conceivable fast food and retail shop in between.

As I neared the convent of the Sisters of Charity of Nazareth just north of Bardstown, my spirit rose, as it always does. I turned right into the convent's drive to visit relatives buried near the motherhouse. I probably have fifty pictures of Mother Catherine Spalding's grave. It is simple and starkly beautiful. I took another shot.

The Bardstown library moved a couple of years ago. I was not sure of its new location. I ducked into a bookstore to ask for directions, and to hunt around. An hour or so later I brought a stack of books to the man working a crossword puzzle behind the counter. But he did not work there, he explained. He was just a regular visitor. He nonetheless did admire my selection of books, all on Catholic history. The man was a priest, he explained, the chaplain to the Sisters of Charity of Nazareth.

About the time the owner appeared, I asked the priest about Bardstown. I always considered it an incredibly historic and cute small town, full of antebellum structures, many beautifully maintained. I wondered how much the new Walmart had changed things. "We are losing what makes us special. We are losing our holiness," the priest lamented. The owner agreed. "This place is for sale," she added. "Are you interested?"

After a few hours in the Bardstown library, I had figured that General Israel Putnam had been awarded for his military service land some fifty miles east of Bardstown in Lexington, Kentucky. His grandson, Joseph, claimed the land. Joseph's son, Joseph W., married a woman from Taylor County, south of Bardstown. Their son was my great-grandfather, Nathan Henry Putnam.

None of these Putnams were Catholic, that is, until Nathan Henry met Anna Edward "Nannie" Spalding, the very Catholic sister of Bishop John Lancaster Spalding. Bishop Spalding baptized Nathan Henry shortly before performing his and Nannie's wedding at Saint Augustine's Church just north of Taylor County in Lebanon, Kentucky, where the Spaldings lived. Ned has some silver that someone gave Nathan and Nannie as a wedding present.

I do not foresee myself ever owning a bookstore. But I certainly hope to keep writing books that tell the stories of Catholic people. Faith-filled stories define Catholicism and keep the community alive. At the Bardstown bookstore I picked up an old copy of Anna Melville's biography of Elizabeth Ann Seton. I started reading it the other night. Ned is meanwhile doing remarkably well some six months into his treatment. He will have to take medicine the rest of his life, which I hope will be a long, long time.

CHAPTER ONE

1. Pope Alexander VI, Bull *Inter Caetera*, May 4, 1493, reprinted and translated in *European Treaties bearing on the History of the United States and its Dependencies to 1648*, ed. Frances Gardiner Davenport (Washington, D.C.: Carnegie Institution of Washington, 1917), 17.

2. Columbus to Raphael Sanchez, treasurer of Ferdinand and Isabella, March 14, 1493, in *Select Letters of Christopher Columbus, with Original Documents, Relating to his Four Voyages to the New World*, R.H. Major, ed. (Surrey, U.K.: Ashgate, 2010), 10 and 11.

3. Columbus to Raphael Sanchez, 15; and an adventurer quoted in Jay Dolan, *The American Catholic Experience—A History from Colonial Times to the Present* (Garden City, N.Y.: Doubleday, 1985), 20.

4. Robert H. Fuson, *Juan Ponce de León and the Spanish Discovery of Puerto Rico and Florida* (Granville, Ohio: McDonald & Woodward, 2000), 63; and Hatuey, quoted in José Barreiro, "A Note on Tainos: *Whither Progress?*" from *Northeast Indian Quarterly* (Fall 1990), 75.

5. Bartolome de las Casas to Ferdinand, quoted in Mark A. Noll and Edwin S. Gaustad, *A Documentary History of Religion in America to 1877* third edition (Grand Rapids: Eerdmans, 2003), 25.

6. Samuel Turner, "Juan Ponce de León and the Discovery of Florida Reconsidered," *Florida Historical Quarterly* 92, no. 1 (2013), 11 (translation of Herrera text); and Fuson, 106 (quoting Herrera account).

7. Contract between Ponce de León and Ferdinand, September 27, 1514, translated into English and quoted by Fuson, 130.

8. Paul III, *Sublimis Deus*, 1537, quoted in Gaustad and Noll, 25.

9. Garcilaso de la Vega, *The Florida of the Inca—The Fabulous De Soto Story*, trans. John and Jeannette Varner (1605; Austin: University of Texas, 1951), 281.

10. Vega, 298 and 130; and a soldier quoted in Alan Taylor, *American Colonies—The Settling of North America* (New York: Penguin, 2001), 72.

11. Vega, 380, 639, and 499; and las Casas, quoted in Taylor, 73.

12. Vega, 509, 134, 118, 314.

13. Fuson, 212.

14. Menéndez, quoted in Taylor, 78.
15. "Royal Orders for New Discoveries," (1573), quoted in Taylor, 79; Oñate, quoted in Taylor, 81; and a Franciscan quoted in Gaustad and Noll, 32.
16. Taylor, 89.
17. John Gilmary Shea, *The Cross and The Flag—Our Church and Country* (1900), 115; and John Lancaster Spalding, "The Catholic Church in the United States, 1776–1876," *Catholic World* 23 (July 1876), 436.
18. "The Homily by Pope John Paul II in Port-au-Prince, Haiti: The Need for Social Change," *Origins* 12, no. 14 (March 24, 1983); and John Paul II and Alfretta Antone, quoted in Clyde Crews, *American & Catholic—A Popular History of Catholicism in the United States,* 2nd ed. (Cincinnati: St. Anthony Messenger Press, 2004), 11.
19. "1992: A Time for Remembering, Reconciling, and Recommitting Ourselves as a People," National Conference of Catholic Bishops (November 1991), 1 and 2.
20. National Conference of Catholic Bishops, *Native American Catholics at the Millennium—A Report on a Survey of the United States Conference of Catholic Bishops' Ad Hoc Committee on Native American Catholics* (Washington, D.C.: United States Catholic Conference, 2002), 2 and 20.
21. *Tico Times*, February 20, 2014.

CHAPTER TWO

1. Reuben Gold Thwaites, introduction to Edna Kenton, ed., *The Jesuit Relations and Allied Documents* (New York: Albert & Charles Boni, 1925), xx.
2. Montagnais hunter quoted in Paul Le Jeune, "Relation of what occurred in New France on the great river of St. Lawrence, in the year One Thousand Six Hundred Thirty-Four," in Kenton, 65.
3. Le Jeune, 56.
4. Kenton, 23 n. 1.
5. Thwaites, xxiv.
6. Brébeuf, "Instructions for the Fathers of Our Society who shall be sent to the Hurons," (1637), quoted in Kenton, 118; *Relation de la Novvelle France, de fes Terres, Natvvel dv Païs, & de fes Habitans*, Pierre Biard, Lyons, 1616, in *Jesuit Relations*, vol. 6, 111 and 117. (The *Jesuit Relations* is a multi-volume collection that Kenton, and others, have condensed into smaller books.)
7. Paul Le Jeune and Jean de Brébeuf, "Relation of what occurred in New France, in the year 1635," in Kenton, 94; Brébeuf, "Relation of what

occurred among the Hurons in the year 1635," in Kenton, 103.

8. Jérôme Lalement, "Relation of 1640," *Jesuit Relations*, 19:93.

9. Jogues, quoted in "How Father Jogues was taken by the Iroquois, and what he suffered on his first entrance into their country," (from Relation of 1647), in Kenton, 191.

10. Jogues to Monsieur the Governor, June 30, 1643; reprinted in Kenton, 185.

11. Jogues, quoted in "How Father Jogues was taken by the Iroquois," in Kenton, 200.

12. John Paul II, "Address at the Martyrs' Shrine at Huronia," September 15, 1985, Saints.SQPN.com, http://saints.sqpn.com/pope-john-paul-ii-address-at-the-martyrs-shrine-at-huronia/.

13. "Letter of Father Paul Ragueneau to the Very Reverend Father Vincent Caraffa, General of the Society of Jesus, at Rome (1649)" reprinted in Kenton, 216; and Allan Greer, *Mohawk Saint—Catherine Tekakwitha and the Jesuits* (New York, Oxford University Press, 2005), 16.

14. Christophe Regnaut, "A Veritable Account of the Martyrdom and Blessed Death of Father Jean de Breboeuf and of Father Gabriel L'Alemant, in New France, in the country of the Hurons, by the Iroquois, enemies of the faith," in Kenton, 220 and 221. Gabriel Lalemant was the nephew of Jerome and Charles Lalemant, two other Jesuit missionaries to New France.

15. Regnaut, 221.

16. Regnaut, 222.

17. Paul Ragueneau, "Of the Removal of the House of Sainte Marie to the Island of St. Joseph…," (from the Relation of 1649–1650) in Kenton, 226.

18. Ragueneau, 229 and 230.

19. Ragueneau, 238.

20. Chabanel, quoted in *Martyrs' Shrine Message* 74, no. 1 (2009); and Chabanel to Pierre Chabanel, S.J., quoted in Kenton, 242.

21. Greer, 126 and 132.

22. Greer, 133.

23. Pierre Cholenec, S.J., to (unnamed) Jesuit Superior at Quebec, February 1680; quoted in Greer, 145.

24. The Martyrs' Shrine currently houses relics of Brébeuf, Lalemant, Garnier, and Tekakwitha.

25. John Paul II, quoted in Crews, *American & Catholic*, 12; and John Paul II, "Address at the Martyrs' Shrine at Huronia."

CHAPTER THREE

1. Stock to Cardinal Ottavio Bandini, Member of Propaganda in Rome, May 10, 1625, London, in Luca Codignola, *The Coldest Harbour of the Land: Simon Stock and Lord Baltimore's Colony in Newfoundland, 1621–1649*, trans. Anita Weston (Kingston and Montreal: McGill-Queen's University Press, 1988), 81.

2. Stock to Cardinal Ottavio Bandini, in Codignola, 81.

3. Calvert, quoted in Morris Radoff, ed., *The Old State Line—A History of Maryland* (Baltimore, Md.: Hall of Records Commission, 1971), 3.

4. Charles I, quoted in Cogdignola, 54.

5. Maryland Land Office (Patent Record) 1646–1657, liber ABH, folio 65, Maryland State Archives S920–4, 1/29/2/45.

6. Quoted in James Hennesey, "Roman Catholicism: the Maryland Tradition," *Thought* 51 (September, 1976), 284.

7. Quoted in James Hennesey, *American Catholics: A History of the Roman Catholic Community in the United States* (New York: Oxford University, 1981), 39.

8. Andrew White, quoted in Radoff, 8.

9. "Diary of Br. Joseph Mobberly," Maryland Province Archives, vol. 1, 17.

10. Assembly and Jesuits quoted in Edward Terrar, "Was There a Separation between Church and State in Mid-17th Century England and Colonial Maryland?" *Journal of Church and State* 35 (Winter 1993), 63 and 66.

11. Brent, quoted in Lois Green Carr, "Margaret Brent—A Brief History," Maryland State Archives (2002).

12. Relation for 1655 and 1656, quoted in Thomas Hughes, *History of the Society of Jesus in North America—Colonial and Federal*, Text II (New York: Longmans, 1917), 59.

13. Jowett descendant quoted in Joseph Zwinge, "The Jesuit Farms in Maryland: Facts and Anecdotes, the Negro Slaves," *Woodstock Letters* 41, no. 3 (1912), 195.

14. Quoted in Ross Kimmel, "Slave Freedom Petitions in the Courts of Colonial Maryland," (unpublished manuscript), Maryland State Archives, G1239, 1.

15. Quoted in Kimmel, 35.

16. *Wikipedia*, s.v. "Doughoregan Manor," accessed August 27, 2014, http://en.wikipedia.org/wiki/Doughoregan_Manor.

CHAPTER FOUR

1. Zwinge, 199.

2. Francis Neale to Dzierozynski, January 10, 1826, Maryland Province Archives, vol. 61, 9.

3. Francis Neale, 1814, quoted in Zwinge, 200.

4. George Hunter, S.J., *Retreat* (1749), quoted in Zwinge, 218.

5. "Old St. Joseph's in the 18th Century," Old St. Joseph's Church, accessed September 2, 2014, http://oldstjoseph.org/blog/about-osj/history/18th-century/.

6. Zwinge, 209.

7. Joseph Mosely, S.J., to his sister, June 5, 1772, Tuckahoe, Maryland, reprinted in *Woodstock Letters*, 35 (1906), 54.

8. (Probably) John Boone, sometime between 1765 and 1770, and John Lewis, before 1761, both in Georgetown University Archives, Sermon Collection.

9. John Carroll to Benjamin Franklin, January 18, 1778, in *John Carroll Papers*, ed. Thomas O'Brien Hanley (Notre Dame: University of Notre Dame Press, 1976), vol. 1, 50.

10. Letter of T. Stone, April 8, 1781, quoted in Edward Beitzell, *The Jesuit Missions of St. Mary's County, Maryland* (private publication, 1976), 73.

11. John Carroll to Leonardo Antonelli, August 5, 1789, in *John Carroll Papers*, vol. I, 376; and "The address of the Roman Catholics to George Washington, Esq., President of the United States, 1790," *John Carroll Papers*, vol. I, 410.

12. Quoted in *The Carmelite Adventure—Clare Joseph Dickinson's Journal of a Trip to America and Other Documents*, ed. Constance Fitzgerald (Private Publication of Carmelite Sisters, Maryland, 1990), 14–15.

13. Patrick Smythe, *The Present State of the Catholic Mission, Conducted by the Ex-Jesuits in North America* (Dublin, 1788), 18.

14. "Unpublished Reply by Rev. John Carroll, 1788," *American Catholic Historical Researches* 1, no. 3 (July 1905), 202.

15. Margaret K. Fresco, *Doctors of St. Mary's County, 1634–1900* (private publication, 1992), 90.

16. John Carroll to Leonardo Antonelli, August 5, 1789, in *John Carroll Papers*, vol. 1, 376.

17. Boston *Herald of Freedom*, August 31, 1790.

18. Carroll to Charles Plowden, June 11, 1791, Fordham Archives, 202, B–36.

19. Carroll to Gallitzin, October 20, 1798 (paraphrase of editor), in Thomas Spalding, *John Carroll Recovered* (Baltimore: Cathedral Foundation Press, 2000), 30.

20. John Lancaster Spalding, speech delivered at the Cooper Institute, New York City, June 4, 1879, quoted in *Ave Maria* 15, no. 19 (July 19, 1879), 576.

21. Jay Dolan, *The Immigrant Church—New York's Irish and German Catholics, 1815–1865* (1975; Notre Dame, Ind.: University of Notre Dame Press, 1983), 3.

22. Thomas Spalding, *The Premier See—A History of the Archdiocese of Baltimore, 1789–1989* (Baltimore: John Hopkins University Press, 1989), 17.

CHAPTER FIVE

1. Benedict Webb, *The Centenary of Catholicity in Kentucky* (Louisville, Ky.: Webb, 1884), 106.

2. Hughes Spalding, *The Spalding Family of Maryland, Kentucky, and Georgia from 1658 to 1963* (private publication, 1963), 21.

3. Badin to Carroll, June 28, 1796, Archives of the Archdiocese of Baltimore, 1–E2.

4. Martin Spalding, *Sketches of the Early Missions of Kentucky; From their Commencement in 1787, to the Jubilee of 1826–7* (Louisville, Ky.: Webb, 1844), 113.

5. Webb, 86 and 87.

6. Badin to Carroll, August 29, 1808, Archives of the Archdiocese of Baltimore, 1–I–10.

7. Badin, quoted in Martin Spalding, *Sketches*, 67.

8. Webb, 177.

9. Martin Spalding, *Sketches*, 116.

10. April 11, 1796 Badin to Carroll, Archives of the Archdiocese of Baltimore, 1–E–1.

11. Martin Spalding, *Sketches*, 76.

12. Badin to Carroll, May 5, 1801, Archives of the Archdiocese of Baltimore, Special Collection, A–H–2.

13. Badin to Carroll, June 18, 1801, Archives of the Archdiocese of Baltimore, Special Collection, A–H–1.

14. Florence Wolff, *With Captain Dogwood* (Sisters of Loretto private publication, 1986), 4.

15. Badin to Carroll, July 17, 1806, Archives of the Archdiocese of Baltimore, SPA–N–2.

16. Badin to Carroll, July 17, 1806.

17. Badin to Carroll, July 17, 1806.

18. *Catholic Miscellany*, December 4, 1830; quoted in Webb, 456; and Badin, quoted in Webb, 457n.

19. Quoted in Webb, 471n.

CHAPTER SIX

1. Seton, quoted in C. Bernard Ruffin, *Profiles of Faith—The Religious Beliefs of Eminent Americans* (Missouri: Liguori, 1997), 86.

2. "1817 Sisters of Charity Act of Incorporation," quoted in James Rada Jr., *Battlefield Angels—The Daughters of Charity Work as Civil War Nurses* (Gettysburg, Pa.: Legacy, 2011), 11.

3. Seton, quoted in Ruffin, 86–87, and 88.

4. Flaget cited in Clyde Crews, *An American Holy Land: A History of the Archdiocese of Louisville* (Delaware: Michael Glazier, 1987), 75.

5. Sisters of Charity Archives, Duplicate Early Annals, 19–20, reprinted in Mary Ellen Doyle, *Pioneer Spirit—Catherine Spalding Sister of Charity of Nazareth* (Lexington, Ky.: University Press of Kentucky, 2006), 98.

6. "St. Rose Philippine Duchesne (1769–1852)," AmericanCatholic.org, Franciscan Media, accessed November 25, 2014, http://www.american-catholic.org/features/saints/saint.aspx?id=1205.

7. Peter Verhaegen, *History of the Missouri Mission of the Society of Jesus* (unpublished document), English translation, Personnel File, Missouri Province, Midwest Jesuit Archives, Foundational Documents of the Missouri Province (004) Bin 0028.

8. Felix L. Verreydt, "The Memoirs of Felix L. Verreydt, S.J." (unpublished manuscript, 1874), 49, Personnel File, Missouri Province, Midwest Jesuit Archives, "Memoirs."

9. De Smet, quoted in Jacqueline Peterson, *Sacred Encounters—Father DeSmet and the Indians of the Rocky Mountain West* (Norman, Okla.: University of Oklahoma Press, 1993), 22.

10. John Ireland, introduction to Samuel Mazzuchelli, *Memoirs, Historical and Edifying of a Missionary Apostolic of the Order of Saint Dominic Among Various Indian Tribes and Among the Catholics and Protestants in the United States of America* (Chicago, 1915), viii.

11. Diane Batts Morrow, *Persons of Color and Religious at the Same Time—The Oblate Sisters of Providence, 1828–1860* (Chapel Hill, N.C.: University of North Carolina Press, 2002), 5; and "Original Rule," quoted in Morrow, 1.

12. Pope John XXIII, quoted in "St. Elizabeth Ann Seton Parish," accessed September 2, 2014 http://www.parishesonline.com/scripts/HostedSites/

org.asp?p=21&ID=6239; Pope Paul VI, quoted in "Biography of St. Elizabeth Ann Seton," The National Shrine of St. Elizabeth Ann Seton, accessed September 2, 2014, http://www.setonheritage.org/learn-and-explore/resources/mother-seton-bio/.

CHAPTER SEVEN

1. John O'Raw, Charleston, South Carolina, to Bryan and Nellie O'Raw, April 1, 1809, in *Irish Immigrants in the Land of Canaan: Letters and Memoirs from Colonial and Revolutionary America, 1675–1815*, Kerby A. Miller, Arnold Schrier, Bruce D. Boling, and David N. Doyle, eds., (New York: Oxford University Press, 2004), 95.

2. "Archbishop Ambrose Maréchal's Views on the Irish, 1818," in Jeffrey Burns et al., *Keeping Faith—European and Asian Catholic Immigrants* (New York: Orbis, 2000), 4.

3. Lyman Beecher, *Plea for the West* (Cincinnati: Truman and Smith, 1835), 61.

4. *The Awful Disclosures of Maria Monk, as Exhibited in a Narrative of Her Sufferings During a Residence of Five Years as a Novice and Two Years as a Black Nun, in the Hotel Dieu Nunnery in Montreal* (New York: Howe and Bates, 1836), 47.

5. Gilbert J. Garraghan, "The Mission of Central Missouri, 1837–1861," *Saint Louis Catholic Historical Review* 11, no. 4 (1920), 165.

6. Quoted in John Lamott, *History of the Archdiocese of Cincinnati, 1821–1921* (New York: F. Pustet 1921), 139, n. 79.

7. Hannah Curtis to John Curtis, November 24, 1845, and William Dunne to John Curtis, April 25, 1846, both in Pennsylvania Historical Society, Philadelphia, Pennsylvania.

8. Hannah Curtis to John Curtis, April 2, 1847, Pennsylvania Historical Society.

9. "German Immigration to the U.S. in the 1800s," quoted in John Gurda, *The Making of Milwaukee* (Milwaukee: The Milwaukee County Historical Society, 1999), 74.

10. Quoted in Coleman Barry, *The Catholic Church and German Americans* (Milwaukee: Bruce, 1953), 11 and 10.

11. Simon Bruté, quoted in Albert Kleber, *Saint Joseph Parish, Jasper, Indiana, Diocese of Indianapolis (1834–1898, Diocese of Vincennes) Centenary 1837–1937* (Saint Meinrad, Ind.: St. Meinrad Abbey Press, 1937), 15.

12. Bede O'Connor, O.S.B., to Abbot Heinrich, February 27, 1853, quoted in Peter Yock, "The Role of Saint Meinrad Abbey in the Formation of

Catholic Identity in the Diocese of Vincennes, 1853–1898" (PhD dissertation for Pontificia Universitate Gregoriana, Evansville Bindery, 2001), 1.

13. Bede O'Connor to (unnamed) dean of Maria Einsiedeln Abbey, July 12, 1854, reprinted in Burns et al., 58 and 59.

14. "Adolph Kolping," Kolping International, accessed September 16, 2014 http://www.kolping.net/en/who_we_are/adolph_kolping.html.

CHAPTER EIGHT

1. Richard Caton, "A Brief Statement of Facts in the Management of the Late Mr. Carroll of Carrollton's Moneyed Estate," December 11, 1832, Maryland Historical Society, quoted in Scott McDermott, *Charles Carroll of Carrollton—Faithful Revolutionary* (New York: Scepter, 2002), 243.

2. Martin Spalding, *Sketches*, 123–124 (emphasis his).

3. Badin to Cardinal Prefect of Propaganda Fide, no date (though probably c. 1805), Archives of the Propaganda Fide, America III, 227, reprinted in part in Mary Ramona Mattingly, *The Catholic Church on the Kentucky Frontier (1785–1812)* (Washington, D.C.: Catholic University of America, 1936), 173.

4. J.J. Peemans (quoting Nerinckx) to Propaganda Fide, September 28, 1806, in *Documents, Nerinckx—Kentucky—Loretto, 1804–1851 in Archives Propaganda Fide, Rome*, eds. Augustin Ward and M. Lilliana Owens (St. Louis: Mary Loretto, 1972), 32.

5. Flaget cited in Charles Lemarié, *A Biography of Msgr. Benedict Joseph Flaget*, trans. Mary Wedding (private publication of the Sisters of Charity of Nazareth, undated), 108.

6. John England, quoted in Hennesey, *American Catholics*, 146.

7. Roothaan to Kenney, July 3, 1830, Maryland Province Archives 500.61.

8. Dzierozynski to Roothaan, January 28, 1831, Jesuit Archives in Rome, Maryland 4.i.5.

9. Carbery cited in John LaFarge, *The Manner is Ordinary* (New York: Harcourt, 1954), 189.

10. Thomas Lilly to Roothaan, July 2, 1838, Jesuit Archives in Rome, Maryland 7 II 7; and Peter Havermans to Roothaan, October 20, 1838, Jesuit Archives in Rome, Maryland 7 I 9.

11. Purcell, quoted in *Catholic Telegraph* (Cincinnati), October 11, 1838.

12. Pope Gregory XVI, "Concerning the Not Carrying on the Trade of Negroes," December 3, 1839.

13. John England, *Letters of the Late Bishop England to the Hon. John Forsyth on the Subject of Domestic Slavery: to which are Prefixed Copies, in Latin*

and English, of the Pope's Apostolic Letter, Concerning the African Slave Trade, with Some Introductory Remarks, Etc. (Baltimore: John Murphy, 1844), 23.

14. Mother Catherine Spalding to Sister Claudia Elliot, June 17, 1851, Archives of the Sisters of Charity of Nazareth, NLB 71.

15. F.P. Kenrick, *Theologia Moralis*, vol. 1, translated from Latin (1843; Mechliniae: H. Dessain, 1861), 255.

16. Saint Rose Register, March 29, 1843, 137.

17. For "oats," etc., see, for example, *Catholic Advocate*, September 29, 1838.

18. *Bardstown Herald*, September 29, 1832, and February 17, 1836; *Catholic Advocate*, April 1, 1837.

19. Harry Smith, *Fifty Years of Slavery in the United States of America* (originally published by the Grand Rapids, Michigan, Printing Company, 1891), 12.

20. Isaac Johnson, *Slavery Days in Old Kentucky* (originally published by Canton, N.Y.: Friends of the Owen D. Young Library: St. Lawrence County Historical Association, 1901; redistributed by Syracuse University Press, 1994), 13–14.

21. Johnson, *Slavery Days in Old Kentucky*, 24–25.

22. Johnson, *Slavery Days in Old Kentucky*, 25–26, and 31.

23. Johnson, *Slavery Days in Old Kentucky*, 5.

24. Charles Stonestreet and Angelo Paresce, "Missions for the Tertians for 1851," reprinted in Robert Emmett Curran, ed., *American Jesuit Spirituality—The Maryland Tradition, 1634–1900* (New York: Paulist, 1988), 212; Diary of Father Roger T. Dietz, S.J., April 28, 1854, reprinted in *Early Records of the White Marsh Church, Prince George's County, Maryland*, compiled by the Publications Committee of the Prince George's County Genealogical Society, 2005 (private publication, 2005).

25. Interview of Charles Coles, November 15, 1937, recorded in Maryland section of *The American Slave: A Composite Biography*, vol. 16, Kansas, Kentucky, Maryland, Ohio, Virginia, and Tennessee Narratives, ed. George P. Rawick (1941; Portsmouth, N.H.: Greenwood, 1972), 4–5; and Charles Stonestreet and Angelo Paresce, "Missions for the Tertians for 1851," reprinted in Curran, *American Jesuit Spirituality*, 212.

26. *Litterae Annuae*, 1864–1866, quoted in Gilbert Garraghan, *The Jesuits of the Middle United States*, vol. 3 (Chicago: Loyola University Press, 1984), 330.

27. Peter Kenrick to Francis Kenrick, cited in "Archdiocese of St. Louis: 1843–1903: The Immigrant Church," Archdiocese of St. Louis, accessed September 17, 2014, http://archstl.org/archives/page/1843-1903-immigrant-church-0.

28. Purcell, quoted in Mary Agnes McCann, *Archbishop Purcell and the Archdiocese of Cincinnati: A Study Based on Original Sources* (Washington, D.C.: Catholic University of America Press, 1918), 78; and William Barry, quoted in Hennesey, *American Catholics*, 151–152.

29. Unnamed woman working at Paducah, Kentucky, hospital, quoted in Ellen Ryan Jolly, *Nuns of the Battlefield* (Providence: Providence Visitor, 1927), 7.

30. Purcell in *Baltimore Catholic Mirror*, February 25, 1862; and Hughes, quoted in Rada, 47.

31. Euphemia Blenkinsop, quoted in Rada, 67 and 73.

32. Purcell, quoted in Jolly, 41.

33. Witness (Francis Burlando), quoted in Rada, 132; O'Connell quoted in Jolly, 45; unnamed Shiloh man quoted in Rada, 58; and Jolly, 46.

34. Unnamed soldier quoted in Rada, 139.

35. Unnamed soldier referred to in Ignatius Sumner, "Register of the Events from the Foundation of the Convent of the Sisters of Mercy, Vicksburg, Mississippi, c. 1828–1895," in Mary Paulinus Oakes, ed., *Angels of Mercy—An Eyewitness Account of Civil War and Yellow Fever by a Sister of Mercy* (Baltimore: Cathedral Foundation Press, 1998), 21.

36. Unnamed soldier quoted in Rada, 53.

37. Purcell, quoted in Anthony Deye, "Archbishop John Purcell and the Civil War," (master's thesis, University of Cincinnati, 1944), 33.

38. Martin Spalding, in David Spalding, "Martin John Spalding's 'Dissertation on the American Civil War,'" *Catholic Historical Review* 52, no. 1 (April 1966), 80.

39. David Spalding, "Martin John Spalding's 'Dissertation,'" 76.

40. Lincoln, quoted in Oakes, xiii.

41. *Chicago Tribune*, July 10, 1897.

42. Lafarge, 184.

43. *America*, April 17, 1909 (first issue), quoted in Raymond Schroth, *The American Jesuits—A History* (New York: New York University Press, 2007), 115–116; and Anthony Maas to LaFarge, quoted in Schroth, *American Jesuits*, 118.

44. Schroth, *American Jesuits*, 120.

45. William Markoe, quoted in Schroth, *American Jesuits*, 121.

46. Unnamed women quoted in LaFarge, 190

47. Oakes, ix.

48. "An Interracial Role: Memoirs of Rev. Wm. M. Markoe, S.J., 1900–1966," 168, Slaves/Slavery, Missouri Province Collection, III–B Florissant-Saint Stanislaus Seminary, Midwest Jesuit Archives.

49. Cardinal George, quoted in "Cardinal's Network Archive—Fr. Augustus Tolton," Archdiocese of Chicago, March 1, 2010, accessed September 27, 2014, http://www.archchicago.org/cardinalsnetwork/archive.aspx?id=49.

CHAPTER NINE

1. Ireland, quoted in Marvin O'Connell, *John Ireland and the American Catholic Church* (St. Paul, Minn.: Minnesota Historical Society Press, 1988), 194.

2. Mary Onahan Gallery, "Monsignor Daniel J. Riordan," *Illinois Catholic Historical Review* 4 (January, 1922), 328; and Hennesey, *American Catholics*, 180.

3. Spalding, in *Saint Raphaels Blatt*, 6 (August–October, 1891), 63, quoted in Coleman Barry, 167.

4. Cabrini, quoted in Mary Louise Sullivan, M.S.C., "Cabrini, Frances Xavier (1850–1917)," in *Encyclopedia of American Catholic History* (Collegeville, Minn.: Liturgical, 1997), 182.

5. Quoted in John Tracy Ellis, *The Life of James Cardinal Gibbons, Archbishop of Baltimore, 1834–1921*, vol. 1 (Milwaukee: Bruce, 1952), 489.

6. Ellis, 509.

7. Ellis, 529.

8. Leo XIII, *Rerum Novarum*, May 15, 1891, n. 28.

9. (St. Louis) *Chronicle*, December 16, 1892.

10. "Oath of American Protective Association, 1893," reprinted in Burns et al., 85.

11. J.L. Spalding, "Catholicism and APAism," *North American Review* 159 (September 1894), 282 and 283.

12. Leo XII, quoted in Gerald Fogarty, *The Vatican and the American Hierarchy from 1870 to 1965* (Collegeville, Minn.: Liturgical, 1982), 178.

13. Rosemary Skinner, ed., *Encyclopedia of Women and Religion in North America* (Bloomington, Ind.: Indiana University Press, 2006), 877.

14. "Reflections of Father Walter Elliot, St. Bede College, Peru, Illinois, June 26, 1900," Archives Propaganda Fide, Americanism file (for first part of the conversation); and O'Connell to Ireland, March 23, 1900, Archives of the Archdiocese of Saint Paul (for second part of conversation).

15. Riordan to O'Connell, Rome, August 31, 1902, Archives of the Diocese of Richmond.

16. Mary Harris Jones, quoted in Elliot J. Gorn, *Mother Jones* (May/June 2001), accessed September 24, 2014, http://www.motherjones.com/politics/2001/05/mother-jones-woman.

17. Sandra L. Ballard and Patricia L. Hudson, *Listen Here: Women Writing in Appalachia* (Lexington, Ky.: University Press of Kentucky, 2013), 307.
18. Pope Pius X, *Acerbo Nimis* (1905)
19. His Holiness Pope St. Pius X, "The Oath Against Modernism," September 1, 1910, Papal Encyclicals Online, http://www.papalencyclicals.net/Pius10/p10moath.htm.

CHAPTER TEN

1. Quoted in Christopher Kauffman, "Knights of Columbus," *Encyclopedia of American Catholic History*, 769.
2. *Cincinnati Post*, Nov. 23, 1931.
3. *Our Bishops Speak, Bishops' Program of Social Reconstruction*, 243. After WWI the NCWC became the National Catholic Welfare Council, which soon became the National Catholic Welfare Conference, which after Vatican II became the National Conference of Catholic Bishops, and then the United States Catholic Conference, which is what the body is called today.
4. Ryan, quoted in Jeffrey M. Burns, "Ryan, John Augustine (1865–1945)," *Encyclopedia of American Catholic History*, 1228.
5. Leo XIII, *Rerum Novarum*, May 15, 1891, n. 36.
6. André Siegfried, 1927, quoted in Al Smith, *Up to Now—An Autobiography* (New York: Viking Press, 1929).
7. Leonard, "Address to Southern Baptist Leaders," quoted in Corwin Smidt, et al., *The Disappearing God Gap? Religion in the 2008 Presidential Election* (New York: Oxford University Press, 2010), 21; and Al Smith, "Address at Oklahoma City," September 20, 1928, reprinted in *Campaign Addresses—Governor Alfred E. Smith, 1928* (Washington, D.C.: Democratic National Committee, 1929), 57.
8. Day, quoted in Jim Forest, "Dorothy Day (1897–1980)," *Encyclopedia of American Catholic History*, 414.
9. Dorothy Day, *The Long Loneliness—The Autobiography of the Legendary Catholic Social Activist* (New York: Harper One, 1952), 45.
10. Quoted in Jim Forest, "Dorothy Day," *Encyclopedia of American Catholic History*, 415.
11. Quoted in Burns, "John Augustine Ryan (1865–1945)," *Encyclopedia of American Catholic History*, 1228.
12. Father Coughlin, "Anti-Semitism," Old Time Radio, accessed June 12, 2013, http://www.fathercoughlin.org/father-coughlin-anti-semitism.html; and Al Smith, quoted in James Fisher, *Communion of Immigrants—A*

History of Catholics in America (New York: Oxford University Press, 2008), 102.

13. Unnamed USO official, quoted in Julia M.H. Carson, *Home Away From Home—The Story of the USO* (New York: Harper Brothers, 1946), 26; and *Cincinnati Post*, Dec. 4, 1942.

14. Quoted in George Sirgiovanni, "World War II and American Catholics," *Encyclopedia of American Catholic History*, 1520.

15. *Cincinnati Post*, Dec. 4, 1942.

16. John R. Satterfield, *We Band of Brothers: The Sullivans & World War II* (Parkersburg, Ia.: Mid-Prairie, 1995), 5.

17. Quoted in Sirgiovanni, 1521.

18. Sirgiovanni, 1522.

19. *Cincinnati Enquirer*, July 13, 17, 1945; and *Cincinnati Post*, May 18, 1944.

20. "Peace and Unity—The Hope of Mankind," November 15, 1956, and "A Statement on Freedom and Peace," November 19, 1959, both in Hugh Nolan, ed., *Pastoral Letters of the United States Catholic Bishops*, vol. 2, 1941–1961 (Washington, D.C.: USCC, 2005), 187, 188, and 215.

21. Quoted in James Terence Fisher, "Vietnam War and American Catholics," in *Encyclopedia of American Catholic History*, 1437.

22. Fisher, "Vietnam War and American Catholics," 1439.

23. "Statement on Iraq, 2002," United States Conference of Catholic Bishops, November 13, 2002.

CHAPTER ELEVEN

1. Sheen, quoted in Thomas J. McSweeney, "Fulton John Sheen (1895–1979), *Encyclopedia of American Catholic History* (Collegeville, Minn.: Liturgical, 1997), 1287.

2. Ellis and unnamed source, quoted in Thomas J. McSweeney, "Fulton John Sheen (1895–1979), *Encyclopedia of American Catholic History* (Collegeville, Minn.: Liturgical, 1997), 1286.

3. Anne Heagney, *The Magic Pen* (Milwaukee: Bruce, 1949), dust jacket.

4. *The Book of Catholic Authors*, Walter Romig, ed., 6th series (Ann Arbor, Mich.: Braun-Brumfield, 1960), 155; and Joseph Dever, *No Lasting Home* (Milwaukee: Bruce, 1947), dust jacket.

5. Sylvester, *Moon Gaffney* (New York: H. Holt and Company, 1947), 85, 13 n. 2, and 12.

6. Sylvester, 56; and Philip Jenkins, "Who is Harry Sylvester," *First Things* (March 2007), 18.

7. "Religion: Merton's Mountainous Legacy," *Time*, December 31, 1984.

8. Merton, quoted in Joel Wells, "Mary Flannery O'Connor (1925–1964)," *Encyclopedia of American Catholic History*, 1074.

9. Paul Blanshard, *American Freedom and Catholic Power* (Boston: Beacon, 1950), 3 and 4.

10. Ellis's address, "American Catholics and the Intellectual Life" at the annual meeting of the Catholic Commission on Intellectual and Cultural Affairs at Maryville College in St. Louis which proved to be the most famous of his career, was initially read, and later published in *Thought* 30 (1955), 351–88, and has reappeared numerous times, including in *American Catholic History—A Documentary Reader*, ed. Mark Massa, S.J. (New York: New York University Press, 2008), 95–101, quote from 97.

11. "To Be Catholic and American," *Time*, December 12, 1960.

12. Isabel Green to Katie Putnam, February 10, 1948, Nazareth, Kentucky. Isabel Green is the aunt of the author of this article, who inherited her correspondence.

13. Richard McBrien, "The 'good old '50s aren't what they used to be," *Messenger* (Covington, Kentucky), February 25, 1994.

14. McBrien, "The 'good old '50s aren't what they used to be."

15. "Walker Percy, A Documentary Film," PBS, accessed November 24, 2014, http://www.pbs.org/program/walker-percy/.

16. James Farl Powers, *Morte d'Urban* (New York: Doubleday, 1962), dust jacket and 20.

17. Thomas Merton, *No Man is an Island* (New York: Harcourt, 1955), 123.

18. Foreword to Gordon Oyer, *Pursuing the Spiritual Roots of Protest—Merton, Berrigan, Yoder, and Muste at the Gethsemani Abbey Peacemakers Retreat* (Eugene, Ore.: Cascade, 2014), xi.

19. "Statement from Arturo S. Rodriguez, President United Farm Workers of America, AFL-CIO, Celebrating Cesar Chavez's Birthday, March 31, 1998," United Farm Workers, accessed January 1, 2015, http://www.ufw.org/_board.php?mode=view&b_code=news_press&b_no=185&page=16&field=&key=&n=53.

20. Mary Gordon, "Getting Here from There: A Writer's Reflections on a Religious Past," in *Good Boys and Dead Girls, and Other Essays* (New York: Penguin, 1992), 174 and 175.

21. Bernard Häring, "A Contemplative House—Notes From a Discussion Held at Notre Dame," *Review for Religious* 26 (September, 1967), 772.

22. Häring, quoted in Ann Chester, *My Journey in the House of Prayer* (Monroe, Mich.: Pathways, 1991), 42.

23. Isabel Green, (unpublished) Open letter of solicitation for "testimonials," November 1973, Ann to Isabel Green, January 22, 1975, and Green, quoted in Gloucester *Community News*, "Nuns Rise at Dawn for Daily Yoga," November 21, 1975.

24. Gordon, "More Catholic than the Pope," in *Good Boys and Dead Girls, and Other Essays* (New York: Penguin, 1992), 180 (emphasis mine).

25. Gordon, "More Catholic than the Pope," 197.

26. "History of the Fellowship," Fellowship of Catholic Scholars, accessed November 12, 2014, http://www.catholicscholars.org/.

27. "Statement of Purpose," Fellowship of Catholic Scholars, accessed November 12, 2014, http://www.catholicscholars.org/.

28. "About Edwina," Edwina Gateley, accessed November 24, 2014, http://edwinagateley.com/about/.

CHAPTER TWELVE

1. *Catholic Telegraph* (Cincinnati), Aug. 13 and Dec. 10, 1965.

2. *Catholic Telegraph* (Cincinnati), March 20 and April 10, 1970.

3. "Patty Crowley Addresses the Papal Birth Control Commission (1965)," in *American Catholic History—A Documentary Reader*, ed. Mark Massa, S.J. (New York: New York University Press, 2008), 74.

4. "Patty Crowley Addresses the Papal Birth Control Commission (1965)," 74 and 75. Some thirty years before, the Church had introduced the Rhythm method as a calendar-based form of birth control. In the 1950s, more biologically based fertility awareness techniques began to emerge, and though these techniques were not incorporated into the approved Rhythm method of the 1960s, they eventually contributed to today's approved Natural Family Planning.

5. Alter, quoted in Roger Fortin, *Faith and Action—A History of the Catholic Archdiocese of Cincinnati, 1821–1996* (Columbus, Ohio: Ohio State University Press, 2002), 353.

6. "The 'Land O'Lakes' Statement on American Catholic Universities (1967)," in *American Catholic History*, 110 and 112.

7. John J. Egan, Peggy Roach, and Philip Murnion, "Catholic Committee on Urban Ministry: Ministry to Ministers," *Review of Religious Research* 20, no. 3 (summer 1979), 279.

8. Bernard Marthaler, quoted in Leslie Woodcock Tentler, *Catholics and Contraception—An American History* (Ithaca, N.Y.: Cornell University Press), 265.

9. Lyman Stebbins, "The Essential Meaning and Purpose of Catholics United for the Faith," Catholics United for the Faith,

accessed November 24, 2014, http://www.cuf.org/2012/10/
the-essential-meaning-and-purpose-of-catholics-united-for-the-faith/.

10. Lawrence Lucas, *Black Priest/White Church* (New York: Random House, 1970), 43 ("Newark priest statement"), 233, and 114.

11. National Office for Black Catholics, Mission Statement, *St. Thomas University*, accessed November 24, 2014, http://www.stu.edu/lib/LibraryServices/ArchivesSpecialCollections/NationalOfficeofBlackCatholics/tabid/5739/Default.aspx.

12. *About CCHD*, Catholic Campaign for Human Development, United States Conference of Catholic Bishops, 2009, revised 2011, accessed November 24, 2014, http://www.usccb.org/about/catholic-campaign-for-human-development/Who-We-Are/upload/ABOUT-CCHD.pdf, emphasis in original.

13. John J. Egan, Peggy Roach, and Philip Murnion, "Catholic Committee on Urban Ministry: Ministry to Ministers," *Review of Religious Research* 20, no. 3 (summer 1979), 287.

14. National Conference of Catholic Bishops, "Statement on Abortion," April 22, 1970, in *Public Voices—Catholics in the American Context*, eds. Steven Avella and Elizabeth McKeown (Maryknoll, N.Y.: Maryknoll, 1999), 344.

15. For statistics, see *Catholic Telegraph* (Cincinnati), June 26 and December 25, 1970; and Fortin, 365.

16. Andrew Greeley, W. McCready, and K. McCourt, *Catholic Schools in a Declining Church* (Kansas City, Mo.: Sheed and Ward, 1976), 152 (2), 153.

17. Greeley et al., 153 and 152; and McCready and Greeley, "The Ultimate Values of Americans," cited in *Catholic Telegraph*, February 14, 1975.

18. Bernardin, "My dear friends," (in response to accusations of CUF) April 1, 1975, reprinted in *Office of Religious Education Newsletter* 12, no. 6 (April 1975).

19. *Catholic Telegraph* (Cincinnati), February 14, 1975.

20. *Inter Insigniores*, Declaration on the Question of Admission of Women to the Ministerial Priesthood Sacred Congregation for the Doctrine of the Faith, October 15, 1976.

21. "Our Story—Developments of the Mission, Key Turning Points," Women's Ordination Conference (2014), accessed November 24, 2014, http://www.womensordination.org/about-us/our-story/.

22. "Our Story—Developments of the Mission, Key Turning Points."

23. Pope John Paul II, *Ordinatio Sacerdotalis* (1994), 3 and 4; and Cardinal Joseph Ratzinger, *Responsum ad Dubium*, Concerning the Teaching

Contained in *Ordinatio Sacerdotalis* (1995). Also see Pope John Paul II, Apostolic Letter *Motu Proprio Ad Tuendam Fidem*, by which certain norms are inserted into the *Code of Canon Law* and into the *Code of Canons of the Eastern Churches* (1998).

24. McBrien and Pilla, quoted in Peter Steinfels, "Vatican Says the Ban on Women As Priests Is 'Infallible' Doctrine," *New York Times*, November 19, 1995.

25. *Catholic Telegraph* (Cincinnati), April 14, and January 11, 1980.

26. *Catholic Telegraph* (Cincinnati), January 27, 1995.

27. *Catholic Telegraph* (Cincinnati), January 29, 1988.

28. Paul Galloway, "Bernardin, Ex-accuser Reconcile—Cardinal Describes Apology As 'Direct, Deeply Moving,'" *Chicago Tribune*, January 5, 1995.

29. "Our Beginnings," Voice of the Faithful, accessed November 24, 2014, http://www.votf.org/whoweare/our-beginnings/101.

30. "Who We Are," Voice of the Faithful, accessed November 24, 2014, http://www.votf.org/whoweare/who-we-are/100.

31. "Number of Priests Accused of Sexually Abusing Children as Reported by the U.S. Conference of Catholic Bishops with Numbers of Persons Alleging Abuse," compiled by BishopAccountability.org from reports commissioned by the USCCB, March 28, 2014, accessed November 24, 2014, http://www.bishop-accountability.org/AtAGlance/USCCB_Yearly_Data_on_Accused_Priests.htm.

32. Dan Horn, "Clergy Abuse His Biggest Challenge—Interview with Archbishop Pilarczyk," *Cincinnati Enquirer*, December 21, 2009. Pilarczyk served as president of the National Conference of Catholic Bishops from 1989 to 1992.

33. Horn, "Clergy Abuse His Biggest Challenge."

34. *Ex Corde Ecclesiae*, Association of Jesuit Colleges and Universities, accessed November 24, 2014, http://ajcunet.edu/ECE.

35. "The Mandatum," *Ex Corde Ecclesiae*, Association of Jesuit Colleges and Universities, accessed November 24, 2014, http://ajcunet.edu/ECE.

36. "John Paul II and Youth Day," Resources for Christian Living, accessed November 24, 2014, http://www.faithfirst.com/html/popeJohn/youth/youth.html.

37. Crews, *American & Catholic*, 156.

38. Cardinal John O'Connor, *Catholic New York*, June 20, 1996.

39. Cecil Janson, quoted in *Cincinnati Enquirer*, July 14, 1994.

40. William Buckley, *Nearer, My God—An Autobiography of Faith* (New York: Doubleday, 1997), 37.

41. Bernardin, *The Gift of Peace* (New York: Doubleday, 1997), xi–xiii.

42. "Slain Priest: 'Bury His Heart, Not His Love,'" NPR, September 9, 2011, accessed November 24, 2014, http://www.npr.org/2011/09/09/140293993/slain-priest-bury-his-heart-but-not-his-love.

43. Anthony Ruff, O.S.B., "Open Letter to the U.S. Catholic Bishops," quoted in *America* (February 14, 2011), 6.

44. USCCB, "Federal Budget Choices Must Protect Poor, Vulnerable People, Says U.S. Bishops' Conference," April 17, 2012, accessed November 24, 2014, http://www.usccb.org/news/2012/12-063.cfm.

45. Congregatio pro Doctrina Fidei, "Doctrinal Assessment of the Leadership Conference of Women Religious," April 18, 2012.

46. Quoted in Kenneth Overberg, S.J., "Faithful Creativity," *Ministry and Liturgy* 41, no. 9 (November 2014), 24.

47. "Transcript of Simone Campbell Remarks as Prepared for Delivery, Democratic National Convention," Daily Kos, September 5, 2012, accessed November 24, 2014, http://www.dailykos.com/story/2012/09/05/1128209/-Transcript-of-Simone-Campbell-remarks-as-prepared-for-delivery-Democratic-National-Convention.

48. USCCB, "USCCB Migration Chairman Welcomes Obama Administration Announcement of Relief for Immigrant Families, USCCB President Cites Urgent Pastoral Need for a More Humane View of Immigrants," November 20, 2014, accessed November 24, 2014, http://www.usccb.org/news/2014/14-196.cfm.

49. Rick Hampson, "What to Think of Francis—American Catholics are Trying to Discern Exactly what this Pope is Bringing to the Church," *USA Today*, November 2, 2014.

Avella, Steven M., and Elizabeth McKeown, eds. *Public Voices—Catholics in the American Context* (New York: Orbis, 1999).

Ballard, Sandra L., and Patricia L. Hudson. *Listen Here: Women Writing in Appalachia* (Lexington: University Press of Kentucky, 2013).

Baraga, Frederic. *The Diary of Bishop Frederic Baraga: First Bishop of Marquette, Michigan,* trans. Joseph Gregorich and Rev. Paul Prud'homme, S.J. (Detroit: Wayne State University Press, 1990).

Barry, Colman J. *The Catholic Church and German Americans* (Milwaukee: Bruce, 1953).

Beitzell, Edwin Warfield. *The Jesuit Missions of St. Mary's County, Maryland,* second edition (n.p.: private publication, 1976).

Bernardin, Cardinal Joseph. *The Gift of Peace* (New York: Doubleday, 1997).

Blanshard, Paul. *American Freedom and Catholic Power,* second edition (Boston: Beacon, 1958).

Bogen, David S. "Mathias de Sousa: Maryland's First Colonist of African Descent," *Maryland Historical Magazine*, vol. 96, no. 1 (Spring 2001), 68–85.

Bossy, John. *The English Catholic Community 1570–1850* (New York: Oxford University Press, 1976).

Buckley, William F. *Nearer, My God—An Autobiography of Faith* (New York: Doubleday, 1997).

Burns, Jeffrey M., Ellen Skerrett, and Joseph M. White, eds. *Keeping Faith—European and Asian Catholic Immigrants* (New York: Orbis, 2000).

Callan, Louise. *Philippine Duchesne—Frontier Missionary of the Sacred Heart, 1769–1852* (Westminster, Md.: Newman, 1957).

Carey, Patrick. *People, Priests, and Prelates—Ecclesiastical Democracy and the Tensions of Trusteeism* (South Bend, Ind.: University of Notre Dame Press, 1987).

———. *The Roman Catholics* (Westport, Conn.: Greenwood, 1993).

Carson, Julia M.H. *Home Away From Home—The Story of the USO* (New York: Harper, 1946).

Chester, Ann. *My Journey in the House of Prayer* (Monroe, Mich.: Pathways, 199)1.

Codignola, Luca. *The Coldest Harbour of the Land: Simon Stock and Lord Baltimore's Colony in Newfoundland, 1621–1649*, trans. Anita Weston (Montreal: McGill-Queen's University Press, 1988).

Crews, Clyde. *American & Catholic—A Popular History of Catholicism in the United States,* second edition (Cincinnati: St. Anthony Messenger Press, 2004).

———. *An American Holy Land: A History of the Archdiocese of Louisville* (Delaware: Michael Glazier, 1987).

Curran, Robert. *American Jesuit Spirituality: The Maryland Tradition, 1634-1900* (New York: Paulist, 1988).

Day, Dorothy. *The Long Loneliness—The Autobiography of the Legendary Catholic Social Activist* (New York: Harper, 1980), originally published in 1952.

de la Vega, Garcilaso. *The Florida of the Inca—The Fabulous De Soto Story* trans. John and Jeannette Varner (Austin, Tx.: University of Texas, 1951), originally published in 1605.

Dever, Joseph. *No Lasting Home* (Milwaukee: Bruce, 1947).

Diner, Hasia R. *Erin's Daughters in America: Irish Immigrant Women in the Nineteenth Century* (Baltimore: Johns Hopkins University Press, 1983).

Dolan, Jay. *The Immigrant Church—New York's Irish and German Catholics, 1815–1865* (Notre Dame, Ind.: University of Notre Dame Press, 1983), originally published in 1975.

———. *The American Catholic Experience—A History From Colonial Times to the Present* (Garden City, N.Y.: Doubleday, 1985).

Doyle, Mary Ellen. *Pioneer Spirit—Catherine Spalding Sister of Charity of Nazareth* (Lexington: University Press of Kentucky, 2006).

Ellis, John Tracy. *The Life of James Cardinal Gibbons, Archbishop of Baltimore, 1834–1921*, two volumes (Milwaukee: Bruce, 1952).

———. *American Catholicism* (Chicago: University of Chicago, 1956).

England, John. *Letters of the Late Bishop England to the Hon. John Forsyth on the Subject of Domestic Slavery: to which are Prefixed Copies, in Latin and English, of the Pope's Apostolic Letter, Concerning the African Slave Trade, with Some Introductory Remarks, Etc.* (Baltimore: John Murphy, 1844).

Fisher, James T. *Communion of Immigrants—A History of Catholics in America* (New York: Oxford University Press, 2008).

Fitzgerald, Constance, ed. *The Carmelite Adventure—Clare Joseph Dickinson's Journal of a Trip to America and Other Documents* (Private Publication of Carmelite Sisters, Maryland, 1990).

Fogarty, Gerald P. *The Vatican and the American Hierarchy from 1870 to 1965* (Collegeville, Minn.: Liturgical, 1985).

Fortin, Roger. *Faith and Action—A History of the Catholic Archdiocese of Cincinnati, 1821–1996* (Columbus: Ohio State University Press, 2002).

Fuson, Robert H. *Juan Ponce de León and the Spanish Discovery of Puerto Rico and Florida* (Blacksburg, Va.: McDonald & Woodward, 2000).

Garraghan, Gilbert J. *The Jesuits of the Middle United States*, 3 volumes (Chicago: Loyola University Press, 1984).

Gaustad, Edwin S., and Mark A. Noll. *A Documentary History of Religion in America to 1877*, third edition (Grand Rapids: Eerdmans, 2003).

Glazier, Michael, and Thomas J. Shelley, *Encyclopedia of American Catholic History* (Collegeville, Minn.: Liturgical, 1997).

Gleason, Philip, ed. *Catholicism in America* (New York: Harper & Row, 1970).

Gordon, Mary. *Good Boys and Dead Girls, and Other Essays* (New York: Penguin, 1991).

Greeley, Andrew, William C. McGready, and Kathleen McCourt. *Catholic Schools in a Declining Church* (Kansas City: Sheed and Ward, 1976).

Greer, Allan. *Mohawk Saint—Catherine Tekakwitha and the Jesuits* (New York: Oxford University Press, 2005).

Gurda, John. *The Making of Milwaukee* (Milwaukee: Milwaukee County Historical Society, 1999).

Gurn, Joseph. *Charles Carroll of Carrollton, 1737–1832* (New York: P.J. Kenedy & Sons, 1932).

Hammett, Regina Combs. *History of St. Mary's County, Maryland, 1634–1990* (n.p.: private publication, 1991).

Hanley, Thomas O'Brien, ed. *John Carroll Papers*, 3 volumes (South Bend, Ind.: University of Notre Dame Press, 1976).

Heagney, Anne. *Charity Goes to War* (Milwaukee: Bruce, 1961).

———. *The Magic Pen* (Milwaukee: Bruce, 1949).

Hennesey, James. *American Catholics—A History of the Roman Catholic Community in the United States* (New York: Oxford University Press, 1981).

———. "Roman Catholicism: the Maryland Tradition," *Thought* (September 1976), 282–295.

Higman, B.W. *A Concise History of the Caribbean* (Oxford: Cambridge University Press, 201), 1.

Hoffman, Ronald. *Princes of Ireland, Planters of Maryland—A Carroll Saga, 1500–1782* (Chapel Hill, N.C.: University of North Carolina Press, 2000).

Huber, Raphael M. ed. *Our Bishops Speak—National Pastorals and Annual Statements of the Hierarchy of the United States, Resolutions of Episcopal Committees and Communications of the Administrative Board of the National Catholic Welfare Conference, 1919-1951* (Milwaukee: Bruce, 1952).

Hughes, Thomas. *History of the Society of Jesus in North America—Colonial and Federal*, four volumes (New York: Longmans, 1908–1917).

Hunt, Thomas C., David J. O'Brien, and Timothy Walch, eds. *Urban Catholic Education—The Best of Times, the Worst of Times* (New York: Peter Lang, 2013).

Johnson, Isaac. *Slavery Days in Old Kentucky* (Canton, N.Y.: Friends of the Owen D. Young Library and the St. Lawrence County Historical Society, 1994), facsimile of the original 1901 edition.

Jolly, Ellen Ryan. *Nuns of the Battlefield* (Providence: Providence Visitor, 1927).

Kenton, Edna ed. *The Jesuit Relations and Allied Documents* (New York: Albert & Charles Boni, 1925).

Kleber, Albert. *Saint Joseph Parish, Jasper, Indiana, Diocese of Indianapolis (1834-1898, Diocese of Vincennes) Centenary 1837-1937* (Saint Meinrad, Ind.: Saint Meinrad, 1937).

Krugler, John D. "'Our Trusty and Well-beloved Councillor': The Parliamentary Career of Sir George Calvert, 1609-1624," *Maryland Historical Magazine*, vol. 72 (1977), 470–491.

————. "Sir George Calvert's Resignation as Secretary of State and the Founding of Maryland," *Maryland Historical Magazine*, vol. 68 (1973), 234–254.

————. "'The Face of a Protestant and the Heart of a Papist': A Re-examination of Sir George Calvert's Conversion to Roman Catholicism," *Journal of Church and State*, vol. 20 (1978), 507–532.

————. "'With Promise of Liberty in Religion': The Catholic Lords Baltimore and Toleration in Seventeenth-Century Maryland, 1634–1692," *Maryland Historical Magazine*, vol. 79 (1984), 21–43

————. "Lord Baltimore, Roman Catholics and Toleration; Religious Policy in Maryland During the Early Catholic Years, 1634–1649," *Catholic Historical Review*, vol. 65 (January 1979), 49–75.

LaFarge, John. "The Survival of the Catholic Faith in Southern Maryland," *Catholic Historical Review*, vol. 21 (April 1935), 1–20.

————. *Manner is Ordinary* (New York: Harcourt, 1954).

Lahey, Raymond J. "The Role of Religion in Lord Baltimore's Colonial Enterprise," *Maryland Historical Magazine*, vol. 72 (1977), 492–493.

Lamott, John. *History of the Archdiocese of Cincinnati, 1821–1921* (Cincinnati, 1921).

Lemarié, Charles. *A Biography of Msgr. Benedict Joseph Flaget*, translated from the French by Mary Wedding (private publication of the Sisters of Charity of Nazareth), undated.

Light, Dale. *Rome and the New Republic—Conflict and Community in Philadelphia Catholicism between the Revolution and the Civil War* (South Bend, Ind.: University of Notre Dame Press, 1996).

Lucas, Lawrence. *Black Priest/White Church—Catholics and Racism* (New York: Random House, 1970).

Major, R.H. ed. *Select Letters of Christopher Columbus, with Original Documents, Relating to his Four Voyages to the New World* (Burlington, Vt.: Ashgate, 2010), originally published in 1848.

Massa, Mark, ed. *American Catholic History—A Documentary Reader* (New York: New York University Press, 2008).

Mattingly, Mary Ramona. *The Catholic Church on the Kentucky Frontier (1785–1812)* (Washington, D.C.: Catholic University of America, 1936).

McAvoy, Thomas. "The Formation of the Catholic Minority in the United States, 1820–1860," *The Review of Politics*, (January 1948), 13–34.

McCann, Mary Agnes. *Archbishop Purcell and the Archdiocese of Cincinnati: A Study Based on Original Sources* (Washington, D.C.: Catholic University of America, 1918).

McDermott, Scott. *Charles Carroll of Carrollton—Faithful Revolutionary* (New York: Scepter, 2002).

Mann, Charles C. *1491—New Revelations of the Americas Before Columbus* (New York: Knopf, 2006).

———. *1493—Uncovering the New World Columbus Created* (New York: Knopf, 2011).

Mazzuchelli, Samuel. *Memoirs, Historical and Edifying of a Missionary Apostolic of the Order of Saint Dominic Among Various Indian Tribes and Among the Catholics and Protestants in the United States of America* (Chicago: W.F. Hall, 1915).

Melville, Annabelle M. *Elizabeth Bayley Seton, 1774–1821* (New York: Jove, 1985), originally published in 1951.

Merton, Thomas. *No Man is an Island* (New York: Harcourt, 1955).

———. *The Seven Storey Mountain—An Autobiography of Faith* (New York: Harcourt, 1998), originally published in 1948.

Miller, Kerby A. Arnold Schrier, Bruce D. Boling, and David N. Doyle, eds., *Irish Immigrants in the Land of Canaan: Letters and Memoirs from Colonial and Revolutionary America, 1675–1815*, (New York: Oxford University Press, 2004).

Miller, Randall M., and Jon L. Wakelyn. *Catholics in the Old South: Essays on Church and Culture* (Macon, Ga.: Mercer University Press, 1983).

Minogue, Anna C. *Pages from a Hundred Years of Dominican History—The Story of the Congregation of Saint Catharine of Siena* (New York: Frederick Pustet, 1921).

Morrow, Diane Batts. *Persons of Color and Religious at the Same Time—The Oblate Sisters of Providence, 1828-1860* (Chapel Hill, N.C.: University of North Carolina Press, 2002).

National Conference of Catholic Bishops. "1992: A Time for Remembering, Reconciling, and Recommitting Ourselves as a People" (Washington, D.C.: United States Catholic Conference, 1991).

————. *Economic Justice for All—Pastoral Letter on Catholic Social Teaching and the U.S. Economy* (Washington, D.C.: United States Catholic Conference, 1986).

————. *Heritage and Hope: Evangelization in the United States* (Washington, D.C.: United States Catholic Conference, 1991).

————. *Native American Catholics at the Millennium—A Report on a Survey of the United States Conference of Catholic Bishops' Ad Hoc Committee on Native American Catholics* (Washington, D.C.: United States Catholic Conference, 2002).

————. *Pastoral Letters of the United States Catholic Bishops*, volume II, 1941–1961 (Washington, D.C.: United States Catholic Conference, 1984).

Nolan, Charles E. *A History of the Archdiocese of New Orleans* (Strasbourg, France: Éditions du Signe, 2000).

————. *The Old Ursuline Convent, New Orleans, Louisiana* (Strasbourg, France: Éditions du Signe, 2011).

Noll, Mark. *The Old Religion in A New World—The History of North American Christianity* (Grand Rapids: Eerdmans, 2002).

Noonan, Pachala. *Signadou—History of the Kentucky Dominican Sisters* (Manhasset, N.Y.: Brookville, 1997).

Oakes, Mary Paulinus. *Angels of Mercy—An Eyewitness Account of the Civil War and Yellow Fever, by a Sister of Mercy* (Baltimore: Cathedral Foundation Press, 1998).

O'Connell, Marvin R. *John Ireland and the American Catholic Church* (St. Paul, Minn.: Minnesota Historical Society, 1988).

O'Toole, James M. *The Faithful—A History of Catholics in America* (Cambridge, Mass.: Harvard University Press, 2008).

Overberg, Kenneth R. *An Inconsistent Ethic? Teachings of the American Catholic Bishops* (Lanham, Md.: University Press of America, 1980).

Oyer, Gordon. *Pursuing the Spiritual Roots of Protest—Merton, Berrigan, Yoder, and Muste at the Gethsemani Abbey Peacemakers Retreat* (Eugene, Oreg.: Cascade, 2014).

Pané, Fray Ramón. *An Account of the Antiquities of the Indians*, translated into Spanish by José Juan Arrom, and into English by Susan E. Griswold (Durham, N.C.: Duke University Press, 1999).

Peterson, Jacqueline. *Sacred Encounters—Father DeSmet and the Indians of the Rocky Mountain West* (Norman, Okla.: University of Oklahoma Press, 1993).

Powers, James Farl. *Morte d'Urban* (New York: Doubleday, 1962).

Putz, Louis J. ed. *The Catholic Church, U.S.A.* (Chicago: Fides, 1956).

Rada, James, Jr., *Battlefield Angels—The Daughters of Charity Work as Civil War Nurses* (Gettysburg, Penn.: Legacy, 2011).

Radoff, Morris, ed. *The Old State Line—A History of Maryland* (Baltimore: Hall of Records Commission, 1971).

Romig, Walter. *The Book of Catholic Authors* (sixth series) (Grosse Pointe, Mich.: Walter Romig, 1960).

Ruffin, C. Bernard. *Profiles of Faith—The Religious Beliefs of Eminent Americans* (Liguori, Mo.: Liguori/Triumph, 1997).

Satterfield, John R. *We Band of Brothers: The Sullivans & World War II* (Parkersburg, Ia.: Mid-Prairie), 1995.

Schroth, Raymond A. *The American Jesuits—A History* (New York: New York University Press, 2007).

Shea, John Gilmary. *The Cross and The Flag—Our Church and Country* (New York: Office of Catholic Publications, 1900).

Skinner, Rosemary, ed. *Encyclopedia of Women and Religion in North America* (Bloomington, Ind.: Indiana University Press, 2006).

Smith, Al. *Up to Now—An Autobiography* (New York: Viking, 1929).

Smith, Harry. *Fifty Years of Slavery in the United States of America* (Grand Rapids: Grand Rapids, Michigan Printing Company, 1891), reprinted by the Clarke Historical Library.

Smythe, Patrick. *The Present State of the Catholic Mission, Conducted by the Ex-Jesuits in North America* (Dublin, n.p., 1788).

Spalding, Hughes. *The Spalding Family of Maryland, Kentucky, and Georgia from 1658 to 1963* (n.p.: private publication, 1963).

Spalding, John Lancaster. "The Catholic Church in the United States, 1776-1876," *Catholic World* vol. 23 (July 1876), 434–452.

———. "Columbus," *Catholic World*, vol. 56 (October 1892), 1–16.

Spalding, Martin John. *Sketches of the Early Missions of Kentucky; From their Commencement in 1787, to the Jubilee of 1826–7* (Louisville: Webb, 1844).

Spalding, Thomas W. *John Carroll Recovered* (Baltimore: Cathedral Foundation, 2000).

———— *The Premier See—A History of the Archdiocese of Baltimore, 1789–1989* (Baltimore: John Hopkins University Press, 1989).

Sweeney, David Francis. *The Life of John Lancaster Spalding—First Bishop of Peoria, 1840–1916* (New York: Herder and Herder, 1965).

Sylvester, Harry. *Moon Gaffney* (New York: H. Holt, 1947).

Taylor, Alan. *American Colonies—The Settling of North America* (New York: Penguin, 2001).

Tentler, Leslie Woodcock. *Catholics and Contraception—An American History* (New York: Cornell University Press, 2004).

Terrar, Edward "Was There a Separation between Church and State in Mid-17th–Century England and Colonial Maryland?" *Journal of Church and State*, vol. 35 (Winter 1993), 61–82.

Tinker, George E. *American Indian Liberation—A Theology of Sovereignty* (New York: Orbis, 2008).

Trisco, Robert, ed. *Catholics in America, 1776-1976* (Washington, D.C.: United States Catholic Conference, 1976).

Turner, Samuel. "Juan Ponce de León and the Discovery of Florida Reconsidered," *Florida Historical Quarterly*, vol. 92, issue 1 (2013), 1-31.

Ward, Augustin, and M. Lilliana Owens, eds. *Documents, Nerinckx—Kentucky—Loretto, 1804-1851 in Archives Propaganda Fide, Rome*, (St. Louis, Mo.: Mary Loretto, 1972).

Webb, Benedict. *The Centenary of Catholicity in Kentucky* (Louisville: Webb, 1884).

Wills, Gary. *Head and Heart—A History of Christianity in America* (New York: Penguin, 2007).

Wolff, Florence. *With Captain Dogwood* (n.p.: private publication, Sisters of Loretto, 1986).

Zwinge, Joseph. "Jesuit Farms in Maryland—Facts and Anecdotes, The Negro Slaves," *Woodstock Letters*, volume 41, number 3 (1912), 275–291.

About this Author

C. Walker Gollar is a professor of Catholic history and theology at Xavier University in Cincinnati. He holds a Ph.D. in historical theology from the University of Saint Michael's College, Toronto; an M.A. in theological studies from the University of Dayton; and a B.S. in psychology from Xavier University. He has published extensively in academic journals and historical publications, and speaks widely on topics relevant to both history and Catholicism.